Media Globalization and the Discovery Channel Networks

This book is about the relationship between media and globalization, explored through the unique study of the global expansion of Discovery Communications, spearheaded by the Discovery Channel, one of the world's largest providers of factual television programming and media content. The book argues that the study of Discovery's relationship with globalization provides both a specific and a more general practical and theoretical understanding of how the processes of increased linking and interweaving of media and communications unfold and develop, as well as some of the consequences of this.

Ole J. Mjos is a Post Doctoral Fellow at the Department of Information Science and Media Studies, University of Bergen, Norway. He completed his PhD at the University of Westminster, UK, in 2007. His previous professional experience in the media and creative industries includes work in television documentary production, and contributions on many records within the wide genre of electronic music.

Routledge Advances in Internationalizing Media Studies

**1. Media Consumption and
Everyday Life in Asia**
Edited by Youna Kim

2. Internationalizing Internet Studies
Beyond Anglophone Paradigms
Edited by Gerard Goggin and
Mark McLelland

3. Iranian Media
The Paradox Modernity
Gholam Khiabany

**4. Media Globalization and the
Discovery Channel Networks**
Ole J. Mjos

Media Globalization and the Discovery Channel Networks

Ole J. Mjos

Routledge
Taylor & Francis Group
New York   London

First published 2010
by Routledge
711 Third Avenue, New York, NY 10017

Simultaneously published in the UK
by Routledge
2 Park Square, Milton Park, Abingdon, Oxfordshire OX14 4RN

Routledge is an imprint of the Taylor & Francis Group, an informa business

First published in paperback 2011

© 2010 Taylor & Francis

Typeset in Sabon by IBT Global.

Library of Congress Cataloging in Publication Data

Mjos, Ole J., 1970–
  Media globalization and the Discovery Channel networks / by Ole J. Mjos.
    p. cm. — (Routledge advances in internationalizing media studies ; 4)
  Includes bibliographical references and index.
  1. Discovery Channel (Firm) 2. Television and globalization. I. Title.
  PN1992.92.D57M56 2009
  384.55'5 — dc22
  2009005679

ISBN13: 978 0 415 99246 6 (hbk)
ISBN13: 978-0415-80900-9 (pbk)
ISBN13: 978-0-203-87294-9 (ebk)

Contents

List of Tables   vii
List of Figures   ix
Acknowledgments   xi

1   Media Globalization and Televisual Culture   1

2   The Rise of Discovery: 'The world's number one non-fiction
    media company'   19

3   Discovery the Brand: Image, Reputation, Promise   49

4   The Globalization of Factual Entertainment   73

5   Discovery's Localization Strategies   96

6   Global Resonance: Television Programing for the World   118

7   Negotiating the Global and the National through Televisual
    Culture   132

8   The Duality of Globalization in Discovery   145

Appendices   153
Bibliography   199
Index   217

Tables

2.1	Subscribers to Discovery Networks US	23
2.2	The Roll-out of Discovery in Europe	28
2.3	Indian Television's Triumvirate	31
2.4	Subscribers to Discovery Networks International	33
2.5	Global Revenue	34
2.6	The Five Television Channels with the Largest Market Shares	35
2.7	Network Viewer Product Usage/Lifestyle Profile	38
2.8	Demographic Targeted Programming	39
2.9	Discovery's Nine Branded YouTube Destinations	44
3.1	Documentary Channels in the US	52
3.2	Top 25 Television Network Brands Ranked by Quality Score, 2006	53
3.3	Top 25 Online Brands Ranked by Quality Score, 2006	54
3.4	Discovery International's Presence	58
3.5	Discovery International's Television Channels	59
3.6	Discovery Global Businesses and Brands	63
3.7	Interbrand: Best Global Brands 2005	64
4.1	Number of BBC and Discovery Co-productions Presented in BBC Worldwide Program Sales: 2002—2006	88

4.2   The Walking with . . . Factual Brand   92

4.3   The Ten Most Memorable Factual Programs, 2003   95

5.1   European Growth of Channels by Genre:
        Documentary Channels   99

5.2   Documentary Programming (hours) on Public-service
        Channels in Europe, 2002—2004   100

5.3   Hours of Factual and Learning on BBC Television
        Channels   100

5.4   All Feeds—Discovery Europe Networks   106

5.5   Discovery Channel UK: Percentage of Content in
        Categories   110

5.6   Discovery Channel Norway: Percentage of Content in
        Categories   110

5.7   Main Language of Programing   111

5.8   Total Number of Programs Broadcast in Thematic
        Categories   112

5.9   Ofcom, Factual Television Genre Definitions   113

6.1   Market Share by Genre   120

6.2   List of Discovery's Global Specials for 2004   123

Figure

5.1   Discovery Networks Europe regional structure:
the Nordic region   105

Acknowledgments

Various individuals have contributed in different ways in making this book possible. I thank, in particular, Daya K. Thussu, Colin Sparks, and Annette Hill, all at the University of Westminster, UK, and Tehri Rantanen, of London School of Economics. At the University of Bergen, Norway, I want to express my gratitude to Knut Helland, Hallvard Moe, Lars Nyre, Jostein Gripsrud, and Torny E. Aarbakke.

I am grateful to everyone who kindly let me interview them for this project as well as to Erica Wetter my editor at Routledge, and to Elizabeth Thussu for help with editing.

Finally, I thank my mother Kari, father Ole, and my sisters Hilde and Elisabeth Mjos, and all my dear friends for continuous support and encouragement.

1 Media Globalization and Televisual Culture

> (A) principle is to think globally and to act locally. The new technologies give us the chance to span the world and tie it together in ways never before imagined. The goal is not to export one culture in an effort to dominate and denigrate others. It is to showcase a mosaic of influences—to venerate the best of many cultures in hopes of forming a truly global culture.
>
> (Hendricks, founder and chairman of
> Discovery Communications, 1999)

INTRODUCTION

This book is about the relationship between media and globalization, explored through the study of the global expansion of Discovery Communications, spearheaded by the Discovery Channel, one of the world's largest providers of factual television programing and media content. The book argues that the study of Discovery's relationship with globalization provides both a specific and a more general practical and theoretical understanding of how the processes of increased linking and interweaving of media and communications unfold and develop, as well as some of the consequences of this.

The term 'globalization' has spread rapidly throughout the world. From only being used by a few economists, it was increasingly adopted by the public throughout the 1990s and 'skyrocketed to terminological stardom' (Osterhammel and Petersson, 2005: 1). However, despite its widespread use, the meaning, significance, and nature of globalization are fiercely disputed. The term is praised by some for describing developments in society in a concise way; others consider it an inaccurate term or even hype. Some claim to be pro-globalization while others are anti-globalization. The very moment one attempts to define globalization, the contested and confusing nature of the concept emerges.

Sociologist Anthony Giddens describes globalization as a 'portmanteau term' lacking a common definition (Giddens quoted in Rantanen, 2005b:

67). Similarly, fellow sociologist Bauman argues that: 'Globalization is on everybody's lips; a fad word fast turning into a shibboleth, a magic incantation, a pass-key meant to unlock the gates to all present and future mysteries' (Bauman, 1998: 1). Also, Nederveen Pieterse (2004: 8) points to the complicated character of the concept: 'Globalization invites more to controversy than consensus, and the areas of consensus are narrow by comparison to the controversies.' Media scholar Sparks echoes this view, and argues that: 'Opinions differ as to whether globalization is a positive or a negative development, but there is general agreement that whatever is going on is either a symptom or a consequence of globalization.' Furthermore, Sparks sums up: 'There is no single theory of globalization upon which all social scientists, let alone everybody else, are agreed' (2005: 20). A consequence of the incompatible understandings and definitions of globalization is that: 'many globalization debates are stalemated from the outset' (Scholte, 2000: 17).

This book does not set out to solve the 'riddle of globalization' once and for all. Instead, it narrows and focuses its enquiry with the aim to advance the knowledge of the connections between media and globalization. This relationship is explored through an empirical and theoretical investigation of the worldwide expansion of Discovery Communications' television networks and key ventures into new media. This approach attempts to illuminate and give insight into the more general phenomenon of media globalization: the characteristics, intensity, and limits of the activity in an increasingly interwoven and connected global media and communications landscape and infrastructure.

The focus of the book is to examine the globalization of Discovery's televisual culture as the enterprise has expanded from its US origins into Europe, Asia, and Latin America. The concept of televisual culture embodies the processes of producing and distributing television programing through cable, satellite, or online; the marketing of programs and television and other media outlets; and the impact these actions have on the programing and media content. The concept of televisual culture thus serves as a focal entity of the book for the investigation of Discovery's relationship with media globalization. This concept also provides a way of connecting with theoretical discourses on the connection between media and globalization, and also the wider debate on the globalization of culture.

Discovery's rapid worldwide expansion provides an opportunity for scrutinizing the progress and characteristics of media globalization. Discovery Communications' first television channel, the Discovery Channel, was launched in the US in 1985, 'designed to provide high quality documentary programming' to 156,000 subscribers (Discovery, 2006a). In 1993, the founder and chairman of the company, John Hendricks, pronounced: 'We hope to blanket the world by late 1995 or early 1996' (Hendricks quoted in Brown, 1993: 38). The company's television channels, fronted by the Discovery Channel, were about to expand worldwide. In 2006, Discovery

Communications Inc. (DCI) claimed that Discovery Channel is 'the most widely distributed television brand in the world, reaching 475 million homes in more than 160 countries' (Discovery, 2006a). By 2008, Discovery's tier of television channel brands reached a total of over 1.5 billion cumulative subscribers (i.e., one home with television channels Discovery Channel and Discovery Civilization counts as two cumulative subscribers) in over 170 countries. Having expanded into education; cinema; e-commerce; and digital media content distribution platforms such as mobile telephony, the Internet, and video-on-demand, DCI claims to be 'the world's number one nonfiction media company' (Discovery, 2008a).

Discovery has had a pioneering role in the narrowcasting of popularized factual television themes such as science, engineering, technical issues, archeology, and wildlife. Television programing recently distributed worldwide throughout Discovery Channel's network include the series *MythBusters*, *American Chopper*, *Deadliest Catch*, *The Greatest Ever: Bombers, and FBI Files*. Furthermore, Discovery and BBC Worldwide, the commercial arm of BBC, have together introduced the blockbuster logic to the factual genre by creating global factual cross-media brands such as *Walking with Dinosaurs*, and the natural history series *Planet Earth* and *Blue Planet*.

This book investigates how Discovery's globalizing televisual culture navigates in intricate ways between the global and national to construct a global, regional, and national factual television and media platform. This first chapter presents the main theoretical framework of the book, which uses three key theoretical concepts: *cultural homogenization*, *cultural hybridization*, and *cultural heterogenization*—three different views of how a globalizing televisual culture evolves. The next five chapters investigate the key components of Discovery's televisual culture, its operations, and its characteristics, which, in the last two chapters, are analysed and articulated in terms of the theoretical framework.

Chapter 2 examines how global television and media enterprises such as Discovery have first consolidated their activities and operations in the US, and then expanded into Europe, Latin America, and Asia. Discovery and other global media entities have harnessed the political, economic, and technological developments associated with media globalization to develop a worldwide presence. Through the take-up of satellite and cable and digital distribution technology, targeting of niche audiences, economies of scale, and the replication of its US television network structure throughout the world, the media enterprise has been able to establish an increasingly worldwide presence as it attempts to 'blanket the world'.

Chapter 3 analyses the roles of branding and marketing, which have played an immensely important role for Discovery, CNN, Disney, BBC, and other global media enterprises. Discovery has rapidly expanded the development and dissemination of its brands, from that of the company to specific television programs and media brands. Branding is considered as a key means for enterprises and organizations to navigate and achieve their aims, whether this is profit, support, or recognition. The branding process attempts to manage the relationship between an organization and the environment in which it operates, and serves to create ties and bonds with consumers, individuals, groups, or other organizations. Furthermore, brands are increasingly considered as contributors to the overall financial value of media companies, and provide protection when the company expands globally.

Chapter 4 explores how aspects of the globalization of production have reached the film and television industry, and are influencing, and have been adopted by, Discovery in television program production. The globalization of production has been most visible within the manufacturing industry, but now extends across many industry sectors as enterprises search for opportunities outside their national territories, create cross-national alliances, and spread production across the globe.

Chapter 5 maps the imperatives for global media outlets to localize their programing and media content, and aims to understand why and how Discovery localizes media content to reach national segments of the world's television audience.

In contrast, Chapter 6 focuses on global programing. In parallel with localization strategies, Discovery creates and provides programing for worldwide circulation and global audience appeal. The key characteristics of this kind of media content are scrutinized, including an examination of how Discovery's approaches to the popularization of factual themes and use of elements of infotainment influence the treatment and presentation of the real world. Furthermore, the chapter shows how central economic and cultural dynamics of the general global television programing export market and its power relations are also found and are embedded within Discovery's globalizing televisual culture. Discovery draws on the characteristics of various programing genres to make its media content able to travel worldwide across cultural and political borders.

In Chapter 7, the relationship between the components of Discovery's televisual culture and the ongoing theoretical debate on globalization of culture in its televisual form is examined. Discovery's televisual culture attempts to create global, regional, and national factual television and media platforms. This process can be viewed in terms of the theoretical framework provided by the concepts of cultural homogenization, cultural hybridization, and cultural heterogenization. This chapter demonstrates how the three concepts penetrate and are embedded within a globalizing televisual culture in general, and also in Discovery's televisual culture in particular, in complex and overlapping ways. The concluding Chapter 8 shows how Discovery's televisual culture has a dual relationship with media globalization, as it both harnesses and contributes to the process. Furthermore, the nature of its televisual culture makes it able to simultaneously operate on a global and local level. This suggests that, on one level, Discovery's televisual culture may be theoretically explained by the seemingly contradictory processes of *standardize to globalize and standardize to localize.*

MEDIA GLOBALIZATION AND TELEVISUAL CULTURE

Despite the disagreement surrounding the term 'globalization', it is possible to locate a certain interdisciplinary consensus among scholars on the relationship between media and globalization, which can form a basis for reaching a closer understanding of the concept of media globalization. A key starting point is to recognize how scholars agree that the development of a global media and communications infrastructure through cable, satellite, telecommunications, and the Internet has increased possibilities for distribution of media content and information across national borders and continents. Media and communications scholar, Thussu, underlines how: 'The coming of satellites for communications and broadcasting and the development of global information (and control) systems opened up infinite scope for the delivery of electronic goods, transcending physical and political constraints' (Thussu, 1998: 2). Similarly, Katz points out how globalization is tied to the increased possibility for the worldwide distribution of media content: 'The concept of globalization refers to the transmission of television signals across cultures and continents, involving commercial and transnational proliferation of information, entertainment, and advertising' (Katz, 2005: 9). Kraidy, argues in a similar vein, and draws attention to the possible 'asymmetry' of this development:

> In the last two decades, information technologies have overcome many restraints on terrestrial broadcasting. The advent of geo-stationary satellites, whose orbit is calculated to follow Earth's movements in order to keep the coverage area, or footprint, constant has decreased the technical laboriousness and financial cost of television coverage. Global information networks have mitigated time and space restrictions, albeit selectively and asymmetrically. (Kraidy, 2005: 98)

In addition, scholars outside the media and communications discipline point to the central role of communications in the globalization process (Held and McGrew, 2007; Ohmae, 2005: Nederveen Pieterse, 2004). The developments have created and facilitated increased possibilities for global communication. Rantanen (2005a: 8) argues that media and communication are so central in the globalization process that one should refer 'explicitly to them' in the definition of globalization: 'Globalization is a process in which worldwide economic, political, cultural, and social relations have become increasingly mediated across time and space.' However, how is this condition created, and to what extent, and how, are the possibilities for global mediation and communication utilised? This book draws on Tomlinson suggestion that:

'the broad task of globalization theory is both to understand the sources of this condition of complex connectivity and to interpret its implications across the various spheres of social existence' (1999: 2). This book, therefore, proposes that one may explore how the phenomenon of media globalization unfolds and develops by studying the economic, political, and technological processes creating an increasingly global media and communication infrastructure and, through the exploration of Discovery's televisual culture, investigate the characteristics of parts of the activity within this media and communications infrastructure.

Televisual culture is a key concept of this book. Caldwell defines the term 'televisual' as the shift in look, style and the aesthetics in American television in the 1980s (Caldwell, 1995). This was: 'an important historical moment in television's presentational manner, one defined by excessive stylization and visual exhibitionism' (1995: 352). Although this book explores aspects of the style and aesthetics of television programing, it uses the term 'televisual' in a wider context by defining televisual culture as:

> The practices and rituals in the production and distribution of television programing and media content, including the marketing and branding activities by television channels and other media outlets, and the outcome of these complex activities on the form and content of programing and media content.

Although televisual culture includes the aesthetics of television programing and media content, the concept resembles Caldwell's idea of the study of 'deep texts'. These are: 'visual icons, social and professional rituals, demotapes, recurrent trade and union narrativizations, and machine designs, that *audiences and viewers never see*' as they 'precede and prefigure the kinds of film/television screen forms that scholars typically analyze' (Caldwell, 2004: 165). These texts serve as 'user-guides and road maps for practitioners' (Caldwell, 2004: 185). However, this book examines a wider and more extensive range of 'texts' that influence, create and characterize Discovery's televisual culture, but the idea of investigating 'deep texts' resonates with this book's utilization of the term 'televisual culture'. The inquiry into the nature and characteristics of Discovery's televisual culture, as it navigates in an increasingly globally linked and interwoven media and communications landscape, will exemplify, illuminate, and give insight into how media globalization proceeds and develops.

MAPPING GLOBALIZING TELEVISUAL CULTURE: A THEORETICAL FRAMEWORK

How can one best theoretically conceptualize Discovery's aim of 'blanketing the world'? This book argues that these negotiations can be expressed through the theoretical concepts of cultural homogenization, cultural hybridization and cultural heterogenization. These concepts penetrate and are embedded within a general globalizing televisual culture and also Discovery's globalizing televisual culture. Discovery's televisual culture's operations are characterized by the interplay between these three theoretical concepts in a variety of forms. The theoretical framework articulates Discovery's televisual culture negotiation between the global and the national, between globalizing trends and appealing to culturally and linguistically diverse markets.

Several scholars have drawn attention to these theoretical concepts, and how they relate to each other. Rantanen points to the two central paradigms for explaining the consequences of globalization—cultural homogenization and heterogenization—and points out the complexity of applying these paradigms as 'the consequence of globalization is neither homogenization nor heterogenization, but both of these, either simultaneously or sequentially' (Rantanen, 2005a: 116). Similarly, Morley and Robins have described how two 'seemingly divergent' processes are emerging:

> On the one hand, technological and market shifts are leading to the emergence of global image industries and world markets; we are witnessing the 'deterritorialisation' of audiovisual production and the elaboration of transnational systems of delivery. On the other hand, however, there have been significant developments towards local production and local distribution networks. (Morley and Robins, 1995: 1–2)

However, they argue that: 'The issue is not one of global media or local media, but of how global and local are articulated' (Morley and Robins, 1995: 2). This resonates with Thussu's point: 'It has been argued that international communication and media are leading to the homogenization of culture, but the patterns of global/national/local interactions may be more complex' (Thussu, 2000: 166).

Nederveen Pieterse's three theoretical classifications of 'cultural difference' give an overview of the relationship between culture and globalization—referred to as the increased worldwide interconnectedness. This provides a theoretical analogy to the way this book analyses Discovery's televisual culture. Each of the three perspectives argue for specific 'futures' of how the relationship between culture and globalization evolve: 1) the 'cultural convergence' view emphasizes how cultural centers such as the West or the US dominates; 2) the 'cultural differentialism' view sees globalization as 'a surface phenomenon only', as territorial culture is still dominating; and 3) the perspective of 'cultural mixing' describes a process of continuous cultural mixing (Nederveen Pieterse, 2004: 55–57). In a similar way, although limited to televisual culture, this book shows how the chosen theoretical framework relates to—and manifests itself in—several dimensions within a globalizing televisual culture. These dimensions are mapped out in the following, and they are then revisited and applied to the various components of Discovery's globalizing televisual culture in the last two chapters of the book. The aim is to articulate both an empirical and theoretical understanding of how Discovery's globalizing televisual culture navigates to construct a worldwide factual television and media platform.

GLOBALIZATION OF TELEVISUAL CULTURE THROUGH HOMOGENIZATION AND STANDARDIZATION

One of the most popular views is that globalization of culture is characterized by processes of cultural homogenization or standardization. Traditionally, these processes have been considered to create cultural sameness in contrast to cultural diversity in the world society. A commonly held understanding of the consequence of globalization is that the world's society is 'becoming more uniform and standardized, through a technological, commercial and cultural synchronization emanating from the West' (Nederveen Pieterse, 2004: 59). What is the relationship between the concepts of cultural homogenization and standardization and televisual culture? These concepts relate to—and manifest themselves in—developments and practices within the process of globalization of televisual culture in a variety of forms; in the uneven power in the television program market, in the global cable and satellite broadcasters' programing content, in the branding of these broadcasters, and in the marketing and advertising distributed by these broadcasters.

The argument of homogenization of culture relates to the cultural imperialism thesis. Originally, proponents of the thesis emphasize the dominant position of USA media over the local culture of Third World countries (Tunstall, 1977: 57). The process of cultural synchronization is part of cultural imperialism. Hamelink pointed out in the 1980s that the process involves:

> that the decisions regarding the cultural development in a given country are made in accordance with the interests and needs of a powerful central nation and imposed with subtle but devastating effectiveness without regard for the adaptive necessities of the dependent nation. The principal agents of cultural synchronization today are transnational corporations, largely based in the United States, which are developing a global investment and marketing strategy. The transnational corporations which are most directly involved with the cultural component of this global expansion are the international communications firms. (Hamelink, 1983: 22–23)

Although the cultural imperialism thesis and cultural synchronization argument focused on the US/Third World-relationship, Schiller warned against the consequences of the uneven cultural power between USA and Western Europe (1985, 11). A similar view was expressed from within the European Commission in the mid-1980s. American films and television programs dominated the European media space, creating 'a certain uniformity' on television screens (European Commission, 1984: 47). However, the forceful argument of cultural imperialism has increasingly been criticized for several reasons. Sreberny criticizes the 'cultural imperialism' thesis for expressing ideas of hegemonic media that are 'frozen in the realities of the 1970s, now a bygone era' (2000: 96). Others point out that 'imperialism' is inaccurate, as: 'The model needs to take account of audiences, audience preferences; audience consumption of specified cultural products as a proportion of total media and non-media consumption' (Boyd-Barrett, 1998: 168). The idea of imperialism also fails to take into account: 'the counter-flow generated by burgeoning regional television exporters in various other parts of the world', but even so, Morley continues, 'world trade in TV and film is still largely dominated by Anglo-American producers' (Morley, 2006: 35). The cultural imperialism thesis has far less support today, but the continuing differences seen in the trade of film and television programing reminds us of uneven power relations existing within parts of the media industry.

Global Television Channels

When satellite television emerged in the 1980s in Europe, some considered it as a possible danger to national public service broadcasters, as well as to the presence of national European programing on television channels monopolies (Collins, 2002: 9). However, warnings against the possible threat posed by satellite television channels have also been expressed throughout the 1990s and 2000s. Price points out how: 'polished global services by satellite, dilute any competitive domestic political voice at home as much as they weaken the controlled voice of the state itself' (Price, 1995: 38). This view resonates with Schlesinger, who warns that:

> Transnationally broadcast television (with news and journalism at its center) is part of a global struggle for commercial and political hegemony that certainly needs to be watched, not least because of its perceived impact on national sovereignty and political and cultural identities. (Schlesinger, 2001: 112)

Some claim that Discovery is also part of this 'global struggle'. Discovery is focusing on the non-fiction program genre and themes such as science, nature, travel, and health that have traditionally been associated with the public service broadcaster. A consequence of Discovery's strategies for 'imitating public service broadcasters' is that the media enterprise takes the place once held by public broadcasters who, over the last 20 years: '[have] lost financial, political and ideological support around the globe' (Fursich, 2003: 146). While not claiming that MTV is threatening public service broadcasters, scholars point out that, although the pan-European branch of MTV had to retreat from its original 'One World—One Music' concept due to 'the European cultural and linguistic diversity', aspects of standardization and homogenization are still present within MTV:

> On one level MTV is a spectacular example of the validity of the globalization thesis: first, it uses contemporary technology to deliver essentially the same product (predominantly Anglo-American music video clips) and the same commodity advertisements (cola, sports shoes, jeans, etc.) to the same demographic group all over the world; second, many of the uses and gratifications associated with MTV are in many respects strikingly similar among young people in divergent cultures; and third, MTV has (until now at least) been financially successful in this enterprise. (Roe and De Meyer, 2001: 42)

The characteristics of MTV's operations have resonance with Ritzer's theory of *McDonaldization* (Ritzer, 2004). The principles of efficiency, calculability, predictability, and control originally applied to the fast-food restaurant McDonalds are increasingly introduced to other parts of society, and also the media industry. The global broadcaster CNN introduced 'McDonaldized television news' throughout the world. Although CNN has split its service into regional networks, CNN is still mainly distributing 'the same homogenous product, "sliced and diced" in many different ways' (Ritzer, 2004: 211–212). There are strong arguments for the existence of homogenizing and standardizing forces with a globalizing televisual culture: global television channels challenge or dominate national broadcasters, and both MTV and the news channel CNN distribute similar programing across the world. There are also arguments for the presence of cultural homogenization also within the branding and marketing of these channels.

Global Marketing and Branding

The notion of homogenization or standardization in the market framework was described in Levitt's article, *The Globalisation of Markets* (1983). The argument put forth was that the spread of technology is leading to the globalization of markets. As a consequence, national and regional differences are vanishing: 'Everywhere everything gets more and more like everything else as the world's preference structure is relentlessly homogenized' (Levitt, 1983: 93). In the mid-1990s, Morley and Robins argued that Levitt's logic was present in, for example, the global American box office hits and, at the same time, satellite and cable channels were considered as 'making headway in marketing standardized product worldwide' (Morley and Robins, 1995:

15). Such standardization is also seen in the process of branding of some of these media outlets. The American-originated global television channels have all pursued a strategy of creating a homogeneous global media brand using the same logo and brand name in its expansion. Having established a branded television network model in the US, the broadcaster is replicating this model globally; they have organized themselves in 'international networks' of television channels addressing national preferences in the form of language, advertising, and a varying degree of programing content. While they are targeting national and local audience segments, these television channels are centred around 'a core broadcasting philosophy' manifested in a common global brand (Chalaby, 2005b: 56).

Although these media outlets are addressing national audiences, these are cross-national or global audience segments. Returning to marketing scholar Levitt, Morley and Robins point out that the targeting of segments or 'niche' markets: 'are not denials or contradictions of global homogenisation, but rather its confirmation . . . globalisation does not mean the end of segments. It means, instead, their expansion to worldwide proportions' (Levitt, 1983: 30–1 quoted in Morley and Robins, 1995: 15). This development is seen especially in the pan-European news television channels' efforts to target a wealthy audience. A study of the pan-European television audience by market research company IPSOS in 16 countries showed that the sample average had a yearly income of 78,000 Euros. CNN International was the most watched channel, followed by MTV, Euronews, BBC World, Discovery, and CNBC (Chalaby, 2005b: 52). Global television channels and its pan-European networks have a double function in relation to branding and marketing. Although the networks create a standardized brand of themselves, they also facilitate the same opportunities for their advertisers, allowing them to create uniform brands 'homogeneously across a region' (Chalaby, 2005b: 52; Chalaby, 2002). Global television channels relate to the concept of cultural homogenization through aspects of programing, branding, and marketing, but aspects of cultural homogenization are also present in a globalizing televisual culture through developments taking place specifically within news and factual television programing genres.

News, Factual Television, and Infotainment

The increased focus on entertainment and celebrities within news and factual television (infotainment) has had a significant effect on these programing genres globally (Thussu, 2007). The factual television genre has been characterized by major transformations internationally in the 1980s and 1990s. 'Popular factual television' emerged 'during a period of cross fertilisation with tabloid journalism, documentary television and popular entertainment' (Hill, 2005: 23). The transformation of the factual television genre can, to a certain degree, be explained by the growth of tabloid journalism and popular entertainment, the liberalization and commercialization of the media environment where broadcasters, and cable and satellite television channels fought for the audiences' attention (2005: 15, 23).

Corner suggests several historical 'functions of documentary work', and they help explain the transformations taking place within the factual television genre. These functions have created the 'documentary tradition' across 'national histories of media development' (2002: 258). The three first functions of the genre are 'the project of democratic civics', 'documentary as journalistic inquiry and exposition' and 'documentary as radical interrogation and alternative perspective' (2002: 259). 'Documentary as Diversion' is the fourth function of the documentary, and it relates to the rapid rise of popular factual television. This function, Corner points out, has emerged in the form of 'lightness (of topic and / or treatment)':

> In many countries, it has become a new documentary imperative for the production of "popular factual entertainment." Performing this function, documentary is a vehicle variously for the high-intensity incident (the reconstructed accident, the police raid), for anecdotal knowledge (gossipy first-person accounts), and for snoopy sociability (as an amused bystander to the mixture of mess and routine in other people's working lives. (Corner, 2002: 260)

Compared to the three previous functions, the fourth function increases the 'exchange value'—or commercial value—of the 'documentary', which is 'strategically designed for their competitive strength in the television marketplace' (Corner, 2002: 262). This function also relates to: 'how the drive to entertain in factual output has impacted upon the terms of television documentary ambitions' (Corner and Rosenthal, 2005: 4). This development leads us into the debate on the concept of infotainment within news and the factual genre.

The proliferation of television news channels operating around-the-clock on a national or global scale, and the increased time pressures on these outlets and multimedia journalists, are seen as two of the reasons for the emergence of 'infotainment' within television news (Thussu, 2006: 219–221). Some point out that this development represents major causes for concern as: 'entertainment has superseded the provision of information', and 'traditional news values have been undermined by new values; "infotainment" is rampant' (Franklin, 1997: 4). Parallel to the rapid emergence of the television programing sub-genres 'popular factual programing' and 'factual entertainment', the factual television genre has become included in the 'infotainment' debate. Thussu warns against this worldwide development both within television news and the factual television genre. 'Infotainment' is shaping and influencing media content on a global scale. The definition of 'global infotainment' signals that the term may be understood as a homogenizing force: 'The globalization of US-style ratings-driven television journalism which privileges privatized soft news—about celebrities, crime, corruption and violence—and presents it as a form of spectacle, at the expense of news about political, civic and public affairs' (Thussu, 2007: 8). This definition resonates with the description of Discovery's non-fiction programing:

> To make this genre work across cultures, it has to focus on celebratory accounts and be non-offensive, non-political, non-investigative or culturally constrained. This strategy explains why Discovery connects the term 'entertainment' to its genre of nonfiction or factual programs. Thus, within the category of factual programming, nonfiction entertainment is on the opposite (non-critical) end from investigative journalistic documentaries. (Fursich, 2003: 145)

This indicates that the broadcaster's programing is characterized by entertainment and a non-critical and non-controversial approach to themes, elements that are closely related to the concept of infotainment.

There are several aspects of cultural homogenization and standardization within a globalizing televisual culture. Furthermore, the concept of infotainment seems to represent a worldwide tendency leading to increased focus on certain aspects of reality within news and factual television. This book explores to what extent the concept of cultural homogenization and standardization outlined in this section relate to Discovery's televisual culture.

GLOBALIZATION OF TELEVISUAL CULTURE THROUGH HYBRIDIZATION

The concept of cultural hybridity can be used to explain the process of globalization of culture. In contrast to cultural homogenization and standardization, hybridization implies that the mixing of culture (Nederveen Pieterse, 2004) leads to the emergence of new cultural expressions and forms over time—also within television. Cultural hybridity has a presence within televisual culture as territorial cultures and language are mixed (Kraidy, 2005; Straubhaar and Duarte, 2005; Thussu, 2005), and television genres and production methods are transformed (Hill, 2005; Kilborn, 2003). Cultural hybridizing forces are also present within the transformations of the factual television genre.

The Factual Television Genre and Hybridity

The factual television genre was characterised by major changes internationally in the 1980s and 1990s. Economic, technological, and political changes in the media industry led to a mixing between 'tabloid journalism, documentary television, and popular entertainment'. In an increasingly competitive multichannel environment, television channels were interested in creating low-cost, and frequently locally produced, factual television content that appealed to large or segmented television audiences (Hill, 2005: 23). The term 'hybrid' has been frequently used when describing the mixing of genre conventions as new factual programing forms, such as docu-soap, docu-drama, reality TV, factual formats, lifestyle, and make-over programs, rapidly emerged (Chris, 2007; Hill, 2005; Born, 2004; Kilborn, 2003; Brunsdon, et al., 2001).

The changes within the factual genre show how television genres 'operate in an ongoing historical process of category formation—genres are constantly in flux, and thus their analysis must be historically situated' (Mittell, 2004: xiv). A similar development is also found in art forms and genres, as some artists and writers: 'open the territory of painting or the text so that their language migrates and is crossed with others. But there are constitutionally hybrid genres—for example, graffiti and comic strips' (Garcia Canclini, 1995: 249). The process means that aesthetic borders and categories are leaky, and high and low culture are combined (Nederveen Pieterse, 2001: 238). Thus, the mixing of traditional documentary and more popular television forms shows how the factual television genre is part of the wider process of cultural hybridity. The reality TV genre exemplifies this process as: 'television cannibalises itself in order to survive, drawing on existing genres to create successful hybrid programs, which in turn generate a "new" television genre' (Hill, 2005: 24). The factual television genre is, therefore, an area of the globalizing televisual culture in which the process of cultural hybridity has been highly visible. The factual television format represents an additional form of cultural hybridity. The factual television formats that emerged in the 1980s and 1990s exemplify how national territorial culture and a global television concept are mixed. *Big Brother* (Endemol), *Changing Rooms* (Endemol) and *Who Do You Think You Are* (Wall to Wall, UK) are some of the most well known factual television program formats.

Television formats can be developed by a broadcaster or a producer in one country and then licensed to broadcasters in another country. Although the production arrangements may vary, the copyright holder often enters into 'co-production arrangements with national producers with the intention of producing a national adaptation of a program format that is designed for that particular national market only' (Moran, 1998: 25–26). The adaptation is far more complex than traditional subtitling or dubbing in national language. The global formats represent a cultural product that allows global cultural producers to reach 'differentiated global market' through the 'strategy of glocalisation' (Robertson, 1995: 40). The inserting of national or local content within the global format framework is an attempt to glocalize. Although this means that global media and cultural producers have expanded their ability to reach national or local markets, this also means that preferences for national and local culture needs to be taken into account to succeed.

The process of cultural hybridization thereby challenges the notion of cultural homogenization and synchronization. The development of television program formats shows how this is the case also within a globalizing televisual culture. The concept of globalization of culture is far more complex, Nederveen Pieterse points out, as: 'cultural experiences, past or present, have not been simply moving in the direction of cultural uniformity and standardization' (Nederveen Pieterse, 2004: 69). As a consequence, the idea of 'global cultural synchronisation'—although not being irrelevant—does not properly address the complexity of developments in the world:

> It overlooks the countercurrents—the impact nonwestern cultures have been making on the West. It downplays the ambivalence of the globalizing momentum and ignores the role of local reception of western culture—for example, the indigenization of western elements. It fails to see the influence nonwestern cultures have been exercising on one another. It has no room for crossover culture, as in the development of 'third cultures' such as world music. It overrates the homogeniety of western culture and overlooks the fact that many of the standards exported by the West and its cultural industries themselves turn out to be of culturally mixed character if we examine their cultural lineages. (Nederveen Pieterse, 2004: 69)

This mixing and morphing of Western and non-Western cultural categories is evident in the Indian television channel Zee TV's use of a mix of Hindi and English—Hinglish. This hybrid language has been increasingly taken up by young Indians and is considered a key reason for the success of Zee TV and Indian television beyond India (Thussu, 2000; Thussu, 2005: 162). Furthermore, the Latin-American television soap *Telenovela* is considered as a classic example of cultural hybridity within television programing (Tunstall, 1977: 59; Straubhaar and Duarte, 2005: 223). The genre is characterized as a mix of Latin American cultural codes and conventions of the North American soap television. Cultural hybridization emerges within a globalizing televisual culture in factual television genre and in television formats, as will be seen in relation to Discovery's televisual culture.

GLOBALIZATION OF TELEVISUAL CULTURE THROUGH HETEROGENIZATION

Although some give emphasis to the significance of cultural homogenization and cultural hybridization in the process of globalization of televisual culture, others draw attention to the strength of the concept of cultural heterogenization. The presence of cultural heterogenization is evident, proponents argue, as national and local cultural and linguistic preferences among people are developed over time and remain strong. This corresponds with Nederveen Pieterse's description of the third paradigm of 'cultural difference' in relation to the globalization of culture. The 'cultural differentialism' perspective underlines how differences in territorial culture, language, and religion create: 'A mosaic of immutably different cultures and civilizations' (Nederveen Pieterse, 2004: 55). The concept of cultural heterogenization relates to several developments and practices within a globalizing televisual culture. The significance of this concept is demonstrated by the fact that television channels and media outlets that focus on national culture and language continue to have appeal among television audiences around the world.

THE POWER OF THE 'NATIONAL'

The deregulation and commercialization of European television in the 1990s led to a proliferation of television channels; since then, the number of satellite channels in Europe has exploded from around 100 to almost 1600 (*Screen Digest*, 2005). Morgas Spá and Lopez argue that the growth in television channels has led to the increase of regional and local television channels in many European countries: 'What is observed nowadays in Europe is a panorama of multiple forms and models of stations trying to adapt themselves and give an answer to the existent diversity (cultural, linguistic, political, demographic, geographic)' (Moragas Spa and Lopez, 2000: 43). However, already in 1990, Collins pointed out that differences in language and also culture complicated the creation of a transnational television and its audience (Collins, 1990b: 3-4). As a result of competitors launching local imitations towards the second half of the 1990s, the American thematic cable and satellite television channels have been forced to localize and adapt to local audiences (Chalaby, 2002: 192).

The argument of cultural heterogenization is closely tied to critiques of the globalization debate. Although the participants of this debate come from different academic disciplines or schools, most of them agree that 'globalization is eclipsing the nation' (Curran, 2002: 182). This view leads to a 'shared bias', Curran warns, as the discourse focuses on the exploration of how globalization is leading to change, and thereby 'understate—despite the occasional caveat—the extent of continuity with the past' (2002: 182). The national specificities are still present in the current media landscape: 'Nations have different languages, political systems, power structures, cultural traditions, economies, international links and histories. These find continuing expression in the media of different nation states' (2002: 183). It could be argued, then, that the significance of the 'national' has thereby not been sufficiently addressed in the globalization debate. Hafez picks up on this view in his critique of media globalization, pointing out that national and regional media enterprises have been 'ignored almost entirely in the globalization literature.' This, in spite of the fact that they are 'in no way inferior to the global companies and in most cases are in fact superior to them' (Hafez, 2007: 162). The cultural heterogenization argument is further supported by the fact that the national terrestrial television channels in the Nordic countries, Germany, the UK, and in other parts of the world still attract a significant share of national television audiences.

The significance of the 'national' connects with the Smith's view that the history of national cultures is of continuing significance as 'cultures are historically specific, and so is their imagery' (1995: 23). Developments within factual television programing on British national terrestrial channels show the significance of cultural heterogenization in the form of continuity with national mediated culture and its 'imagery'. *The Third World and Environment Broadcasting Project* has been examining 'non-news factual international programming' since 1989. The analysis *The World on The Box: International Issues in News and Factual Programs on UK Television 1975–2003*, showed a 40 per cent decrease in factual international programing on the four largest terrestrial channels in 2003 compared to in 1989–90:

> The decline began in the early 1990s and, although levels of total output have remained fairly consistent since then, the type of coverage offered to viewers has changed. Increasingly prominent within factual international programming are genres that reveal little about the realities of life for non-British people living outside this country: travel programmes; series following British adventurers; documentaries about 'Brits abroad' and reality game-shows in 'exotic' locations. (*Third World and Environment Broadcasting Project*, 2003)

Furthermore, the amount of factual programing on developing countries was 49 per cent lower on all UK terrestrial television in 2003—the lowest figures since 1989–90 (*Third World and Environment Broadcasting Project*, 2003). Media users' preference for national or local media content is also observed in the mobile television industry. A commercial mobile TV study conducted in Finland showed that well-known television programs offered by Finnish television channels were preferred ahead of sports and news television channels such as CNN, BBC World, and Euronews (MobileTV Nokia, 2005).

The themed pan-European television channels have been forced to address these preferences for national and local culture. The complexity of targeting a large geographical region is exemplified by how local competition limited MTV Europe's original ambitions. The pan-European television channel experienced fierce local competition in Germany and Low Countries (Belgium, Netherlands, and Luxembourg) (Roe and De Meyer, 2001: 42). Similarly, as the youth music channel The Voice was introduced in Norway with Norwegian-speaking hosts, MTV Nordic split into MTV Norway, MTV Sweden, and MTV Denmark. The splitting of video signals has allowed pan-European television channels to insert programing and advertising for specific countries, in contrast to the whole European territory. However, Chalaby points out that such localization is a strategy that 'accelerates the process of globalization', as global media enterprises are able to operate cross-nationally despite national cultural differences. The global players can thereby establish themselves in a number of markets, and compete with national television channels (Chalaby, 2002: 199). These television channels are, therefore, seen as a link, letting the local be reached by the global: 'Localised channels have an ambivalent relationship to the local. They incorporate some elements of local culture but within an international framework. While adapting to local tastes they also make global culture (and/or American in the case of MTV, CNN or Fox Kids) more accessible to local audiences' (Chalaby, 2002: 200).

MTV's original approach had limited success, and this fact leads scholars to make a more general statement: 'If the "universal language of music" has been unable fully to deliver global homogenization, then it is difficult to see how other types of services can hope to succeed except in a very limited superficial sense' (Roe and De Meyer, 2001: 42). The popularity of national television channels and the global broadcasters' strategy of localization demonstrates the strong interest for mediated national and local territorial culture and language.

2 The Rise of Discovery
'The World's Number One Nonfiction Media Company'

The global media enterprise that is Discovery consists of a range of television channel networks launched in 170 countries, and a growing number of digital media offerings distributed via the Internet and mobile telephony, targeting global segments of the world's television and media audience (Discovery, 2008a). However, its current global operations has evolved from the single cable television channel, the narrowcaster Discovery Channel (originally the Cable Education Network Incorporated), launched in the US in June 1985 to 156,000 homes (Discovery, 2006a; McElvouge, 2000). This chapter maps out how Discovery and other global media players have harnessed the economic, political, and technological developments associated with the increased global linking and intertwining of the media and communications infrastructure and media landscape to expand worldwide. Following the same strategy as other American US-based media players, Discovery first consolidated in the US, and then rapidly advanced into Europe, Latin America, and Asia. Although focusing on Discovery, the tracing of this development provides further insight into the characteristics and intensity of media globalization.

THE RISE AND CONSOLIDATION OF DISCOVERY NETWORKS US

The Discovery Channel emerged in a US media environment characterized by deregulation. By the mid-1980s, cable and satellite channels began to challenge the terrestrial broadcasters, as: 'Part of the Reagan administration's agenda was to *de*-regulate businesses and the media were no exception' (Croteau and Hoynes, 2001: 43). A number of political and economic factors contributed to the changing of the media and communications sector. The traditional broadcasting networks' position gradually weakened as the expansion of cable, new video-delivery technology, as well as rapid VCR penetration increased the fragmentation of the American media audience (Owen and Wildman, 1992: 196; Litman, 1998: 137; Crandall, 1992: 211). These developments had a radical impact as American broadcast networks saw their audience share slide from 90 per cent to under 50 per cent in the period from 1978 to 1997 (Owers et al., 1998: 35). In 2006, the 'big four' broadcasting networks, ABC, NBC, CBS and Fox, had an audience share of less than 50 per cent, and were experiencing continuing decline (Croteau and Hoynes, 2006: 131).

In the 1980s, the documentary genre in the US was perceived as an 'out-of-vogue genre' (Chris, 2002: 7). In 1987, the three major US television networks produced only 31 documentaries (Sterling and Kittross, 2002: 543). Joyce Taylor, former Managing Director, Discovery Networks Europe recalls this period: 'I mean, when John Hendricks started Discovery he was laughed at; they said "nobody watches documentaries", because there were no documentaries, or hardly, in America, you can either see that as a dead end or a huge opportunity. He saw that as a huge opportunity' (Joyce Taylor, former Managing Director, DNE, interview with author, London, 18 June, 2003). Stuart Carter, Managing Director of London-based factual television production company Pioneer Productions also describes an American television landscape lacking documentary programing:

> If you look at the American market in the 1980s, (it) had its funding decimated by Reagan. So there was nobody really in America making factual programs, or serving this need for factual information. The networks there certainly didn't, the PBS was struggling, and still continues to struggle, and it had one or two documentary strands such as *Nova*, the science series there. So, suddenly there was this vacuum and it is a bit like evolution of animals, evolution of channels, that when there is a niche to be filled, somebody comes along and fills it. So, that the problems that PBS was having created a vacuum in which John Hendricks, the founder, (. . .) said (hypothetically and not literally); 'Why don't we have an educational, factual channel?' (. . .) From what we see now, he couldn't have predicted the evolution. I'd be very surprised if he could have done that. (Carter, Managing Director of Pioneer Productions, UK, interview with author, London, 23 March, 2004)

Although Discovery Channel aimed to fill this gap in the television market, the documentary genre was 'believed by most of the industry and potential investors to be irreversibly unprofitable' (Chris, 2002: 9). John Hendricks, the founder of the Discovery Channel, started to promote the plan to create a documentary television channel to potential investors in 1982 (Chris, 2002). Hendricks talked to 211 venture capitalists before bankers Allen & Co, New York, agreed to provide $3 million in funding (Forrester, 2003a). Despite the difficulty in finding funding, Hendricks launched Discovery Channel in June, 1985 to 156,000 homes (Discovery, 2006a; Chris, 2002: 12; Forrester, 2003a).

Only a year after its launch, in 1986, the Discovery Channel was in need of additional funding. Hendricks then sold the majority of the company to

US cable operators: TCI (Tele-Communications, Inc.), Cox Cable Communications, Newhouse Broadcasting, and United Artists Entertainment (later bought by TCI) (Lewyn, 1992). Joyce Taylor, former Managing Director at Discovery Networks Europe underlines the importance of the cable operators' involvement: 'In fact, it wasn't until TCI came in, which was a major cable operator and gave it distribution, that Discovery started to work as a business' (Joyce Taylor, former Managing Director, DNE, interview with author, London, 18 June, 2003).

The biographer of media mogul John Malone (then the owner of TCI, and now a major owner of Discovery through Liberty Media, which is discussed later in this chapter) claims that: 'Hendricks had come to the ideal investor. Malone loved to watch documentaries and nature shows when he had time to watch' (Robichaux, 2002: 60). However, it seems as if it was more than a love for documentaries that motivated the cable operators. Nick Comer-Calder, former Senior VP and General Manager at Discovery Networks Europe, reflects:

> I mean, it is important to remember that when Discovery launched in 1985, cable was still in its infancy in America. It really was a baby-service (. . .). Hendricks ran out of money and essentially went to the cable operators and said: 'Look, I've run out of money' and they said 'Fine we will take over the company'. There was Liberty and Cox, Newhouse . . . but they said: 'Yeah, OK fine. We'll give you distribution on all of our networks. We'll own the company. You carry on.' Because it was great for them because they were then able to turn around to the government and authorities and say: 'Look, there is quality on cable. Cable is a good thing. We have the Discovery Channel.' And, that was a very important part of why they started off being so, kind of, government friendly. (Comer-Calder, former Senior VP and General Manager, DNE, interview with author, 4 October, 2004)

This indicates how Discovery was a strategic investment as cable operators wished to grow and solidify their presence and businesses. These powerful industry players were to play a decisive role in Discovery's growth in the US and, eventually, its worldwide expansion.

The investment in the Discovery Channel provided not only funding. In addition, the new owners also 'agreed to carry the network on its systems' (Chris, 2002: 12). The deal, therefore, proved to be of major importance for Discovery's expansion in the US, as these cable providers—Multiple System Operators (MSOs)—control the 'primary access to the audience, (and) no network can survive without substantial MSO commitment or, more commonly, an MSO ownership position ("equity")' (Jacobs and Klein, 1999: 128). With new powerful shareholders, Discovery Channel's subscription base increased substantially. TCI later increased its stake in Discovery Communications by incorporating United Artists Entertainment. By 2003,

John Malone's Liberty Media had a 50 per cent stake in Discovery Com-munications, previously held by TCI, and both Cox and Newhouse Broad-casting Corp. had around 24.8 per cent ownership of the company. The founder of Discovery, John Hendricks, now controlled a minor 3 per cent stake (Forrester, 2003a).

Although Liberty Media was smaller and less well known than con-glomerates such as News Corporation and Viacom, the company had global ambitions. By the end of the 1990s, Tele-communications Inc. (TCI) was the second-largest cable TV company in the US, reaching one-third of American homes. AT&T was the US' largest telecommunications company (Aversa, 1999). In 1998, John Malone sold TCI to AT&T for $48 billion (*The Observer*, 2004). The deal was, amongst others, made possible by the Telecommunications Act of 1996, which facilitated the possibilities for increased convergence between previously separate ser-vices. Cable companies could increasingly expand into telephony, and phone companies get involved in cable service. The TCI and AT&T merger 'helped trigger mergers in Europe' (Tunstall and Machin, 1999: 47, 49). Liberty Media had started as the programing division of TCI. However, later, when AT&T was divided into three parts, Malone bought Liberty Media back (*The Observer*, 2004; Bloomberg, 2006). Since then, Lib-erty Media has grown into an extensive enterprise of holding companies, subsidiaries, and interests in other companies owning cable and satellite channels, and digital distribution platforms internationally.

In 2003, Liberty Media took control over 92 per cent of UnitedGlobal-Com, with more than 9 million subscribers in Europe, Latin America, and the Pacific region (Grover, 2004). Liberty Global was formed in 2005 when Liberty Media International and UnitedGlobalCom were combined. Liberty Global describes itself as: 'the leading international cable opera-tor offering advanced video, telephone, and broadband Internet services.' The company offers broadband networks in 15 countries in Europe, Japan, Chile, and Australia (Liberty Global, 2008).

The Liberty Media conglomerate also had interests in other conglom-erates. Tunstall and Machin describe how Malone applied a 'mogul-to-mogul entrepreneurial style,' by 'placing bets on the success of other entrepreneurs and moguls. Some of Malone's bets were placed on small moguls, while other bets were placed on larger moguls, such as Rupert Murdoch' (Tunstall and Machin, 1999: 259–260). In 2006, Liberty Media was a shareholder of both Time Warner (Auletta, 2006), and News Cor-poration (Mermigas, 2005). However, Liberty Media and News Corpo-ration later agreed to exchange the shares Liberty Media held in News Corporation for a controlling stake in DirectTV from News Corporation (Li, 2006).

In 2005, Discovery Holding Company was incorporated. Discovery Hold-ing Company consisted, amongst others, of Liberty Media's 50 per cent ownership in Discovery Communications (DHC, 2006). In 2007, Discovery Communications swapped its ownership in Travel Media, Inc., including Travel Channel and TravelChannel.com, for Cox Communications 25 per cent ownership in Discovery. Discovery Communications, Inc. was formed as a public company in 2008, and the shareholders now consisted of Discovery Holding Company and Advance/Newhouse Communication (Discovery, 2008a). The commitments from the owners paved the way for Discovery's growth in the US throughout the 1990s (Chris, 2002; 2007). By 2003, Discovery Channel became the most widely distributed cable network in the US, reaching 88.6 million households, and by 2008 the channel reached 97 million homes (PWC, 2005: 16; Discovery, 2008b).

In contrast to other commercial companies, Discovery claims to have: 'used all of its available cash in the expansion of its business and to service its debt obligations' (DHC, 2006: 14). The revenues from the Discovery Channel US provided the necessary funding to launch new channels. In 1999, US trade magazine *Broadcasting & Cable* reported that the Animal Planet network in the US was expected to break even in 2000, but would have cost $250 million. The Discovery Health Channel was estimated to cost between $300 and $350 million to establish, and The Travel Channel a reported $270 million (Higgins, 1999). Table 2.1 illustrates the number of channels and subscribers to Discovery's television channels in the US by 2008.

Table 2.1   Subscribers to Discovery Networks US (In Millions)

Discovery Networks US	
Discovery Channel	97m
TLC	96m
Animal Planet	93m
Discovery Health	67m
Discovery Kids	59m
Science Channel	54m
Planet Green	50m
ID: Investigation Discovery	50m
Military Channel	51m
FitTV	43m
HD Theater	15m
Discovery en Espanol	8m
Discovery Familia	1m

(Source: Discovery, 2008b)

Cable and satellite television channels are often referred to as competitors to the terrestrial television channels. However, consolidation in the US media industry has led to a situation where terrestrial television channels and cable and satellite channels have the same owners. As Viacom and CBS merged in 1999, the network now has the same owner as cable channels such as MTV and Nickelodeon (Croteau and Hoynes, 2006: 85). National Geographic Television and NBC formed a joint venture company in 1996 to launch the National Geographic Channel globally (National Geographic Channel, 2006). News Corporation now owns 67 per cent of the National Geographic Channel US and around 52 per cent of National Geographic Channel International (News Corporation, 2008). After the NBC merger with Vivendi Universal, NBC Universal owned the television channels Bravo, USA, and Sci-Fi (PWC, 2005: 15). Disney, owner of Disney Channel and ESPN, bought Capital Cities/American Broadcasting Corporation (ABC) in 1995 (Croteau and Hoynes, 2006: 44). In 2006, History Channel was co-owned by Disney, General Electric/NBC, and Hearst (Croteau and Hoynes, 2006: 175). Furthermore, when examining these ownership structures, Liberty Media was formerly an indirect part owner of one of Discovery's cable television channel competitor, the National Geographic Channel, through its shareholdings in News Corporation.

DISCOVERY NETWORKS ROLLING OUT: EUROPE, LATIN AMERICA, ASIA

The Discovery Channel US went into profit in the 1980s and sought new international markets (Chris, 2002). US-originated media enterprises have had the 'capital, corporate ethos, expertise and content library,' needed to expand outside the US (Chalaby, 2002: 187). Throughout the 1990s and 2000s Discovery expanded into Europe, Latin America, and Asia.

In the 1980s and 1990s, national deregulation, privatization, and liberalization of cross border activity and ownership rules were the dominating trends in the European broadcast industry (Barker, 1999; Curran, 2002; Dahlgren, 2000; Thussu, 2000; Tunstall and Machin, 1999). These developments helped facilitate the entry of the American-originated cable and satellite television channels. In the early 1990s, trade magazine *Variety* announced that Europe was 'the next market ripe for expansion' for US cable television channels (Pedleton, 1992). At the time, a Discovery Communications spokesman pointed out the lack of possibilities in the US: 'for rapid growth we've experienced in the past,' explaining that 'European cable is at a similar place as cable was in the US' in the late 1970s (Pedleton, 1992).

In 1992, Discovery Communications, Inc. held a 20 per cent stake in Discovery Channel Europe, and the majority of the European arm was controlled by the Tele-Communications, Inc.-owned United Artists Programming Entertainment (Pedleton, 1992). Adam Singer had returned from

Tele-Communications, Inc. (TCI) in the US to manage United Artists—the joint venture that launched Discovery in Europe. Singer reflects on the American cable channels' belief that Europe, and especially the UK, was similar to their country of origin:

> The (US) market was slowly getting more mature—there had been a huge round of franchising and acquisition and consolidation of cable in the late seventies and early eighties. So, the question for a number of US cable companies was, were else could they get cheap subscribers and build them up into this kind of value? The UK seemed like an obvious place to go. They (the Brits) spoke something that approximated to a similar language, it wasn't a bad place to go, shopping wasn't too terrible, the food wasn't too awful, so they turned up and invested.
>
> They invested very much on the basis that they were building classic US cable businesses. They were not at all aware of the nature of British television but the one thing they did believe, very passionately, was that there is no difference between a US consumer and a UK consumer and that everybody wants, essentially, more television, more choice from their box. So they just saw this as a dead straight extension of the US cable model. (Singer quoted in Bonner and Aston, 2003: 420)

United Artists launched Discovery in 1989 to around 120,000, mainly UK, homes, but was soon distributed to homes in the Netherlands and Scandinavian through cable (Brown, 1998; *Variety*, 1993). But, US cable television companies experienced major differences between the US and UK: 'US cable had been built on a huge infrastructure base. Over 20 million homes had been built (out of range of a clear terrestrial signal) on the basis of a relayed television signal. That didn't exist here' (Singer quoted in Bonner and Aston, 2003: 420). The satellite channels experienced a number of difficulties such as: 'poor satellite transmissions, expensive home reception equipment, governments reluctant to grant access to their market, and a reception universe that was too small to attract advertisers and cover costs' (Chalaby, 2005b: 44). Former Managing Director at Discovery Networks Europe, Joyce Taylor, reflects on this early period:

> We (Discovery) really launched into a tiny market place. There was no satellite distribution, only cable distribution, which was minute. The first thing you have to do is to get distribution and I think we launched into 120,000 homes . . . a few in the UK and a handful in Scandinavia. We launched with acquired programing, to be perfectly honest, botched together, very low quality, but we got a service on the air, and that was the important thing. We got a service on the air, and we were charging a subscription fee and the basis of Discovery business, compared to some of the others that came later, was that this was

a dual revenue stream with subscription as the basis of the business, and, later advertising once we had enough distribution. There were other channels that came along and said: "No we will just go out free and make money from advertising." We could see that that would not work. (Joyce Taylor, former Managing Director, DNE, interview with author, London, 18 June, 2003)

However, several of the pioneering cross-border television channels had to close their services or were reestablished under a new name with new owners (Chalaby, 2005b). One of Discovery's financial advantages was that, becausee it was a private company, it could 'reinvest in new brands that do not make money in year one or two', according to Dave Leavy, Senior Vice President of corporate affairs, Discovery (Leavy quoted in Clarke, 2003: 10). This point is also emphasized by the former Managing Director of BBC Worldwide, Dick Emery:

> Because it is not a public company, and particularly because Liberty (49 per cent ownership) were interested in asset growth, not short term profit, Discovery were able to reinvest their profits in growing the business, so you had a fairly unique situation. I mean if you think about today, if you pick up a news paper or listen to the business news, business is just so short term, so that people do not get an opportunity to reinvest their profit in growing a business long term. It is all about what you can do now and that limits the ambition. And, I think that Discovery had that wonderful opportunity of shareholders who were really interested in long-term value creation, rather than short-term profit. (Emery, Former Managing Director, BBC Worldwide, interview with author, London, 16 May 2003)

The financial strength in the US allowed Discovery's international operations to overcome the high entry costs. *Variety* reported that the Discovery networks being launched in Latin America, Asia, India, and Germany lost a total of $133.6 million in 1995 (Peers, 1997). The European operation alone lost a total of $100 million in the six years from the start up in 1989 and until it went into profit in 1995 (McElvouge, 1998b). The joint venture television channel Animal Planet broke even in Europe in 2004/2005 (BBC Worldwide, 2005d). The distribution and revenues in the US was key to Discovery's international growth: 'If you get US distribution you've got a money-making machine (. . .) which helps, in essence, to build business because you will get economies of scale from having this American business to help you run your European or international business' (Joyce Taylor, former Managing Director, DNE, interview with author, London, 18 June, 2003).

In September 1993, Discovery Networks Europe launched on Sky's Astra 1C direct-to-home-satellite with a single feed for Europe (Brown,

1998; Taylor, former Managing Director, DNE, interview with author, London, 18 June, 2003). Satellite distribution gave Discovery access to another 2.5 million British homes (*Variety*, 1993). As Joyce Taylor, former senior executive at Discovery Networks Europe, remarks: 'What built our business up was the growth of Sky Television in the UK, because cable was always bumbling along; it was never taking off' (Joyce Taylor, former Managing Director, DNE, interview with author, London, 18 June, 2003). The London-based Discovery Europe could now offer one feed of eight hours of Discovery Channel programing daily to viewers in the UK, Ireland, Belgium, Denmark, Finland, Holland, Norway, and Sweden via both cable and satellite (Dawtrey, 1993).

In the next phase, new channels were introduced. The Learning Channel, later renamed Discovery Home & Leisure, was launched in the UK in 1994. After reaching profit in 1995 (McElvouge, 1998b), Discovery Networks in Europe, UK, Middle East, and Africa (EMEA) has experienced rapid growth, and by 2008 had 69 million subscribers (Discovery, 2008b). The arrival of digital satellite in 1996 allowed for increased possibility for localization though the introduction of program opt-outs, local advertising and local on-air presentation into the feeds (Brown, 1998). From 1996, Discovery Networks Europe rapidly fragmented into localized channels (*see* Table 2.2).

In addition, Discovery has launched Discovery Channel in Bulgaria; Discovery Channel and Discovery Science in Hungary; and Discovery Channel, Discovery Civilization, Discovery Sci-Trek, and Discovery Travel & Adventure in Russia. Discovery' channels in Spain and Portugal are not included in this list. These channels are not part of Discovery Networks Europe, and are served by separate feeds from the Discovery Networks Latin America/Iberia (DNLA/I) centre in Miami, US.

In Norway, Discovery Channel, Discovery Civilization, Discovery Science, and Discovery Travel & Living are—amongst others—distributed by the cable and satellite distributor Canal Digital.

Discovery Channel Germany was launched in July 1996, and Discovery Geschichte (Discovery History) was launched in 2005 in co-operation with Spiegel TV, who provides local content (Clarke, 2003; Telecoms, 2005). Meanwhile, trade magazine *Variety* announced that Discovery had made a deal with the French cable and satellite channel, Voyage, for a 'twice-weekly co-produced and co-branded programming block' (Williams, 1998). In 2004, the French platform Canalsatellite launched the 24-hour Discovery Channel in France to its 2.75 million subscribers: 'The channel in France will be created for the French market and will be French-language customised,' according to Paxton, and: 'It will follow a similar format to our other international channels by having a mix of original programming, coproductions and acquisitions' (Paxton quoted in C21 Media, 2004a).

Table 2.2   The Roll-out of Discovery in Europe

Year Launch	Channel	Platform
1987	D+	Sky Digital
1989	Discovery+1	Multi
1996	Discovery Channel	Premier
1996	Discovery Channel Czech Republic	Telepiu
1996	Discovery Channel Espana	Canal Digital
1997	Discovery Channel Europe	Sky Digital
1997	Discovery Channel France	Sky Digital
1998	Discovery Channel Germany	None
1998	Discovery Channel Greece	Polsat
1998	Discovery Channel Italia	Canal Digital
1998	Discovery Channel Polska	Sky Digital
1998	Discovery Channel Turkey	Sky Digital
1998	Discovery Civilization	Polsat
1998	Discovery Civilization	Canal Digital
1998	Discovery Civilization	Sky Digital
1998	Discovery Denmark	Polsat
1998	Discovery Health	Canal Digital
1998	Discovery Home & Leisure	Sky Digital
1998	Discovery Home & Leisure UK+1	Sky Digital
1999	Discovery Kids	CS Digital
1999	Discovery Sci-Trek	Cyfra Plus
1999	Discovery Sci-Trek	Canal Digital
2000	Discovery Sci-Trek	None
2000	Discovery Travel & Adventure	Nova Greece
2000	Discovery Travel & Adventure	Sky Digital
2001	Discovery Travel & Adventure	Sky Digital
2002	Discovery Wings	Sky Digital
2003	Discovery Channel Italy	Sky Italy
2003	Discovery Science Italy	Sky Italy
2003	Discovery Travel & Adventure It.	Sky Italy
2003	Discovery Science Italy	Sky Italy
2004	Discovery Channel France	
2005	Discovery Germany Geschicte	

(continued)

Table 2.2   continued

Year Launch	Channel	Platform
2005	Discovery Travel & Living UK	
2005	Discovery Home & Health UK	
2005	Discovery Real Time UK	
2005	Discovery Real Time France	
2005	Discovery Real Time Italy	
2005	Discovery Real Time France	
2005	Discovery HD Germany	
2006	Discovery HD UK	
2006/2007	Discovery HD Poland	DTH, ITI platform
2006/2007	Discovery Historia Poland	DTH, ITI platform

(Source: Discovery, 2003a, Screen Digest, 2003a; Screen Digest, 2003b; Ascentmedia, 2005; Informa Media, 2006)

LATIN AMERICA

In the 1990s, most of Latin American countries began to deregulate its economies. This came as a result of trade pacts such as NAFTA and MERCO-SUR, and included a gradual liberalization of restrictions on cable and satellite television and foreign ownership of media. Several major American media enterprises expanded into Latin America, either by collaborating with large local Latin American media companies, or through acquisitions of local media players. News Corporation's pan-regional satellite network Sky became allied with Televisa in Mexico and Globo in Brazil. The US-based satellite platform DirectTV bought local companies in both of these countries (Straubhaar and Duarte, 2005: 225; Sinclair, 2005: 201). Discovery launched the television channel Discovery Latin America in 1994, followed by Discovery Kids in 1996 (Straubhaar and Duarte, 2005). The two Discovery channels were launched via satellite from Miami, USA. By 1999, Discovery Communications Latin America/Iberia programed 11 channels from the company's Miami headquarters (Whitefield, 1999). The American city has become the bridgehead for Discovery's—and other satellite channels'—expansion not only into Latin America and Central America, but also the Iberian peninsula:

> Miami-based Discovery Networks Latin America/Iberia, launched in 1994, has grown to encompass a family of high-quality brands that reach more than 65 million total subscribers in five languages. Operating in 34 countries with 15 satellite feeds, Discovery Network

Latin America/Iberia oversees six brands throughout Central America, South America and the Iberian Peninsula: Discovery Channel, Discovery Kids, Animal Planet, Discovery Health, Discovery Travel & Adventure and People+Arts. (Discovery, 2008c)

Miami has a 'strategic attraction' for the television industry. Sinclair points out that the market for Spanish-speaking television programing is more regional than national, and reaches 'across both continents of the Americas and across the borders of their constituent nation-states' (Sinclair, 2003: 221). The expanding television channels Animal Planet and People+Arts (distributed in Latin America/Iberia) emerged in 1997 in the region as a result of the channel and program joint venture between BBC Worldwide and Discovery. Olga Edridge, Director Joint Ventures, BBC Worldwide, points out how the two media players have been complementing each other: 'To take two new channels so far in just five years reflects the quality of the programming supplied by the BBC and the marketing and distribution skills of Discovery. Working in partnership with Discovery has given us a major foothold in an immensely important market' (Edrige, cited in BBC, 2002b).

By 2005, the American media conglomerates Time Warner, Discovery Communications, News Corp, Viacom, and Disney had rolled out many of their global television channels in Latin America. However, despite the American presence, the large Latin American media groups such as Globo (Brazil), Televisa (Mexico), and Cisneros (Venezuela) offer competition. Their television channels offer a large amount of local programing. Also, television channels created by 'local and national cable systems' represent competition (Straubhaar and Duarte, 2005: 241–242). However, Discovery has been able to attract 'middle class viewers' in Latin America (Straubhaar and Duarte, 2005: 229).

INDIA

In 1991, Indian television consisted of one channel, Doordarshan. A combination of the emergence of satellite distribution technology, a growing national economy, and gradual integration into the global market, coupled with an expanding middle class with money to spend, have made India a particularly large and attractive market also for US-originated satellite television channels. In 1998, almost 70 cable and satellite television channels had been launched in India. Among these were the large media and television operators STAR, BBC, Discovery, MTV, Sony, and Disney (Thussu, 1999). Discovery took advantage of these new opportunities and launched in India in 1995 (Thussu, 2006). Animal Planet was introduced to the Indian television market in 1998, and Discovery Travel and Living started in 2004 (Pinto, 2005). By 2007, India had become one of the largest television markets in the world and Discovery's television channels formed part of the total of the more than 300 digital channels operating in India (Thussu, 2007). Several of these channels are part of joint ventures and collaborations between Indian and large global and international media conglomerates (Thussu, 2006). One of the significant partnerships was formed in 2002 when Sony Entertainment Television and Discovery formalized 'The One Alliance'—a major television joint venture:

> To expand its nationwide distribution network, the company initiated a strategic partnership with another leading channel, Sony Entertainment Television India to form the One Alliance. The One Alliance substantially strengthened Discovery's cable distribution throughout the geographical landscape of India. (IBEF, 2005)

The powerful 'One Alliance' distributes the three Discovery channels and Sony Entertainment Television's channels, as well as MTV. The current Indian television market is dominated by a television 'triumvirate', of which the Sony/Discovery joint venture is part (*see* Table 2.3).

ASIA AND CHINA

Discovery Networks Asia launched in 1994, the same year as the network's debut in Latin America. Since then, Discovery's television channels have increased their presence and distribution in South East Asia region rapidly. By 2008, Discovery Networks Asia's television channels targeted 23 countries in the region, with 16 different feeds in eight languages reaching

Table 2.3　Indian Television's Triumvirate

Star Bouquet	Sony/Discovery	Zee-Turner
Star Plus	SET MAX	Zee TV
Star News	Discovery	Zee Cinema
Star Movies	Animal Planet	Zee News
Star World	CNBC	Cartoon Network
Star Gold	AXN	CNN
Star Sport	NDTV	HBO
Vijay		
Channel (V) India		
National Geographic		
Adventure One		
ESPN		

(Source: Thussu, 2006: 163)

a cumulative audience of 325 million subscribers (Discovery Channel Asia, 2008). According to trade magazine *Variety*, Liberty Media, the co-owner of Discovery, has been contributing to the television networks expansion in Asia: 'Liberty's 45% stake in jupiter Telecommunications has given Discovery cable distribution in Japan and other Asian territories' (Freeman, 2004). The television industry in Asian countries has been subject to similar transformations in the form of deregulation and privatization as seen in Latin America and Europe. Transnational corporations expanded into these new markets through collaborations and joint-ventures with national and regional media companies (Jin, 2007: 193). Although global television channels have entered and consolidated their presence in most countries in South East Asia, mainland China has proved a more difficult territory to enter.

News Corporation's Star TV entered China in 1996 via investments in the joint venture Phoenix TV. Since then, Star TV has expanded, and also launched a 24-hour television entertainment channel, Xing Kong Wei Shi, in Guangdong. This was made possible partly due to News Corporation's distribution of China Central Television's English-language channel, CCTV 9, on Fox Cable Network in the USA (Chan, 2005: 181–182). Chinese authorities have gradually reduced control over the media system: International satellite channels are, to a certain degree, allowed to broadcast into China, and international media enterprises can invest in the Chinese media industry under certain conditions (Jin, 2007). However, Shi points out that 'the direct, legalized access to global media like CNN or MTV is restricted either to some peripheral 'experimental zones' (Guangdong province) or to privileged locations (such as five-star hotels)' (Shi, 2005: 34). Similarly, Chen points out, television channels such as BBC World, Discovery Channel, MTV Mandarin, and CNN are distributed in Greater China, but have 'landing rights in three-star or better hotels and selected entities in China' (Chan, 2005: 181). Already in 1995, Discovery–branded programs were broadcast on China Central Television (CCTV) as part of a programing partnership (Burgi, 1995). A key strategy for Discovery has been to place Discovery branded programs on Chinese cable systems. According to trade magazine *Variety*, Discovery has two-hour program blocks on 22 regional cable television systems in Chinese cities, reaching over 45 millions households (Osborne, 2002). Programing blocks from Animal Planet reach 35 million households. Furthermore, Discovery Networks Asia announced the opening of an office in Beijing in 2002 (Guider, 2002). The Discovery Networks Asia has collaborated with the major Chinese media corporation Shanghai Media Group (SMG). MTV Networks, CNBC, Universal Music Group, and Sony also have business relationships with SMG (Siklos, 2006). Discovery and SMG organized the First-Time Filmmakers project in China, and the China HDTV Industry Development Forum in 2006 (Borton, 2004; China Daily, 2006). *Forbes* reported that the two media companies have held talks to form a joint venture to create digital cable television networks across China (Forbes, 2005).

US VS. INTERNATIONAL

Discovery Communications, Inc. argues that they seek growth mainly outside the US. According to McCall, president of Discovery Networks International: 'The intent is that the international piece of the business will overtake the US in revenue and profitability in another 10–12 years' (McCall quoted in Thal-Larsen, 2003). By 2008, Discovery's television channels outside the US had the numbers of subscribers shown in Table 2.4.

Jonathan Hewes, Deputy Chief Executive and Head of International Production at the London-based factual television production company, Wall to Wall, explains how international growth is becoming increasingly important:

> In terms of business, I think they've (Discovery) been phenomenally successful in terms of growth. It is quite testing times for them (. . .). One of the problems they face is that when you are growing, particularly in America, when you are growing your cable universe, every year you grow the number of households you're in, and your share goes up and the audience goes up. Then you hit a peak where you can't be in any more homes, you've hit the . . . ceiling, you know (. . .). As a business it is still expected to set aggressive growth targets, and so how do they achieve that? (Hewes, Deputy Chief Executive and Head of International Production, UK, interview with author, London, 23 March, 2004)

Table 2.4   Subscribers to Discovery Networks International (in Millions)

Discovery Channel	252m
Animal Planet	222m
Discovery Travel & Living	166m
Discovery Home & Health	33m
Discovery Science	33m
DMAX Germany/UK	41m
Discovery Kids	23m
Discovery real Time/Real Time Extra	30m
People+Arts	21m
Discovery World	17m
Discovery Turbo	11m
TLC Canada	8m
Discovery HD	4m
Discovery Geschichte/Historia	2m
Discovery Civilisation	2m

(Discovery, 2008b)

Viacom shares a similar optimism in relation to MTV's international expansion. According to CEO of Viacom, Tom Freston: 'The average cable and satellite penetration in the international market place is about 35 to 40 per cent, where the US market was in the mid-1980s' (Freston quoted in Gunther, 2006: 80). Table 2.5 shows the revenues for Discovery's revenue in the US and internationally.

The *Financial Times* reported that Discovery's international side of the business grew faster than in the US (Thal-Larsen, 2003). In 2004, international revenues were 25 per cent, and in 2005 overseas revenues accounted for 27 per cent of total revenue (DHC, 2006). Discovery has expanded through securing as broad a subscriber base as possible for each of its channels by entering into affiliation agreements. The strong financial position in the US proves to be crucial also in this, as: 'In certain cases, Discovery has made cash payments to distributors in exchange for carriage or has entered into contractual arrangements that allow the distributors to show certain of Discovery's channels for extended free periods' (DHC, 2006).

Although Discovery is rolling out its television channel brands across the world, the audience ratings and market shares of pan-European television channels are small compared to the terrestrial broadcasters. For example, Discovery Channel had a share of 1.9 per cent of the total weekly television audience in Norway in week 38, 2008. During this week, the Discovery Channel television series *Mythbusters* was the most popular of the channel's programs, with an audience of 41,000. In comparison, the Norwegian public service broadcaster's main television channel, NRK1, had an audience share of 28.2 per cent the same week, and the most watched program on the channel achieved over 1.1 million viewers (TNS-Gallup, 2008). Similarly, in Denmark, Discovery Channel had a market share of 1 per cent of the total daily television audience during week 38 in 2008. The main Danish national public service television channel DR1 had a total daily audience share of 23 per cent during the same week (TNS-Gallup TV-Meter, 2008). However, it is by considering the combined weight of the multi-channels that shows the impact on the broadcasting environment. Table 2.6 shows the development in the Nordic countries from 1997 to 2007. The terrestrial

Table 2.5   Global Revenue (In Million Dollars)

	2001	2002	2003
International networks	345	416	358
International ventures	48	58	51
U.S. networks	992	1.350	1.210
Total global revenue	1.560	1.999	1.710
International as % of total revenue	22%	24%	24%

(Source: Liberty Media Annual Reports quoted in Freeman, 2004)

Table 2.6   The Five Television Channels With the Largest Market Shares[a,b], 1997–2007 (Per Cent)

Channel	Status	1997	1998	1999	2000	2001	2002	2003	2004	2005	2006	2007
Denmark												
TV2	Public	39	38	36	36	35	35	35	35	36	34	33
DR1	Public	28	29	28	29	28	28	30	30	28	28	28
DR2	Public	1	2	3	3	3	4	4	4	5	5	5
TV3	Private	11	10	11	9	8	7	7	6	5	5	5
3+	Private	1	2	3	3	4	4	4	4	4	4	4
Other channels		20	19	19 ·	20	22	22	20	21	22	24	25
Total		100	100	100 ·	100	100	100	100	100	100	100	100
Finland												
MTV3	Private	44	42	42	40	39	37	38	35	33	29	26
YLE TV1	Public	24	24	23	23	23	24	23	25	25	24	24
YLE TV2	Public	22	21	20	20	20	22	20	20	19	20	17
Nelonen	Private	2	7	10	12	12	12	11	12	11	12	10
Subtv	Private	*	*	*	1	1	1	2	3	4	5	6
Other channels		5	4	5	6	6	6	6	6	8	8	14
Total		100	100	100	100	100	100	100	100	100	100	100

(continued)

Table 2.6 continued

Iceland

RUV	Public	50	46	43	42	41	41	43	43	35	44	45	49
Stöð 2 2	Private	39	43	40	36	29	29	29	29	36	34	27	31
Skjár 1 3	Private	*	..	2	15	19	20	21	22	22	17	21	18
Other channels	Private	11	11	15	7	11	9	7	7	7	5	7	2
Total		100	100	100	100	100	100	100	100	100	100	100	100

Norway

NRK1	Public	41	38	36	38	39	40	41	40	40	38
TV2	Private	31	30	31	32	32	30	30	29	30	29
TVNorge	Private	8	9	9	10	10	10	10	11	10	9
TV3	Private	7	7	8	7	6	6	6	6	6	5
NRK2	Public	2	3	3	3	3	3	3	4	4	3
Other channels		11	13	13	10	10	10	10	10	10	16
Total		100	100	100	100	100	100	100	100	100	100

Sweden

TV4	Private	27	27	27	28	25	25	25	23	22	22
SVT1	Public	22	22	20	25	27	25	25	24	22	19
SVT2	Public	26	26	24	17	16	15	15	14	14	13
TV3	Private	10	10	11	11	10	10	10	10	10	9
Kanal 5	Private	6	6	6	7	8	8	9	9	9	8
Other channels		9	9	12	12	14	17	16	20	23	29
Total		100	100	100	100	100	100	100	100	100	100

Table 2.6   continued

ᵃDefinition of daily reach: Denmark and Sweden: share of viewers who have watched at least 5 consecutive minutes; Finland: based on one minute's viewing; Norway: at least 30 seconds viewing up to 1999, one minute from year 2000; Iceland: share of respondents who tuned into the stations per day on average (surveys in Oct/Nov, except for 2007:June).
ᵇAge of television audience comprising the market shares: Denmark: age 4+/3+; Finland: age 10+; Iceland: age 12-80; Norway: age 12+; Sweden: age 3+
(Source: Harrie, 2009)

television channels are named and the international and global cable and satellite channels are found in the category 'other channels'.

Although the national broadcasters still have the largest market share when comparing the various television channels, the cable and satellite television channels form a significant part of the television landscape in Nordic countries, especially Sweden and Denmark.

NARROWCASTING TO A FRAGMENTING GLOBAL AUDIENCE

The cable and satellite channel's narrowcasting represented a redefinition of television audience. The general entertainment family broadcaster was described as an 'endangered species', and no new channel was launched in Europe that aimed to follow the conventional general programing diet in 2000 (Papathanassopoulos, 2002: 149). The increased specialization in media content is a result of the growing numbers of media players and advertisers preoccupation with 'targeted demographics'. In contrast to traditional mass media, such as broadcasters, cable and satellite channels are more preoccupied with the mapping of television audience's characteristics, such as earnings, age, and gender (Croteau and Hoynes, 2006: 206–207). Discovery's relationship with its audience—especially a male audience—gives insight into this general shift. Table 2.7 indicates the extent to which Discovery Channel researched its audience in the US in 2005, and describes the interests of this audience which is of great significance to advertisers.

The focus on a male audience is further underlined in the audience survey by Nielsen Media Research: 'Discovery Channel consistently delivers key demographics—Season after season, Discovery Channel proves itself to be one of cable's elite networks. Discovery consistently ranks among the top ten networks for delivery of key Adults and Men 18–49 and 25–54'

Table 2.7   Network viewer product usage/Lifestyle profile

Base: Adults 18+	
Electronics	Index
Household Owns an Audio Equalizer	125
Own a Projection TV Set	122
Own a PDA/Cell Phone Combination	117
Own an HDTV	117
Household Owns a Digital Camera	116
Household Owns a Home Theater/Entertainment System	114
Auto	
Heavy User of Leather & Vinyl Protectants (4+ Times/Last 12 Months)	122
Own a Full-Size Pickup	121
Bought a New Domestic Auto/Last 12 Months	115
Service Your Own Vehicle	114
Own a Luxury Vehicle	113
Home	
Done Woodworking/Last 12 Months	126
Bought a Recliner/Last 12 Months	125
Personally did a Home Improvement Job/Last 12 Months	117
Personally did a Home Remodeling Job/Last 12 Months	114
Bought Home Office Furniture/Last 12 Months	114

(Source: MRI Spring 2005 quoted in One TV World, 2006)

(Nielsen Media Research, 2001-2002 [Season 10/01/01–9/29/02] quoted in One TV World, 2006). Furthermore, five of the eleven programs in Table 2.8 targeting the Men 25–54 demographic have also been scheduled on Discovery Channel UK and Discovery Channel Norway in prime time.

The size of the narrowcaster's audience is far smaller than the mass audience the US broadcasters have traditionally catered for. Discovery Channel US had an average of 1.09 million viewers in prime time in February, 2006. The network's series *Dirty Jobs* had an average rating of 1.7 million, and the series *MythBusters* had an average of 1.4 million viewers per premiere episode. The Learning Channel had an average of 719,000 viewers in prime time in February, 2006 (Crupi, 2006a). Although Discovery Channel is the main television brand, the portfolio of channels attempt to serve as a vehicle for advertisers who wish to target different demographics, explains Judith McHale, President of Discovery Communications:

Table 2.8   Demographic targeted programing

Men 25-54 (years of age)

    Deadliest Catch

    Dirty Jobs

    Going Tribal

    Roush Racing: Driver X

    SOS: Coast Guard Rescue

    American Chopper

    American Hot Rod

    Monster House

    Monster Garage

    Myth Busters

Women 25-54 (years of age)

    The Haunting

    Lived to Tell

    Discovery Daytime

(Source: One TV World, 2006)

> A key part of our strategy is that an advertiser can buy either very targeted audiences—say you are in the science area, you can buy Discovery Science—or you can buy across the portfolio. And on some nights, all our channels together almost exceed a broadcast network's reach, in terms of the demographics and households. So it's as easy to get that broad reach by buying my 14 channels as it is buying one broadcast network. (McHale quoted in Carugati, 2003)

Planet Green is one of the most recent media initiatives, demonstrating how the company targets a specific audience. The Planet Green television channel was launched in 2008 and is described as a '24-hour eco-lifestyle' television channel (formerly known as Discovery Home). The target audience is adults aged 18–54 and 'particularly students, new parents, and young baby boomers'. The initiative includes the Web sites TreeHugger.com and PlanetGreen.com, as well as Discovery Education Green, offering lessons on environmental issues (Discovery, 2008a). The Planet Green television channel offers 'eco-tainment' programing according to Eileen O'Neill, the General Manager of the channel (O'Neill quoted in Stelter, 2008). Program hosts include rock musician Tommy Lee, rapper Chris 'Ludacris' Bridges, and actors Leonardo De Caprio and Adrien Greiner (HBO series, *Entourage*) (Levin, 2008b). The factual program forms include reality and cooking shows and home improvement programs (Leonard, 2008), as well as a weekly news program on environmental issues.

Although Discovery has launched a range of new television channels to appeal to different segments of the television audience, the programing content of these channels is not necessarily new. The control over programing has proved to be a key advantage when launching new digital channels. Each new digital channel in the US had one-tenth of the programing budget compared to the established Discovery and TLC, according to US media consultancy *Kagan Research* (Romano, 2004). These digital channels were branded with the Discovery logo and their media content was, to a large degree, dependent on library programs from Discovery Channel, TLC, Animal Planet, and Travel Channel (Petrozzello, 1998). Although acknowledging that the huge library of programing helped launch the digital channels in the US, President at Discovery Networks US Jonathan Rodgers, claimed that: 'After that, we need to go back into the original programming mode like we do on our analogue channels. But, having this luxury of a huge base of programming allows us to be ahead of most of our competitors.' (Rodger quoted in Petrozzello, 1998).

While bandwidth was the scare resource in the analogue world, people's attention is the scare resource in the digital television environment (Taylor, 2002). Discovery Networks US and Europe address the audience by creating new channels, to 'reach a wider range of viewers by having channels like Discovery Health or Animal Planet, which attract a different audience from Discovery Channel' (Taylor, 2002). However, although taking up as much 'shelf space' as possible to attract the audience may seem to be the best strategy, the risk is that the main channel gets weakened (Davies, 2002). Although Discovery has rapidly expanded into a portfolio of channels, National Geographic launched only one spin-off channel, Adventure One.

The two competitors have chosen a different approach when expanding globally. According to George Jeffrey, Managing Director, National Geographic Europe, the risk of creating a giant footprint model is that:

> if you dilute your inventory to the nth degree then [compromising brand integrity] will happen . . . We were cautious about going down the Discovery track . . . There aren't very many economic advantages to spreading yourself thinly and it might well be you dilute the strong proposition you've currently got. (Jeffrey quoted in *Informa Media*, 2003)

However, the main point is that narrowcasting is a vehicle to target and reach the desired audience. Errol Pretorius, Director of Advertising Sales at the National Geographic Channel's comment highlights the logic of narrowcasting: 'Don't count the people you talk to, talk to the people who count. I'd rather talk to a thousand people who can afford to buy a new Volvo, than talk to a million people who can't' (Pretorius quoted in Chalaby, 2002: 201).

Discovery and National Geographic Channel are the world's main factual television narrowcasters, and major providers of factual media content. Their approach is to address a transnational but targeted audience, reflecting the way in which, through transnational communication, people are 'increasingly being addressed across national boundaries on the basis of their purchasing power' (Thussu, 2000: 79). Similarly, the former Managing Director of BBC Worldwide, Dick Emery, points out that Discovery has 'struck a chord, with a valuable demographic' globally (Emery, Former Managing Director, BBC Worldwide, interview with author, London, 16 May 2003). In Europe, 46 per cent of Discovery's viewers had a high medium income, 23 per cent had a medium income, and only 20 per cent in the category of low income (Discovery Mediapack, 2003d). The total audience in Europe is mixed with only a small skew towards the male audience: 52 per cent male and 48 per cent female (Discovery Mediapack, 2003c). In Latin America, it is the elite that subscribes to MTV, HBO, CNN, Disney, and Discovery, as 'the mass audience not only tolerate, but rather enjoy seeing locally made programming (much of it not at all exportable), material which is nationally produced and distributed' (Sinclair, 2005: 212). This is supported by market research company Synovate, who reports that Discovery Channel is the most-watched television channel by 'affluent adults' in Brazil (23.5 per cent) and Mexico (18.4 per cent), and is the second most watched television channel by this group in Argentina (Marketing Charts, 2007). The Latin American television audience is stratified, and 'partly for this reason, the different levels are not mutually exclusive—that is, the build-up of global channels in Latin America does not drive out local, national, and regional programming, any more than the rise of regional programming could ever have hoped to replace the global' (Sinclair, 2005: 212). As in Latin America, Discovery is targeting the wealthiest audience segment in South East Asia. A marketing research survey conducted in Discovery's 'key markets' Bangkok, Hong Kong, India, Jakarta, Kuala Lumpur, Manila, Seoul, Singapore, Sydney, Taipei, and Tokyo claims that Discovery Channel is the most watched regional channel among: 'Business Decision Makers (BDMs), Professional, Manager, Executive, Business Men (PMEBs) and high net worth individuals. The channel also reaches 30% of top management viewers on a weekly basis' (*Indiantelevision*, 2006).

The consequences of narrowcasting have been especially visible within children's television in many parts of the world. Discovery is also active in this audience segment through its Discovery Kids television channel. The American terrestrial channels had 98 per cent share of the children television audience in the 1980s. This share has been drastically reduced. In 2006, the American terrestrial channels had around 15 per cent of this audience, and the cable channels drew 77 per cent of the youngest audience (Alexander and Owers, 2007: 59). Also in Europe, the themed cable and satellite television channels Cartoon Network, Nickelodeon, and Disney's television channels Disney Channel, Playhouse Disney, Toon Disney, and Jetix (76 per cent owned by Disney) have contributed to the fragmentation of the youngest European television audience. The children's audience has increasingly been considered as a commercially valuable demographic. Television for children plays a more and more central role as a platform for promoting merchandising such as toys, clothes, computer games, books, and DVDs. From the mid-1990s, the introduction of the American originated commercial cable and satellite channels represents the main growth of dedicated children's television channels in Western Europe (Iosifidis, et al., 2005: 145–146).

In Europe, the youngest television audience is moving from the main terrestrial television channels to the dedicated television channels. According to the British regulatory body Ofcom, the traditional national terrestrial channels in the UK, France, Germany, and Sweden, but also Canada, Australia, and USA have difficulty in competing for the youngest television audience. The largest reduction was seen in Sweden, where the share of the children's audience was reduced from 81 to 58 per cent from 2002 to 2006. In the UK, the viewing of the youngest audience on five main terrestrial television channels was reduced from 65 to 46 per cent in the same period. The migration from terrestrial television channels were the lowest in Canada, from 24 to 18 per cent, and in the US, from 28 to 24 per cent. Ofcom points out that in these two countries the 'dedicated channels have long dominated children's viewing.' (Ofcom, 2007: 35) Several of the European terrestrial channels have responded to this competition by launching their own children's channels. The Swedish public service broadcaster launched Barnkanalen; the BBC started CBeeBies and CBBC; KiKa was launched by the German ARD and ZDF, and in late 2007 the Norwegian public service broadcaster launched NRK Super. The trend in Europe is to launch dedicated children's channels instead of showing traditional television programing segments on the main terrestrial channels (Iosifidis, et al., 2005: 145–146). As with the proliferation of cable television channels for adults, the launch of both new national and global dedicated channels and outlets for children has led to a demand for large quantities of television programming. Just as Discovery's library of programing enabled it to diversify via new digital channels to reach a global, but fragmented, audience, so too it provided the content with which to exploit new media technologies such as the Internet and mobile telephony.

DIGITAL DISCOVERY

Although Discovery's global tier of television channels forms the backbone of the company's distribution of media content, at the beginning of the 21st century the company has increased its efforts to position itself in the digital environment such as the Internet and within mobile telephony. This had become a common strategy of all large media enterprises as they attempted to use the Internet to harness the possible benefits of synergy from their various operations (Thussu, 2006: 217). The division Discovery Digital Media consists of Web sites such as Discovery.com, Howstuffworks.com, Petfinder. com, treehugger.com, Discovery Mobile, and Discovery On-Demand. Discovery's video library and television programing is central in the expansion on digital platforms as Discovery aims to 'delivering an extensive library of high-quality programming and footage via the web, mobile devices, video-on-demand and broadband channels' (Discovery, 2008d).

Atlas—a costly, high-profile factual television programing series and media project distributed on a variety of platforms—represented a showcase for Discovery's capabilities in the digital environment. This factual television series was distributed throughout the Discovery Channel and Discovery Channel HD television networks throughout the world, on Blu Ray and HD DVD, and through online retailers iTunes and Amazon. Furthermore, a mobile Atlas Web site and related podcasts were developed, and the Atlas television programing was also incorporated in Discovery's education service, Cosmeo (Klaassen, 2006).

Discovery.com, Discovery's main Web site, features video clips, news, and television schedules for its various channels around the world, and the site also has an important function as a portal for the enterprise's other online services and offerings. One of the key areas of the company's expansion of digital services is through its education division, Discovery Education. One of the range of services it offers is Discovery Education streaming, which has become a major online service within the teaching sector. It offers video-on-demand teaching material of up to 7,700 full-length videos and 77,000 video clips, audio files, and a range of other services used by around one million American teachers (Discovery Education, 2008). Schools pay between $1,500 and $2,000 to get access to Discovery's library of educational material (Barnes, 2006).

The online environment also opens up for new possibilities for collaboration. In 2006, Discovery and the online company Google decided to work together: Discovery provided video segments of American national parks for the Google Earth Internet service. This initiative demonstrated the potential for commercial online partnerships: from Google Earth, users could move to a Web site controlled by Discovery, on which Discovery could sell advertising. Google earned revenue from Google Earth from advertising, and from consumers downloading more advanced versions of the software. Furthermore, Discovery's participation was seen as a way to encourage the use of Google Earth instead of competing mapping services provided by Microsoft and Yahoo (Shin, 2006). The launch of Discovery–branded video channels through Google's subsidiary, YouTube, signals a more aggressive expansion into the online environment (*see* Table 2.9). These online channels have the same brand names as the traditional television channels.

The channels offer short video segments from television programs such as *MythBusters* and *Dirty Jobs*, and Discovery will gradually introduce video clips of programing from the UK, Continental Europe, Latin America, and Asia.

Table 2.9   Discovery's Nine Branded YouTube Destinations

Discovery Channel	youtube.com/discoverychannel
TLC	youtube.com/tlc
Animal Planet	youtube.com/animalplanet
Planet Green	youtube.com/planetgreen
Discovery Health	youtube.com/discoveryhealth
Science Channel	youtube.com/sciencechannel
Military Channel	youtube.com/militarychannel
Investigation Discovery	youtube.com/discoveryid
TURBO	youtube.com/turbochannel

(Discovery, 2008b)

Discovery has also expanded through the acquisition of online services and Web sites. In 2007, Discovery acquired Howstuffworks.com—a Web site with information about the world—for $250 million. Howstuffworks. com has an average of 11 million unique visitors each month. This acquisition is an example of Discovery's strategy to exploit possibilities for synergy between its audiovisual library and articles from Howstuffworks.com. The Howstuffworks.com Web site has the digital rights to 30,000 books, 800,000 images and 180,000 maps; Discovery has a video library of more than 100,000 hours. The aim is to merge the two companies' media content to offer a 'video wikipedia', according to Jeff Arnold, CEO of Howstuffworks.com (Arnold quoted in Discovery, 2007a). The same year, Discovery acquired Treehugger.com which is, according to Discovery 'the leading eco-lifestyle website, dedicated to driving sustainability mainstream'. This site forms part of Discovery's Planet Green project in which the television channel Planet Green in the US also features (Discovery, 2008b).

Major players within the media and communications industry believe the distribution of media content, games and music on mobile telephones has huge financial potential. The number of mobile television subscribers is predicted to reach 462 million globally within 2013. The development of mobile television distribution networks and a predicted increase in the amount of mobile television content will stimulate such growth in subscribers (ABI Research, 2008). The total global mobile entertainment market—consisting of music, games and mobile television—is estimated to increase from $20 billion in 2007 to $64 billion by 2012 (Juniper Research, 2008). Since 2003, media and communications players such as television broadcasters and program producers together with advertisers and mobile phone enterprises have offered television content to users of mobile phones, often focusing their efforts to reach users of 3G phones (Goggin, 2006: 173).

In 2003, the US carrier Sprint pioneered the launch of MobiTV with a number of television channels including MSNBC (Snider, 2008). The collaboration between mobile telephony players and media content providers is no coincidence:

> One area in which the cell phone operators lack experience is cultural content. From the early 1990s telcos have partnered with pay television operators, but with the intensification of the commercial Internet they also developed myriad arrangements with media and entertainment industries and the newer interactive multimedia and Internet industries. Such developments have become more commonplace since 2000 as cell phone operators have sought to 'grow' their markets and find new forms of revenue. As cell phone users have slowly become audiences to entertainment, news, and information, so those who have specialised in shaping and servicing such viewers and readers have come to the fore, such as broadcasters. (Goggin, 2006: 176)

Mobile television is seen as a way to reach the valuable demographic group of 18–34 year-olds for content providers such as broadcasters and cable and satellite television channels, as they are the main users of mobile television (Dawson, 2007: 233; Orgad, 2006).

By 2006, Discovery provided media content for mobile hardware in 11 countries, launched direct-to-consumer WAP (Wireless Application Protocol) portals in the UK and Asia, and a broadband portal in the UK, as well as video-on-demand in 10 countries. Discovery Mobile TV was made available through the telecom Vodafone and its partners in UK, France, Sweden, the Netherlands, Spain, and Portugal, with media content in English, French, Spanish, and Portuguese. Discovery Mobile TV is drawing on television programing from Discovery Channel, Animal Planet, and Discovery Science with the aim to give consumers 'flexibility to enjoy Discovery programming wherever or whenever they choose' (Telecoms, 2006). Nokia is one of the mobile phone producers who have been most active in supporting and encouraging mobile television (Goggin, 2006: 178).

In 2006, Discovery entered into collaboration with Nokia and Discovery's content featured on some of Nokia's mobile telephones (Nokia, 2006). In the US, Discovery offers Discovery Mobile, a 24-hour mobile programing network distributed by most of the mobile carriers in the US. The network offers 'made-for-mobile' shorter or longer program segments from various television program genres (Discovery, 2008d). Both terrestrial and cable and satellite channels are increasingly using the mobile telephony platform. The American telecommunications company AT&T offers distribution of a range of mobile channels such as CBS Mobile, CNBC, Comedy Central, ESPN Mobile TV, FOX Mobile, MSNBC, MTV, NBC2Go, Nickelodeon, and CNN Mobile in the US (AT&T Mobile TV, 2008).

Discovery's attempts to move media content between platforms from television to mobile telephony, video-on-demand, and the Internet reflects their strategy to exploit synergy and to develop commercial digital environments that attract users and advertisers alike. Howstuffworks.com aims to serve both, according to Jeff Arnold, CEO of the company: 'As a result of this acquisition, information-seeking consumers benefit from a richer, multimedia experience, while our advertisers and business partners have new opportunities to reach targeted audiences of engaged consumers' (Arnold quoted in Discovery, 2007a). The expansion of cable and satellite television channels provided the opportunity for advertisers to target more specific markets and online retailing has opened up the possibility to monitor individuals' consumption in a more detailed way (Thussu, 2006: 218).

In 2007, Discovery decided to close its 103 Discovery Channel Stores. This signaled a change in Discovery's retail strategy, which is symptomatic for the increased preoccupation with online retailing: 'By eliminating our owned and operated brick-and-mortar storefronts, which are cost-intensive and complicated businesses, Discovery can focus its efforts on high-growth e-commerce and licensing operations,' according to David Zaslav, President and CEO of Discovery Communications (Discovery 2007b). The online DiscoveryStore.com sells Discovery products such as DVDs, books, toys, and games. The site had more than 12 million visitors in 2007 and has developed partnerships with the giant e-commerce companies Amazon.com and eBay. Amazon is among the online retailers that map customers' buying patterns:

> Many content and technology providers in interactive media, which personalize content for individuals (e.g., TiVo, Amazon.com, nytimes.com) use market basket or shopping cart analysis methods that rely on such associational rules. For example, Amazon.com uses these associational rules to determine what might be of interest to an individual based on the data that they have about people who have purchased or scanned similar products. (Baruh, 2007: 197)

Data on customer and user behavior is collected through the use of 'cookies', information about customers' movements on the Internet. If the customer's web browser prevents the use of 'cookies', he or she is not allowed access to, for example, the New York Times' web site: 'In order to access our Web site, your Web browser must accept cookies from NYTimes.com' (NYTimes, 2008). Similarly, Amazon.com does not permit a customer to make purchases from the site under these circumstances:

> If your web browser is set to refuse cookies from our website, you will not be able to complete a purchase or take advantage of essential website features, such as storing items in your Shopping Basket or receiving personalised recommendations. As a result, we strongly encourage you

to configure your web browser to accept cookies from our website. (Amazon, 2008)

But the digital media user can evade commercial pressures to some extent. Pop-up advertising online can be blocked and TiVo technology challenges the traditional television advertising business model (Thussu, 2006: 219). TiVo technology has been branded as 'Darth Vader' by some people in the advertising sector, fearing the newfound power of television viewers to control their viewing. One way to place advertising within the TiVo environment has been to create an area for watching television advertising 'on-demand' (Turow, 2006: 109). Another corporate strategy to tackle the television viewers' ability to avoid traditional television advertising through TiVo is by linking the advertising closer to the television content, to stop viewers skipping the advertising between programs. Discovery was described in *Adweek* as blurring the boundaries between program and advert with its television program series *Lobster Wars*, which was sponsored by the online recruitment agency Monster.com:

> Earlier this fall, the Discovery Channel made its first foray into the somewhat murky waters of what has come to be known as pod-busting, a catchall for the creative executions networks are experimenting with to keep viewers tuned in during a premiere episode of *Lobster Wars*, viewers were asked to ponder the size of the largest sea-dwelling arthropod on record, a query sponsored by Monster.com. Heading out of the break, Discovery hit viewers with the answer: 44 pounds, 6 ounces and 3 feet, 6 inches long. (Crupi, 2007: 10)

Similarly, the television channel linked an advertisement for the beer brand Guinness with the factual television series *Mythbusters*, according to the *Wall Street Journal*:

> During the broadcast of its program "Mythbusters" last spring, Discovery Channel ran a brief ad for Guinness beer designed to echo the theme of the program, which uses science to test the validity of urban legends. One character in the ad asked another whether it was a "myth that Guinness only has 125 calories." After he is told the calorie count was accurate, a voiceover says: 'Mythbusters,' sponsored by Guinness. (Vranica, 2007)

Because of the TiVo challenge, broadcasters and advertisers are experimenting with new ways of targeting viewers. This mixing exemplifies the tendency for the borders between advertising and television programing to become less clear (Thussu, 2006: 218). Broadcasters and media content producers are attempting to establish a presence on digital platforms and the Internet, in order to create new business and advertising opportunities. However, for Discovery, the television channels and traditional television programs still represent the main distribution outlets, and a powerful source of media content for the new distribution forms, whether it is mobile television, the Internet, or video-on-demand.

Discovery televisual culture has expanded globally by harnessing political, economic, and technological developments associated with the increased connectedness in the media and communications industry. The media enterprise has established a worldwide presence through economies of scale in the form of subsidizing from the US, support from powerful owners, the sharing of programing resources among its global channels and new media outlets, the worldwide replication of its US network structure and television channel brands, and the rapid take-up of new distribution technology. Although cable and satellite channels compete with terrestrial television networks in the US for the share of television audience, these new entrants and the traditional US broadcasting networks often have the same owners. Despite an increasingly global presence, Discovery's television channels have small market shares compared to many national broadcasters in the US, Europe, and other parts of the world.

3 Discovery the Brand
Image, Reputation, Promise

> A brand is a strategic asset and it is the key to the long-term performance of that (BBC) product. The BBC brand is definitely a strategic and long-term asset. For what do we promise? Trust, credibility, balance.
>
> (Jane Gorard, Director of Marketing at the
> global news television channel BBC World, 2004)

> The CNN brand for us is everything—much larger than the sum of all our parts . . . a single, uncluttered brand is the way ahead . . . Our brand—and our reputation built up in those seventeen years since 1980—is, I believe one of the reasons we managed to secure access to people and places where others fail.
>
> (Chris Cramer, President of CNN International,
> quoted in Kung-Shankleman, 2000: 106)

CNN International and BBC World are not alone when expressing a strong belief in the concept of branding. Such conviction has become the norm as branding has increasingly taken the center stage in the running of not only global media enterprises, but within many businesses and organizations. Branding is considered as a key means for enterprises and organizations to achieve their aims, whether this is profit, support, or recognition. The practice of branding attempts to manage the relationship between an organization and the environment in which it operates, and serves to create ties and bonds with consumers, individuals, groups, or other organizations. Furthermore, there is a growing preoccupation with the financial value of brands, and it is increasingly accepted that they contribute to the overall value of companies. Marketing scholar Keller points out that although a brand is a product, the brand: 'adds other dimensions that differentiates it in some way from other products designed to satisfy the same need. These differences may be rational and tangible—related to product performance of the brand—or more symbolic, emotional and intangible—related to what the brand represents' (Keller, 2003: 50).

Since the 1970s, branding has moved from the branding of single 'stand-alone' products to a series of products and services. A further change was seen during the 1980s and 1990s, as corporate branding, 'the branding of a company rather than either particular products or services', became widespread (Lury, 2004: 25, 33). Furthermore, this shift reflected the transformation of the role of larger global companies, for whom branding and marketing—and not just the manufacturing of products—have increasingly become key activities:

> Global brands or logos increasingly roam the globe. They are enormously powerful and ubiquitous. They result from how the most powerful corporations have shifted from manufacturing products to becoming brand producers. Their fluid-like power stems from marketing, design, sponsorship, public relations and advertising expenditures, with such companies becoming 'economies of signs'. Such brands include Nike, Apple, Gap, Pepsi-Cola, Benetton, Body Shop, Virgin, Swatch, Calvin Klein, Sony, Starbucks and so on. (Urry, 2003: 67)

The sports enterprise Nike exemplifies Urry's concept of the 'economy of signs'. The company does not own production facilities and does not, itself, manufacture its products. Instead, Nike's key focus is the co-ordination and protection of the progress and utilization of the company's trademark rights and related logos (Lury, 2004: 122). Jan Lindemann, the Global Managing Director for Brand Value at the brand consultancy Interbrand, emphasizes how: 'The increasing recognition of the value of intangibles came with the continous increase in the gap between companies' book values and their stockmarked valuations' (Lindemann, 2004: 27). The brand is considered as such an 'intangible'. However, how do these developments relate to Discovery's expanding televisual culture? This chapter shows how branding and the related concept of marketing have played an important role for Discovery, and for other global media enterprises. Discovery's televisual culture has rapidly expanded its coordination and cross-national circulation and distribution of company and program brands, logos, and supporting messages, as well as programing content that is closely related to the meanings of these signs and symbols.

BRANDING OF US MEDIA ENTERPRISES

Changes in the US media landscape in the last quarter of the twentieth century accelerated the take-up of—and preoccupation with—these branding practices. Branding increasingly came to the fore in the media landscape as deregulation gradually opened up for investment in the cable television industry. The opening up of markets gave increased access to a media audience that previously had been the monopoly of the big three networks. Cable, broadcasting, telephony and satellites—often considered as separate businesses—increasingly became competitors in the same market (Bellamy and

Chabin, 1999: 213, 216). A raft of cable and satellite channels emerged in the US in the late 1970s and throughout the 1980s and 1990s. The sports cable television channel ESPN launched in 1979, and the first cable television channel for children, Nickelodeon, started the same year (Papathanassopoulos, 2002: 228). These channels were followed by CNN (1980), MTV (1981), Disney Channel (1983) and A&E (1984) (Kalagian, 2007: 150).

The Discovery Channel launched into this media environment in 1985. In contrast to traditional national broadcasters, these cable channels are especially interesting in relation to branding, as they have evolved to become global media brands. Chan–Olmsted and Kim argue that the cable television networks: 'are veterans in branding their media properties. Managers at the Discovery Networks have indicated the necessity of marketing their services as a brand' (Chan–Olmsted and Kim, 2002: 304).

While the broadcaster networks had targeted a general, mainstream audience though a mixed programing fare, the new cable entrants focused on more specific topics and program genres, such as news, sports, and music: 'focused on the interests of demographically specific niche audiences' (Croteau and Hoynes, 2006: 131).

The regulatory changes and the proliferation of new entrants such as the cable television channels led to increased competition for the television audience that, in turn, increased the importance of promotion (Bellamy and Chabin, 1999: 217). In a media environment in which the number of media outlets was increasing, it was important to have a robust 'brand image' (Kung-Shankleman, 2000: 109). This development had consequences for the whole media sector. Both commercial and non-commercial television channels increasingly consider the management of brands as a way of facing growing competition (Chan-Olmsted and Kim, 2002).

DEVELOPING THE DISCOVERY BRAND

As mentioned earlier, the documentary genre in the US was perceived as a fading television genre in the 1980s, and Discovery is claimed to have 'strategically reinvigorated an out-of-vogue TV genre to engineer a niche market' in American television (Chris, 2002: 7). In the early phase, Discovery Channel in the US relied on acquired programing from domestic and foreign producers, such as BBC and National Geographic. By the end of the 1980s, the cable company started producing its own programs (Chris, 2002). In 1993, Discovery produced 295 hours of original television, and Greg Moyer, Senior Vice President of Discovery Communications Inc.'s programing group, proclaimed: 'We think now more than ever it's important to own and control the software. People who rent their programming from someone else could be squeezed out as the business changes.' (Moyer quoted in Mitchell and Granger, 1993: 38) With greater control over its output, Greg Moyer stated: 'We no longer think of ourselves solely as distributors, but that the heart and soul of our business is our brand' (Littleton, 1996). Discovery Channel is the main media outlet fronting the Discovery brand in the US. But, the company has rapidly launched new Discovery branded channels, now comprising a portfolio of television channels. By 2002, Discovery US dominated the thematic factual entertainment/documentary television channels, with a total of at least 11 channels (*see* Table 3.1). The increase in documentary channels in the US in 1996 and 1998 was largely due to Discovery US's digital television expansion.

Discovery US launched with programing that had traditionally been the domain of the American public broadcasting service, PBS. Supported by such programing, and branding and marketing emphasizing a certain 'public service' ethos, Discovery has attempted to compete with PBS. The television programing presented on Discovery Channel belongs to genres traditionally found on the US channel PBS and Discovery's mission statement of the company does have a certain resemblance to 'public-service' broadcasting: 'Discovery is in the business of helping people to explore their world and satisfy their curiosity' (Hendricks, 1996). The public-service image is further stressed by Discovery founder in a speech to the Royal Television Society in London: 'We must focus on empowerment. We must not simply give people more information. We must give them news they can use and tools to help them make the most out of their lives, to make wise business or lifestyle choices and even to improve their health' (Hendricks, 1999). Discovery's position is also emphasized by Chan-Olmsted and Kim, who point out that Discovery Networks niche television channels represent

Table 3.1   Documentary Channels in the US

Year	Number of Channels
1990	1
1991	1
1992	1
1993	1
1994	1
1995	2
1996	7
1997	7
1998	11
1999	11
2000	11
2001	12
2002	13

(Source: Screen Digest, 2002)

Table 3.2   Top 25 Television Network Brands Ranked by Quality Score, 2006

1	Discovery Channel
2	Noggin
3	History Channel
4	National Geographic Channel
5	PBS Kids
6	Discovery Times Channel
7	Weather Channel
8	TLC (The Learning Channel)
9	Food Network
10	PBS (Public Broadcasting Service)
11	Animal Planet
12	A&E
13	AMC Television Network (American Movie Classics)
14	The Science Channel
15	Disney Channel
16	History Channel International
17	Discovery Home Channel
18	Discovery Health Channel
19	Nick Jr.
20	Discovery Kids
21	Playhouse Disney
22	Biography Channel
23	Home & Garden TV (HGTV)
24	Travel Channel
25	USA Network

Note: 69 TV network brands were measured.
(Source: Harris Interactive, 2006)

some of the fiercest competitors to public television (Chan-Olmsted and Kim, 2002).

The increased preoccupation with brands has resulted in the rise of media brand ratings. Market research firms attempting to measure the value of brands in different forms has become important in the competition between companies. Market research firm Harris Interactive conducts the EquiTrend Brand Study perception study in the US, which claims to measure the 'quality' of media brands. According to the study shown in the

Table 3.2, Discovery Channel is the number one 'television network brand' in 'Overall Quality' in 2006 for the tenth consecutive year.

The study also shows that Discovery has the most online brands of any media company in the ranking for 'Quality' (*see* Table 3.3.).

The two ratings indicate a high level of brand recognition of Discovery's media outlets among the US population. Sociologist Celia Lury states that: 'At its most basic, the repetition of a logo—which may be a name (Nike), a graphic image (the Swoosh) or a slogan ("Just do it")—means that when people are asked for examples of brands, most of them are able to give some, displaying what marketers call "brand awareness"' (Lury, 2004: 11). However, according to marketers, the 'awareness' of a brand must be supported by an 'image'. Lury describes the 'image' as: 'the associations that a brand holds for consumers' (Lury, 2004: 12). The brand logo or 'ident' serves as a specular device to magnify 'one set of associations and then another' (Lury, 2004: 12). The Discovery logo is present on-screen 24-hours in the right hand corner, as well as in most non-broadcast initiatives. Julie Willis, Senior Vice President, Discovery Channel Marketing, explains Discovery's attempts to address people's associations:

> What we hear people tell us about the (marketing and branding) campaign is really some of the same things that they're always said about the

Table 3.3 Top 25 Online Brands Ranked by Quality Score, 2006

1	DiscoveryChannel.com
2	Google.com
3	Discovery.com
4	HistoryChannel.com
5	TLC (The Learning Channel) Web site
6	Yahoo!
7	PBS.org
8	Hallmark.com
9	Discovery Health Channel Web site
10	Microsoft.com
11	BarnesAndNoble.com (bn.com)
12	Animal Planet Web site
13	A&E.com
14	Amazon.com
15	eBay

Note: 58 Online brands were measured.
(Source: Harris Interactive, 2006)

network. That its 'high value', 'entertaining', 'quality' . . . all of those things, but on top of that we're starting to hear some of the language that we are aspiring to: 'provocative', 'funny', 'not so didactic', 'not taking it quite so seriously', 'a place where I can have fun', in addition to learning something. We're starting to kind of round up the sense of the brand so that it's maybe a bit less intimidating. (Willis, 2004)

Willis describes how the company attempts to alter associations among its audience and consumers. The aim is to achieve a set of associations or hyperlinks (Lury, 2004) in line with the desired brand perception. Other examples of brand associations include: Disney (fun, magic, family entertainment) and Nike (innovative products and peak athletic performance) (Keller, 2003: 87), as well as determination and competitiveness (Lury, 2004). These are all associations often used when describing a person. Lury points out that personalization of a brand: 'underpins the affective relations between brands and consumers. (. . .) It is nurtured in the marketing practices that build brand relationships and brand loyalty' (Lury, 2004: 12).

The 'public-service' image of the Discovery brand is supported by the study of the perception of the PBS brand in relation to that of cable television brands. This study points out that the Discovery Channel was 'perceived to be the most comparable cable counterpart to PBS' (Chan-Olmsted and Kim, 2002: 309). In Harris Interactive's brand ranking Discovery Channel is ranked number one and PSB is ranked as number ten (*see* Table 3.2.). According to Chan-Olmsted and Kim public television still has: 'a very positive brand image among its viewers in contrast to comparable cable networks, scoring high in areas of "quality," "educational value," and "trustworthiness."' Furthermore, the study points out that the rise of the cable television channels A&E and Discovery 'has not diluted the positive brand perception of public television, nor has it changed significantly the perceived importance of public television and the self-assessed audience viewing behavior' (Chan-Olmsted and Kim, 2002: 315).

BRANDING AND DIVERSIFICATION

Although the concept of branding has, traditionally, within business literature referred to the branding of products, the concept has increasingly come to involve the company and organization behind the product (Balmer and Grey, 2003). Business scholars present several advantages of creating a corporate brand. A central perceived benefit of corporate branding is the 'temporal dimension'. While products may have a shorter life, as they are used to deliver sales, executives hope that corporate brands 'live both in the past and in the future' (Hatch and Schultz, 2003: 1045). The 'Discovery' corporate brand plays a central role in the expansion and diversification of the organization. According to marketing theory, the corporate brand serves as an endorser 'representing an organization that stands behind its products in spirit and substance' (Aaker, 2004: 263). This relates to the claim that the aim is that a corporate brand's stakeholders respond more positively to advertising for a corporate brand, or services with corporate branding, in contrast to similar initiatives by a less familiar enterprise (Keller, 2003: 539).

Since the launch of Discovery Channel in 1985, the company has diversified into a tier of new television channels and new media outlets. The 'Discovery' name has been attached to the majority of these products and services. This follows a branding and marketing strategy described by marketing scholar Aaker as a 'branded house strategy' (Aaker, 2004). Diversification within the television and media industry has relied on the lending of branding approaches from marketing strategies within retail (Chris, 2002: 8). The Virgin brand is used to launch Virgin Airlines, Virgin Express, Virgin Radio, Virgin Rail, Virgin Cola, Virgin Jeans, Virgin Music, and many others (Aaker, 2004: 60).

Similar to Virgin, Discovery used the 'Discovery' brand to diversify and launch new channels, new media outlets, and new consumer products. The ESPN and CNN media brands have followed the same strategy, as have the Internet enterprises Google and Yahoo. Many national public broadcasters such as the BBC and the Norwegian public service broadcaster, NRK, and have adopted the same approach to the branding of television channels and Internet outlets.

Disney has created a corporate brand that is central when extending its brand into consumer products, feature-length films, cruises, and theme parks (Aaker, 1996; Balmer and Grey, 2003: 985). Discovery has emulated Disney by diversification into retail and licensing of products and sales through the Discovery Online Shop or Amazon.com. The company's increasing distribution of content through satellite radio, video-on-demand, and mobile telephony is part of the brand-extending strategy. Discovery Education, for example, is becoming a large provider of educational video and print material. According to DCI, its' products reach 90,000 schools in the US (Discovery, 2006a). In addition, and in line with its public service brand ethos, the company participates in 'public responsibilities' activities throughout the US. These include Discovery Channel Young Scientist Challenge, its partnership in America's National Parks, and the promotion of media literacy.

A corporate brand may also be leveraged through co-branding (Aaker, 1996). A much publicized co-branding venture in the US was Discovery's and *The New York Times'* decision to launch the Discovery Times Channel—formerly known as Discovery Civilization Channel in the US: 'Discovery Times Channel reflects our commitment to bringing together two of the most trusted names in media, *The New York Times* and the Discovery Channel' (The New York Times Company Investor Relations, 2002). This shows how two brands can be bundled in an attempt to combine brand associations, and share brand building costs and the risk of launching a new product (Aaker, 1996: 300). However, in 2006 New York Times Co. decided to sell their share back to Discovery: although the channel reached

39 million subscribers, it was estimated to be watched by fewer than 30,000 viewers each night according to the trade magazine *Mediaweek* (Crupi, 2006b). Instead, The New York Times Co. decided to focus on videos produced for the NYTimes.com Web site (Kehaulani Goo, 2006).

GLOBALIZING THE DISCOVERY BRAND

Branding and marketing had a central role in the development of Discovery in US and have also been vital to its strategy to globalize the brand. As in the US, Discovery has attempted to develop a global corporate brand through its television networks, new media initiatives, joint-ventures, and 'public responsibility' initiatives, in accordance with its 'public service' brand ethos.

In 1996, Discovery's founder Hendricks believed the company was neither 'wed to a particular delivery technology, nor a geographic boundary' (Hendricks, 1996: 4). The same year, Hendricks also emphasized in trade magazine *Multichannel News*: 'The center for our 10-year plan is the concentration of building a brand that has considerable loyalty worldwide' (Hendricks quoted in Katz, 1996: 32). Hendricks' views correspond with the argument that globalization presented the opportunity to expand 'image, product and revenue generation to previously unavailable markets' (Bellamy and Chabin, 1999: 216). This has led to an increased focus on branding of media enterprises across the world. The financial motives for the branding of global media outlets includes the aim to create loyalty among media audiences between media platforms, and the possibilities for achieving cost efficiency 'through synergy effects across borders and technologies' (Fürsich, 2003: 138).

After establishing the Discovery US network, the company focused on 'building the infrastructure worldwide' (Hendricks quoted in O'Shaughnessy, 2002). Today, the company's global network, Discovery Networks International, is split into regional networks, but just as other global television networks operate through a collective visual brand (Chalaby, 2005b: 59). As both Table 3.4 and Table 3.5 show, the Discovery brand name is the same, but the name of region or country is added. The pan-regional television brand Discovery Latin America/Iberia (DLAI), for example, is beamed out from Miami to Spanish- and Portuguese-language viewers in South America, North America, and Europe.

Following the same structure as the US network, each regional network consists of the main brand Discovery Channel, which is gradually expanded into a portfolio of channels, now counting 100 networks (*see* Table 3.5). Discovery's television channels are organized into 'channel conglomerates', which has several advantages. The Discovery tier of channels may be sold jointly in a bundle to cable and satellite operators, and a 'branded environment can be used to sell audiences across channel, platforms and borders to advertisers' (Fürsich, 2003: 140). Furthermore, the various Discovery channels have also generated capital and developed brand names that have made

Table 3.4   Discovery International's Presence

Discovery Español
Discovery Português
Discovery Europe
Discovery Germany
Discovery India
Discovery Asia
Discovery Southeast Asia
Discovery Australia/New Zealand
Discovery Japan
Discovery Channel Middle East
Discovery Canada

(Source: Discovery, 2006a)

it possible to expand into Discovery's 'non-TV ventures' (Chris, 2002: 8). Discovery's 'multiple stream income' also made it possible to launch costly digital channels that would be difficult for independent new entrants to bear (Chris, 2002: 17). Branding creates an umbrella for this process: for example, Disney's Brand Portfolio Strategy 'enables' the various Disney brands to strengthen each other with the aim to create an impact more extensive than just the total of each brand (Aaker, 2004: 42). Discovery is also increasingly expanding into new distribution platforms using the Discovery name. In late 2005, Discovery Communications, Inc. formed the Global New Media Group to manage Discovery's 'worldwide efforts to create content and businesses for new distribution platforms including broadband, wireless and mobile devices, video on demand, the company's websites and satellite radio service and other interactive activities' (Discovery, 2005b). A central factor in this process is also that the cost of producing media content is high but the reproduction or syndication cost is relatively low (Murray, 2005: 431). The CEO of Viacom, Tom Freston describes a similar corporate optimism as the MTV brand expands into new media: 'We go from being TV-centric to brand-centric. Our brands have to prosper on every platform that's out there—TV, digital TV, online, wireless, video on demand, and so forth' (Freston quoted in Gunther, 2006).

GLOBAL ALLIANCES

Global enterprises collaborate through various forms of alliances for mutual benefit. Disney has participated in cross-promotional alliances over

Table 3.5   Discovery International's Television Channels

DISCOVERY ASIA/INDIA

Discovery Channel Southeast Asia

Discovery Channel Taiwan

Discovery Channel New Zealand

Discovery Channel Australia

Discovery Channel Japan

Discovery Channel Korea

Discovery Channel India

Animal Planet Southeast Asia

Animal Planet Taiwan

Animal Planet Australia/New Zealand

Animal Planet Japan

Animal Planet India

Discovery Travel & Living Southeast Asia

Discovery Travel & Living Taiwan

Discovery Travel & Living Australia/New Zealand

Discovery Travel & Living India

Discovery Science Southeast Asia

Discovery Home and Health Southeast Asia

Discovery Real Time Asia

Discovery HD Japan

Total: 20

DISCOVERY UK

Discovery Channel/Discovery Channel +1

Discovery Home & Health/Discovery Home & Health +1

Animal Planet/Animal Planet +1

Discovery Real Time

Discovery Real Time Extra

Discovery Science

Discovery Civilisation

Discovery Travel & Living

Discovery Kids

Discovery Wings

Total: 10

(continued)

Table 3.5   continued

DISCOVERY EUROPE, MIDDLE EAST, AFRICA (EMEA)

Discovery Channel Benelux

Discovery Channel Europe

Discovery Channel Poland

Discovery Channel ME/Africa

Discovery Channel Turkey

Discovery Channel Nordic

Discovery Channel Sweden

Discovery Channel Denmark

Discovery Channel Italy

Discovery Channel France

Discovery Channel Germany

Discovery Channel Hungary

Animal Planet Benelux

Animal Planet Nordic

Animal Planet Europe

Animal Planet Poland

Animal Planet ME/Africa

Animal Planet Germany

Animal Planet Italy

Discovery Science Europe/ME

Discovery Science Italy

Discovery Civilisation Europe

Discovery Civilisation Italy

Discovery Civilisation ME

Discovery Real Time Italy

Discovery Real Time France

Discovery Travel & Living Europe

Discovery Travel & Living Italy

Discovery Geschichte

Total: 29

DISCOVERY LATIN AMERICA/IBERIA

Discovery Channel Latin Americ

Discovery Channel Venezuela

(continued)

Table 3.5   continued

Discovery Channel Mexico

Discovery Channel Brazil

Discovery Channel Argentina

Discovery Channel Iberia (Spain/Portugal)

Animal Planet Latin America/Brazil

Discovery Kids Latin America

Discovery Kids Brazil

Discovery Kids Mexico

People+Arts Argentina

People+Arts Latin America

People+Arts Iberia (Spain/Portugal)

People+Arts Mexico

People+Arts Brazil

Discovery Travel & Living Latin America/Brazil

Discovery Home & Health Latin America

Discovery Science

Discovery Civilization

Discovery Turbo

Total: 20

DISCOVERY CANADA

Discovery Channel

Animal Planet

Discovery Civilization

Discovery Health

Discovery Kids

Discovery HD

Total: 6

(Source: Discovery, 2006a)

many years with the global giants Coca-Cola and McDonalds. Disney and Coca-Cola formed an alliance in 1985. Coca-Cola was given the rights to serve soft drinks in Disney's theme parks, and helped Disney to strengthen its brand in international markets where Coca-Cola had more experience with marketing (Roost, 2005: 264).

Discovery has also formed alliances with well-known companies and orga-nizations. In addition to financial advantages, there is also a potential value to be gained from being associated with other brands. The BBC/Discovery relationship started in the first half of the 1980s as the newly founded Discovery bought the US programing rights for BBC programing. In 1998, a $665 million deal was signed, including co-production and the launch of channels such as Animal Planet globally, and People+Arts in South America, and for the distribution of BBC America in the US. In 2002, the BBC and Discovery extended the deal for another 10 years (Buerkle, 1998: Moss, 2002; BBC, 2002a). The deal gave Discovery global co-branding opportunities with one of the world's best-known media brands. Furthermore, the partnership with the BBC strengthened Discovery's brand in former colonial countries familiar with the British public-service broadcaster (McElvouge, 1998a: 40).

In 2003, Discovery and UNESCO formed a global partnership to 'cele-brate cultural diversity'. Discovery Channel broadcast nine short-form pro-grams about some of the world's threatened languages (Discovery, 2003b; UNESCO, 2003). The Discovery Channel Global Education Partnership (DCGEP), a non-profit charitable organization, has launched learning cen-tres in Africa and South America:

> The Partnership provides schools and community centres in under-re-sourced areas with televisions, VCRs or DVD players, teacher training, satellite technology if possible, and the ongoing delivery of relevant video programming. Today, over 395,000 children plus their commu-nities in 10 countries around the world have access to valuable infor-mation tailored to their needs. (DCGEP, 2006)

In Angola, Discovery formed a partnership with the oil giant ChevronTexaco to launch learning centres. According to Discovery spokesman, David Leavy the DCGEP initiative 'is not about branding at all. (. . .) It is just about help-ing people improve their lives' (Leavy cited in Miller, 2004: 44). Although the initiative undoubtedly does help people, the fact remains that the Discov-ery brand is used as an umbrella for the Discovery Channel Global Education Partnership. And, the company's television programing plays an important role also in this initiative: '70,000 hour library of high quality documentary programing provide us with considerable support for our charitable mission' (DCGEP, 2006). It is important that these initiatives should also be seen in relation to the fact that Africa and South America are large potential media markets. Discovery's global operations are mapped out in Table 3.6.

GLOBAL BRAND VALUE

Each year, the The *Business Week*/Interbrand collaboration presents an Annual Ranking of the 100 Top Global Brands. The ranking attempts to

Table 3.6 Discovery Global Businesses and Brands

Discovery Networks US	Discovery Networks International	Discovery Digital Media
Discovery Channel	Discovery Networks Asia-Pacific	Discovery Online
TLC	Discovery Networks Europe	Discovery Mobile
Animal Planet	Middle East and Africa	Discovery On-Demand
OWN	Discovery Networks UK	
Discovery Kids	Discovery Networks Latin America/U.S Hispanic Group	
Science Channel		
Planet Green		
Investigation Discovery		
Military Channel		
Fit TV		
HD Theater		
Discovery en Espanol		
Discovery Familia		

Discovery Commerce	Discovery Education	Corporate Social Responsibility
DiscoveryStore.com	Discovery Education streaming	Discovery Channel
Discovery Channel Store Catalog	Discovery Education Science	Global Education Partnership
Licensing & Merchandising	Discovery Education Health	
Discovery Education Assessment	AFI/Discovery Channel Documentary Festival	

(Discovery, 2008b)

specify the financial value of the brand as part the overall value of global companies (*see* Table 3.7). The brand value is 'calculated as the net present value of the earnings that the brand is expected to generate and secure in the future for the time frame from July 1, 2004 to June 30, 2005' (Interbrand, 2005).

Table 3.7   Interbrand: Best Global Brands 2005

Rank	Brand	2005 Brand Value $m	Per cent of Market Capitalisation	Country of Origin
1	Coca-Cola	67,525	64%	US
2	Microsoft	59,941	22%	US
3	IBM	53,376	44%	US
4	GE	46,996	12%	US
5	Intel	35,588	21%	US
6	Nokia	26,452	34%	Finland
7	Disney	26,441	46%	US
8	McDonald's	26,014	71%	US
9	Toyota	24,837	19%	Japan
10	Marlboro	21,189	15%	US
. . .				
38	Google	8,461	11%	US
48	MTV	6,647	12%	US
68	Amazon.com	4,248	29%	US

(Source: Interbrand, 2005)

The claimed financial contribution of the global brands is enormous. Disney's brand comprises an estimated 46 per cent of the company's value (market capitalisation) and MTV's brand value equals 12 per cent of its value, and the McDonalds' brand an astounding 71 per cent of the company's value.

Despite the increased preoccupation with valuing brands, Lury points out: 'it is still not possible to recognize the value of brands on balance sheets in the United States and many other places. There is also only a very limited acceptance of the usefulness of brand accounting within many companies. Nevertheless, it is increasingly possible for companies to treat the brand as they do any other form of valuable asset' (Lury, 2004: 121). This point is taken up by marketing scholars who argue that 'brand value' has become central in valuing companies. Since the 1980s, large sums have been paid for brands due to the belief that they can generate additional money, and also because of the 'tremendous difficulty and expense of creating similar brands from scratch' (Kotler and Keller, 2006: 275). Furthermore, the Interbrand rating is widely reported in the financial press (*Business Week*, 2005; Bloomberg, 2005), and may be important information for the ranked companies in their brand-building activities.

In 2003, both *Time Magazine* and the *Financial Times* reported the value of Discovery Communications, Inc. as up to $20 billion (Eisenberg, 2003;

Thal-Larsen, 2003). Neither of them refers explicitly to the brand value of Discovery. However, when comparing the following figures, it is clear that the perceived value of the Discovery brand contributes to the suggested value of the company: Discovery posted a net loss of $48 million in 2002. In 2003 it earned $63 million and $168 in 2004 (*The Washington Post*, 2005). In 2005, Discovery's total assets was valued at $3.1 billion, the company's long term debts at $2.4 billion, and revenues at $1.9 billion (DHC, 2006). André Singer, Creative Director at the factual television production company, West Park Pictures, reflects on Discovery's global brand effort:

> The Discovery brand has become overtly global. They have tried (and succeeded) in generating something where whatever part of the world you're in you'll immediately recognize that brand, and you'll think you know what the product of that brand represents. I think that is different to those companies who have a lot of outlets around the world. This is actually using the globe as part of its process. I can't think of other examples except perhaps National Geographic, where there is a global brand in that sense. You can go to Hong Kong, you can go to Delhi, you can go to Sidney, and you can go to Latin America and you say "Discovery" and people will immediately know what the product is, and will have an idea of its style and content. Sometimes it shifts and is slightly different, but generally it is the same product, the same kind of program. The BBC has a brand that is understood globally, but it is not a global brand. You don't actually have a BBC Australia, BBC Latin America . . . its just that they buy BBC programs; BBC is still a British thing. Discovery is meant to be a global brand. (Singer, Creative Director, West Park Pictures, UK, interview with author, London, 16 June, 2004)

Dick Emery, former Managing Director of BBC Worldwide, describes the Discovery brand:

> Discovery is a strong brand. Discovery is a strong brand in every market. It isn't just a television channel; it is has an atmosphere and aura because they have established that first. They will do well because of that and they will last longer than channels without a brand. And not many television channels have really understood the concept of branding the way that Discovery has. (Emery, former Managing Director, BBC Worldwide, interview with author, London, 16 May 2003)

BRANDING OF DISCOVERY IN EUROPE

While Discovery has attempted to create a brand with a certain 'public-service' resemblance in the US, in Europe, the BBC and other European national public-service terrestrial broadcasters have done this successfully for many decades. Although the factual and documentary television genre had become rare in the 1980s in the US, the genre was available on national television channels throughout Europe. Furthermore, although Discovery in the US could access the best of factual television programing from the BBC, the European branch could not. While not referring to Discovery in Europe explicitly, former Managing Director of BBC Worldwide, Dick Emery, comments on the internationalization of the Discovery brand:

> They took the name (Discovery) to just about every market and they . . . it seemed to me . . . to always establish the brand first. They put money behind marketing the channel first (. . .) and create a name the brand image for the channel. And, once they had done that they really started to put serious money into programing in the local market. (Emery, former Managing Director, BBC Worldwide, interview with author, London, 16 May 2003)

The Discovery brand was unknown when it launched in Europe, according to André Singer:

> Using National Geographic as a comparison: National Geographic had a brand that was already internationally recognizable, because of the magazine and the charity. And, therefore it was easier for them to think globally. In its earlier days, Discovery didn't really have a brand. It was an American cable channel. It had a concept, but it didn't really have a brand outside the US. So, it deliberately took that name Discovery and sold it . . . When it first came to the UK, nobody knew who Discovery was. (. . .) Now, of course, the brand itself works. People know or think they know what Discovery stands for. (Singer, Creative Director, West Park Pictures, UK, interview with author, London, 16 June, 2004)

Former senior executive at Discovery Networks Europe, Nick Comer-Calder, reflects on Discovery's approach in Europe:

> There (was) a huge emphasis on branding. (. . .) It was the Discovery brand that we were creating. And, in a way for me, and I have to stress (. . .) these are my personal opinions, but because my passion was for really good programing that was going to truly open your eyes and tell you something new and tell you something meaningful, this schedule that we actually put out which primarily consisted of really . . . well, lets put it this way: programing that was on the whole not of the level of any of the BBC (or) any of the UK terrestrial channels. And, I suppose my ambitions where that we should have been as good. And, my sense was that if we were really going to live up to the promise of all of our

advertising, and our marketing and this huge thing about the Discovery brand, it was very difficult to do that because we simply hadn't got the quality of product behind it. That focus is very much on the UK. Once you got into Europe, it sort of depended on what territory you where in. I can see that we were pretty attractive compared to a lot of television in say Holland and in Scandinavia, because there the documentary programing did tend to be very serious and very much this kind of model of serious programing where serious people sat down and watched it and it didn't really matter (. . .) whether it was made with a very good story or a sense of drama you sat and watched it. And, I can see that we offered a sort of vibrant alternative to that. (Comer-Calder, former Senior VP and General Manager, DNE, interview with author, 4 October, 2004)

One of the branding initiatives in the UK was a £2 million campaign launched in late 1997. The initiative aimed to strengthen Discovery's position in relation to the new factual television channel competitors National Geographic Channel and UK Horizons, and thereby differentiating the channel's approach to 'factual entertainment'. Focus groups indicated that Discovery was considered 'dry, cold, and scientific', and the branding initiative aimed to change this by 'employing strong, simple and dynamic images designed to convey confidence and warmth, even using humor to engage the interest of the viewers' (Brown, 1998: 23–24). As Discovery UK expanded and Europe's television market matured, market research data became available justifying the launch of pan-European branding initiatives. The campaign with the tagline 'Got to Know' was launched in most of Discovery's international territories apart from the US. The global branding initiative consisted of advertising in traditional and new media together with on-air spots (Major, 2003). In Europe, the campaign was targeting a pan-European audience in the key countries Denmark, Sweden, Italy, Poland, the Netherlands, and Germany in 2004.

The strong emphasis on the regional promotion of the global Discovery brand within Europe is reflected in the job advertising for Channel Directors for three European territories: Nordic (office in Denmark), East Europe (office in Poland), and Italy (office in London). For all three positions, the global/local relationship is central as part responsibilities and duties:

- Develop an articulated perspective on how to develop the Discovery brands in the region,
- Execute the brand strategy set by VP OAP (On-air promotions), EMEA (Europe, Middle East and Africa) in the market,
- Execute global promotables in local markets,
- Manage the communications and listings activities in local market with clear reference to corporate guidelines.

Furthermore, 'required qualifications' include experience in 'managing local expression of global brands' (Discovery. 2004b).

As Discovery's television channels were rolled out in Europe, the company supported the European factual television production community by organizing producer workshops, seminars, and courses. With funding from the EU's Media Program, Discovery Germany, together with non-fiction companies in Europe, initiated the major training initiative *Discovery Campus* for factual and documentary program production. Since its launch in 1998, over 27 open symposia were organized throughout Europe and an estimated 2,000 people from both the public and private part of the European factual and documentary industry (commissioning editors, producers and directors) participated. In addition, the *Discovery Campus Masterschool* offered a professional training course in the production of factual television programing. Tutors included professionals from public and private European and international broadcasters such as ARD (Germany), ARTE (Germany and France), AVRO (Netherlands), BBC (UK), Channel 4 (UK), Discovery Channel (various regions), France 5 (France), HBO (US), Humanistische Omroep (Netherland), ORF (Austria), Spiegel TV (Germany), SVT (Sweden), TVOntario (Canada), VRT Canvas (Belgium), WGBH International (US), YLE (Finland), TV2 (Denmark), and ZDF (Germany). However, although this was a very valuable and popular training initiative, this activity also bears the corporate Discovery logo and was part of the 'public responsibility' initiatives previously described (Discovery Campus, 2006).

BRAND DEFINITIONAL MEDIA CONTENT

A core initiative in developing the Discovery brand and people's perception of Discovery was the case of high budget programing. The BBC/Discovery joint venture resulted in high-budget brand definitional television programing and media content that was distributed worldwide and these productions played an important role in developing the Discovery brand and people's perception of this brand. Traditionally, such 'strategic programming' has delivered large audiences for free-TV channels and drove 'consumer uptake' for pay-TV, as well as press and attention (Humphreys and Lang, 1998:13). The BBC/Discovery partnership will be examined in detail in the next chapter, but this section will introduce the connection between branding and such television programing and media content. The eight-part natural history television programing series *Blue Planet* is an example of brand definitional programing. The series had a budget of £7 million and was produced over five years (Cottle, 2003: 176). The 11-part series *Planet Earth*, costing £1 million an hour, was considered a follow-up to *Blue Planet*. It was financed by BBC's domestic channels, BBC Worldwide, Discovery and NHK (Japan) and was completed by 2006 (Winslow, 2004). Michael Rosenfeld, senior executive producer, National Geographic Channel, claims there is a trend towards what he calls 'event' television within the documentary genre: 'Everybody wants event programming (. . .) that pops out of the schedule.' (Rosenfeld quoted in Forrester, 2003b). These high budget factual programs serve as feature length promo-spots for the channels.

While Discovery could spend a reported $3 million to promote the high-budget documentary *Raising the Mammoth* in the US, the American PBS is not in such a position, according to Carole Feld, PBS's advocate of branding and promotion since 1992: 'We don't have much money, so we can't spread it out so thinly. Every day it's taking more and more to break through' (Feld quoted in Everhart Bedford, 2000). The invention of the Discovery Global Events, *Watch with the World*, is a clever marketing tool for the global reach of Discovery. Since 1999, Discovery has broadcast worldwide the following *Watch With the World* program events: *Raising the Mammoth* (1999), *Cleopatra's Palace: In Search of a Legend* (1999), *Inside the Space Station* (2000) and, in 2005, *The Science of Lance Armstrong*, a major media event around Lance Armstrong of the Discovery Cycling Pro Team in the Tour de France. Discovery claims that 'Our (world) specials are the only media presentations that can deliver a same-day, same-primetime, same-network experience to the entire world' (Grove, 2000: 33). *Cleopatra's Palace: In Search of a Legend* was translated into 23 languages and Discovery used its global distribution network to show the program at 9 p.m. local time around the world. The program was watched by around 30 million people and around 15 million viewers in the US (Reynolds, 2000). Discovery Channel retail stores in the US and Europe supported the telecast with a special collection of books and home videos. A Web site offered additional content (Hall, 2005). The most recent *Watch with the World* went further than the previous events as a global multimedia co-branding initiative. It was based around the Discovery Channel sponsored Discovery Pro Cycling Team and Lance Armstrong, the seven-time winner of the cycling race, the Tour De France. The program *The Science of Lance Armstrong* was broadcast in 160 countries in 35 languages on June 27, 2005. The various elements of the initiative are described in the following way by Discovery:

> Discovery is leveraging all of its global assets to support and promote Armstrong and Team Discovery Channel through the "Chasing #7" initiative. Discovery.com will feature a Tour de France map, event history, rules and dispatches, and will support the online sweepstakes. In addition, Discovery is expanding the www.teamdiscoverychannel.com website to provide fans with news, daily updates from the road, bios of the cyclists, photos and video. This fan-based content is available in 15 languages through the international Discovery Channel websites. Discovery Channel Radio (available on XM, SIRIUS Satellite Radio and AudioFeast) will air daily vignettes and tune-in information, as well as behind-the-scenes interviews with Armstrong, the Team and the Lance Armstrong Foundation. The 120 Discovery Channel Stores

and DiscoveryStore.com will feature merchandise and team apparel; additionally, in-store displays will generate excitement about the programming event and the Team's performance in the Tour de France. Discovery Education will incorporate informational vignettes into Discovery Health Connection—its new online health and prevention curriculum for schools. (Discovery, 2005a)

The initiative shows how Discovery is able to mobilize and coordinate its various media outlets on a global scale. The logic behind Discovery's brand definitional programs, including the *Watch with the World*, is to fund costly programs that the audience remembers and that create an idea of the Discovery brand. The initiatives *Watch with the World* can also be seen as a project that market Discovery as global media company to its stakeholders.

CRITIQUE OF BRANDING

Although the concept of branding is embraced within the corporate world, the practice has been subjected to critique by scholars and activists. Sociologist Celia Lury argues that brands may 'allow markets to be controlled more effectively' as the dominant position of successful brands such as Microsoft, Coca-Cola, and Heinz leads to 'long-standing monopolies or dominance of certain markets and afford protection of long term investment against risk' (Lury, 2004: 71). In a similar vein, Thussu argues that 'synergy' has increased media conglomerates ability to 'promote their products across virtually all media segments', and thereby increase their 'power over global news, information and entertainment' (Thussu, 2000: 128). Furthermore, the branding of a company involves the creation of a 'brand identity', usually by the corporate head office, and this brand identity:

> may be tailored to accommodate local language and cultural preferences (like McDonald's serving pasta in Italy), but its core features— aesthetic, message, logo—remain unchanged. This consistency is what brand managers like to call 'the promise' of a brand: it's a pledge that wherever you go in the world, your experience at Wal-Mart, Holiday Inn, or a Disney theme park, will be comfortable and familiar. Anything that threatens this homogeneity dilutes a company's overall strength. (Klein, 2002)

This critique also extends to the protection of the brand identity through copyright laws. The brand identity is seen as a 'rigorously controlled one-way message' which is 'hermetically sealed off' from any social dialogue' (Klein, 2002). However, marketing scholars point out that registered trademarks can protect a brand name, and the intellectual property rights can provide the necessary security needed for a company to invest in a brand (Kotler and Keller, 2006: 274). The power of copyright and trademark became evident when, in 2002, according to New York-based law firm Shen Law LCC, Discovery Communications sued the China Engineering Drawing Studies Association for infringement of the trademark 'Discovery Channel'. The Chinese association had used the Discovery trademark and design on a magazine they published. Discovery won the case and the Chinese association was 'found to infringe Discovery's trademark rights' (Shen Law firm, 2005).

Deborah Doane, Director of the Transforming Markets program at the New Economics Foundation, draws attention to the methodology used when valuing brands. Interbrand assesses mainly the 'economic use of the brand' when measuring the value of the brand. Doane suggests that 'At least a partial way out of this quagmire is for us to make "brand value" far less dependent on traditional economic intangibles and more dependent on genuine measures of social and environmental performance' (Doane, 2003: 193). However, companies are increasingly taking into account the consequences of their activities. Noreena Hertz points out that the anti-globalization movement's critique of corporations' behavior and production operations has led to concern among corporate management: 'I'm frequently invited to speak to senior executives and board members about these issues. Chief executives are not only worried about how protestors could impact on their brand but also about the impact on institutional investor's perceptions and future liabilities' (Hertz, 2003).

Also, through the Dow Jones Sustainability Indexes, 'corporate sustainability' is measured by assessing, among other things, companies' ability to 'Integrat(e) long-term economic, environmental and social aspects in their business strategies while maintaining global competitiveness and brand reputation' (Dow Jones Sustainability Indexes, 2004). Although companies have given increased attention to these issues, brand consultant Wally Olins emphasized in 1999 that this does not necessarily lead to changes:

> But it is important not to exaggerate the impact of all this on corporate life and the corporate management style. In my experience there are very few large corporations, even the most intelligent and far-sighted, who regard the issues which I have just examined as their highest priority. For the global corporation the core issues remain how to grow, beat the competition and make sense of changes that are taking place around them. (Olins, 1999: 40)

In this respect, it is worth observing how the influential global business consultancy McKinsey suggests that companies may protect their brand, as they may be 'affected by the rising tide of expectations among stakeholders about the social role of business'. According to McKinsey, a company should, as a strategic precaution 'look for signs of emerging hot topics, be ready to respond to them early, and place a series of small strategic bets that will create value if the social and political landscape shifts' (Bonini, et al.: 2006). This resonates with Olin's argument, and gives an indication of the attitude of some corporations when engaging with these issues.

Within its televisual culture, Discovery is increasingly coordinating the cross-national circulation and distribution of media brands and symbols, and programing content. Having established a branded television network model in the US, the media enterprise is replicating this model globally. Through brand and content synergy, cross-promotion, and extensions into new media outlets, Discovery resembles Disney in creating a global media conglomerate. The high-budget brand definitional programing and media content, and 'global events', are distributed throughout its global television networks, also marketing the Discovery brand. The Lance Armstrong-themed global event shows Discovery's televisual culture's ability to exercise its brand and coordinate content across a number of distribution platforms. However, as this study does not explore the audience for this event, it is difficult to assess the actual number of users and viewers of this global initiative. Joint ventures, public relations, but also non-media initiatives are vital parts of Discovery's televisual culture's branding and marketing strategies in making the enterprise known and liked globally. The company attempts to create a homogeneous brand using the same logo and brand name in all its activities, and to some extent attempts to establish an image that has a certain public service ethos. The globalization of Discovery's televisual culture shows how the linking and intertwining of the media and communications landscape have increasingly facilitated the possibilities to distribute logos, symbols, brands, public relations messages, and media content in a multitude of ways.

4 The Globalization of Factual Entertainment

What is the impact of globalization on the production of the factual television and media genre, and how has Discovery responded to it? This chapter explains how processes associated with the globalization of production influenced the production of factual entertainment. The globalization of production has been most visible within manufacturing industry: enterprises search for opportunities outside their national territories; they create cross-national supply chains and alliances, and outsource and spread their production across the globe. Key aspects of this process have also been adopted by the film and television industry, which has both forced and facilitated increased movement and activity on a global scale within the production of television programing in this sector. Practices within the industry reflect this development: for example, producers and broadcasters co-produce television programing across national borders. Furthermore, the globalization of labour extends to the film and television industry as cities, countries, and regions across the world compete to attract film and television productions by offering financial incentives.

As we shall see in this chapter, Discovery has rapidly adapted to these transformations through external and internal co-productions with other broadcasting companies and between the regional Discovery networks. The partnership formed in 1998 between BBC Worldwide and Discovery has harnessed these developments, making it the most extensive factual programing co-production and television channel development partnership in international television history. Parts of the two media organizations have become interwoven in several ways as a result of the collaboration, and they have played a significant part in each other's global expansion. Their global factual brands reach millions of television viewers worldwide and generate large revenues.

When Discovery Channel was launched in the US in 1985, its original mission was to provide factual programing about science, natural history, exploration, and engineering—genres traditionally associated with US public-service broadcasting. However, as we have seen, in the early years Discovery could not afford to produce its own programing and relied entirely on the acquisition of existing programs from 1985 to 1989 (Chris, 2002). The financial start-up backing provided funding for the rights to 4,600 hours of television programing from sources such as the National Geographic Society, the American public broadcaster PBS, and the BBC (Lewyn, 1992). British factual television programing was central to Discovery's acquisition policy: 'originally he (Discovery founder John Hendricks) built his channel by buying cheap British documentaries, or expensive British documentaries that were being sold cheap in to a second window in the United States' (Seidenberg, Documentary television producer, interview with author, London, 14 July, 2003). However, the acquisition policy led to the channel being labeled by some as 'a repository for off-PBS reruns, a showcase of stale fare that nevertheless managed to attract an audience' (Burgi quoted in Chris, 2002: 13). Discovery launched in Europe in 1989, and the situation for the European branch was even more challenging, Joyce Taylor, recalls:

> Discovery, which had begun in the (United) States, had been built from BBC, ITV, and C4 programing, (. . .) but none of these companies would sell to us, because they saw us as competition in their own territory. So, all the material that had built this company was no longer available, and Discovery US had not bought any rights for it outside North America. We had to start from scratch, and all these companies were terrified of this new business, and they thought that if they didn't sell Discovery programing the competition might go away. We bought, basically, poor quality, but what we could get. We bought from Canada, Australia, and other places, but the point was that it was good enough at the time, because there was no competition, and it was a start, and you can't invest more in programing until you've got revenue coming in. (. . .) At that stage, Discovery in the US didn't make any programing, so it didn't own anything. It was 100 per cent acquisitions based. (. . .) (B)ut, then they realized that if they didn't make programing in their own rights, their future was in other people's hands, so they started to build a library of their own programing. (Joyce Taylor, former Managing Director, DNE, interview with author, London, 18 June, 2003)

To launch new channels internationally, the cable and satellite broadcaster began to develop a global programing library. The global programing library was initiated in the mid-1990s:

> Greg Moyer (former executive at Discovery) back in (around) 1994 came up with the idea of a global library and (. . .) he put forward an argument to the Discovery Communications, Inc's board saying: 'In order to really make waves and really be the foremost brand in factual programing in the world, we need to have this library of original programing which we own totally. And, which we can then use to launch all our other channels and they will be the, sort of, jewel in the crown of all of our channels around the world.' And, he got this very substantial

budget. (. . .) Seriously big money. So, then they were able to go out and make (. . .) either big three-part mini-series or very well funded six-part series or these, kind of, one-off global events. So, in that sense, the global library was there to drive the international expansion of Discovery. (Comer-Calder, former Senior VP and General Manager, DNE, interview with author, 4 October, 2004)

Similarly, the National Geographic Channel US could rely on its library of documentaries when launching internationally in 2001 (Beatty, 2001). However, although the global programing library formed a backbone in Discovery's expansion, the growing international 24-hour network required more programing. The deregulation and technological developments had encouraged a rapid increase in television channels in Europe. The competition for advertising and subscription revenues, and thereby funding for television programing, intensified among the plethora of channels (Blind and Hallenberg, 1996; Corner, 2000). This growth in the number of channels also increased the need for all types of television programing, including non-fiction programing (Fürsich, 2003: 141). In the mid-1990s, according to Holtzberg and Rofekamp, the US-based international factual program sales agents: 'due to the continuing rise in popularity of thematic channels and the subsequent increasing global demand for the genre, documentary became a hot commodity' (Holtzberg and Rofekamp, 2002: 4).

In the 1980s, national public television broadcasters had been the main buyers of documentaries internationally, and program licensing was done to defined territories (Holtzberg and Rofekamp, 2002: 3). However, in the early 1990s, the arrival of satellite television enabled private broadcasters to target specific audiences across national boundaries:

> This was due to several factors: Privately owned commercial television started to take off. More important, we witnessed the advent of a totally new phenomenon: thematic specialty channels, which began to spread rather quickly across the globe via cable and satellites. Signals started to reach across national borders. These thematic channels began to segment the market. Instead of offering a broad range of information and entertainment to a large audience, traditionally the task of the public stations, thematic channels introduced narrow, theme-driven programming geared to the specific interest of smaller audiences. (Holtzberg and Rofekamp, 2002: 4)

THE RISE OF FACTUAL ENTERTAINMENT

The rise of thematic channels contributed to the increased global demand for factual programing. In contrast to the US, the factual genre had traditionally had a presence on European public and commercial broadcasters. Stuart Carter, Managing Director of Pioneer Productions, who has produced over a hundred programs for Discovery since 1993, reflects on how Discovery identified a gap in the market:

> So, there was a vacuum there to be filled and at that time. (T)he biggest factual maker in the world was BBC, but not much BBC material was going to America. And, what the BBC was making was very bland, very straight, very old fashioned. Discovery came in, and TLC (The Learning Channel) in the early days, acquiring material (. . .) and then slowly starting to make their own programs and giving them more energy, and better look. So, first of all, I think the positive thing is they suddenly came along and gave factual programing, documentaries, to the American market, which didn't have it. It was a huge benefit for the American market place. And then, I think what they did on a global basis, was they have improved the look and the nature of factual programs. Before that, if you look before about (19)92, you look at BBC programs such as Horizon, they are very slow, very dull, very boring, not doing very well. Discovery ups the amount of energy, the visual look, bringing on popular topics, not just sort of academic topics, so it's a lot more things about sharks, dinosaurs (. . .) things that people are interested in reading about in magazines was suddenly put on to television. (Carter, Managing Director of Pioneer Productions, UK, interview with author, London, March 23, 2004)

Nick Comer-Calder, former Senior VP and General Manager, Discovery Networks Europe, DNE, shares a similar view of Discovery's approach to popularizing the genre:

> (T)here had been a tendency amongst UK terrestrials (. . .) or producers making documentary television for UK terrestrial channels, to take for granted that if they had a great subject, or if they had a subject, which they regarded was very important, they didn't really have to think very much about turning it into a story which would appeal to the audience. (. . .) I think, really, there was some arrogance in the documentary community. It really depended upon the strength of the story. If it was a great story and something they felt really passionate about, then you just went ahead and told it in which ever way you saw fit. (. . .) There was really a tremendous commitment to public service, but at the same time there was also a tremendous commitment, I think, to kind of 'doing your thing' in the way you saw best, and really not paying very much attention to where the audience might coming from. So, I think that Greg (Moyer) and I shared a view that we wanted to sort of change that. That we felt that you could still make really, really good television, but you could make it

in a way which was more accessible, which didn't assume that the viewer had a degree, (. . .) but (. . .) if your motivation was still truly to inform, educate and entertain, then you could produce very fine television. But, I think what happened was that as Discovery grew, it became more and more commercial and as the commercial pressure started to press down on America and then through on to us, that commitment to the sort of higher ground of documentary television really changed. I mean, fairly early on, and I think it was under Greg Moyer's leadership that the term 'factual entertainment' came into being, because there was a sense that the word 'documentary' turned people off. (Comer-Calder, former Senior VP and General Manager, DNE, interview with author, telephone, 4 October, 2004)

This shift was also observed by others working within factual television. The non-fiction television genre developed amongst others due to the fact that themed television channels became increasingly popular and the genre was in demand: 'The terms factual programing and factual entertainment were introduced to reflect this phenomenon. FACTUAL, which for so long was hidden away in the far corner of daytime and late night scheduling became a key word in the international television community' (Holtzberg and Rofekamp, 2002: 4).

In 1993, Discovery's European arm took over the *First Tuesday* documentary series from ITV, who had cancelled the contract (Clarke, 1995). The series was one of ITV's 'very high-quality prestige series', according to Tunstall (Tunstall, 1993: 29). However, after two years, the deal was also cancelled with Discovery:

(T)here was something about the programing being chosen to fit the brand. (. . .) So, there was a restriction on the programing that we would commission or transmit because it had to fit the brand. Many, many documentary producers would come to us with fabulous ideas, and we'd say: 'No, because it doesn't fit the brand.' One of the classics was this strand called *First Tuesday*, which we took over from (ITV in 1993); it was made by Yorkshire Television who at the time had argu-ably one of the UK's finest documentary making teams. (. . .) (I)t was a very heavy hitting, very social concern . . . I mean, like *Panorama* (BBC factual television strand), but much more international in its focus. (. . .) These were heavy hitting programs about big stories around the world of real social concern and they pulled no punches. (. . .) (W)e were paying an absolute fortune, because Greg Moyer was so keen the European channel should have it, because we hoped it would make such a big impact in the UK that we were taking over this prestigious sub-brand of television. But, after about two years the deal was pulled because the kind of programing these documentary filmmakers were making was just not stuff that the Americans could stomach. (Comer-Calder, former Senior VP and General Manager, DNE, interview with author, telephone, 4 October, 2004)

However, Stuart Carter, Managing Director of Pioneer Productions points out that Discovery's approach to the factual genre has been positive:

> So, I think that it (Discovery) had a very positive thing in helping to popularize, certainly in science, which is the area that I know about. Popularizing topics which hadn't been on television before and that people enjoyed watching. So, I think what Discovery has achieved, the BBC would claim a lot of success in this too, but I actually I think it really started because the trigger came from Discovery. (It) was to make popular factual programs that people wanted to watch in large numbers, which hadn't really been happening before. So, I think that, for all factual filmmakers, they've got a lot to thank Discovery for, because without that, the volume of factual material would be a fraction of what it is now. They made it a big part of television. It still is a big part of television. It has evolved now to formats, but it is still factual programing. (Carter, Managing Director of Pioneer Productions, UK, interview with author, London, 23 March, 2004)

However, in the US, Chris argues, 'the repopularization of documentary has been orchestrated at least in part by remaking the genre as simply another style in which dramatic story lines can be delivered.' In support of this argument, Chris points to that Discovery's programs 'have regularly featured natural disasters, unexplained phenomena, . . . forensic science, reality-based crime stories, surgical procedures, or human and animal mating practices' (Chris, 2002: 22).

Although high-budget documentaries such as *Walking with Dinosaurs*, *Blue Planet*, and film director James Cameron's *Bismark* have all achieved record ratings and helped define the Discovery brand globally, *Financial Times* and *Time magazine* have claimed that the flagship channel, Discovery Channel US, was not able to hold the audience on a regular basis (Eisenberg, 2003; Thal-Larsen, 2003). As a response to this development, senior management at Discovery US admits that: 'We had to open up the brand a bit and also make it more entertaining' (Bunting quoted in Thal-Larsen, 2003). The Learning Channel (TLC), owned by Discovery Communications, Inc., became the most active American buyer of British factual television formats. The makeover television format *Changing Rooms* was turned into *Trading Spaces* in 2000 in the US. The format became the highest-rating program in TLC's history, with an audience of 6 million viewers in 2002 (Steemers, 2004). In June 2002, Discovery Channel launched their own hosted factual docu-soap/reality TV series *Monster Garage*, *American Chopper* (the US protagonists are a family building motorcycles), and *MythBusters* (the US hosts are testing myths through trial and error (Hall, 2005). Discovery has been known globally for high budget hour-long traditional documentaries. Such programs are characterized by interviews in the form of 'talking heads', and computer generated graphics. These programs still form a significant part of Discovery's programing offerings. But, partly to differentiate itself from other factual program providers, the broadcaster has also introduced new factual program forms. One way, as we have seen, is by introducing hosts in programs who present themes and involve themselves in the topics (Senior executive (1), DNE, interview with author, London, 12 May, 2004).

GLOBALIZING THE PRODUCTION
OF FACTUAL PROGRAMING

Throughout the 1990s, broadcasters have increasingly searched for funding opportunities outside their national territory (Humphreys and Lang, 1998). International co-production was increasingly seen as an answer to rising production costs in one single territory, and especially in smaller countries (Blind and Hallenberg, 1996; Davis, 1999). Documentary television producer Steven Seidenberg explains how this development relates to the production of the television documentary: 'The driving force behind international co-productions was clearly financial. What happened is that documentaries got too expensive for single broadcasters to be able to afford to make' (Seidenberg, documentary television producer, interview with author, London, 14 July, 2003). Discovery responded to the changes by exploiting cross-border opportunities in several ways, according to Chris Haws, senior executive at Discovery Networks Europe:

> Discovery encourages (. . .) international co-productions, transnational collaborations and imaginative co-funding mechanisms. So, in addition to co-producing locally with BBC, Channel 4, Channel 5 and the ITV regions, we also co-produce with European broadcast partners, such as ZDF, TV2, NRK, and we are developing contacts with FR3 and La Cinquieme. (Haws quoted in Dox, 1997)

Discovery has developed a business model in which it operates as a global television publisher, commissioning, acquiring, and investing in programing. The increasingly commercialized global media industry has created an environment favoring '"lean" management strategies such as out-sourcing, shared financing and synergy,' according to Fürsich. Discovery does not produce in-house, but buys and co-produces (Fürsich, 2003: 142). Discovery's publisher model resembles other global enterprises' role, such as Nike, whose core business is to develop the enterprise's trademarks, logos, and rights (Lury, 2004: 122), and also the design of its branded products. Discovery therefore relies on three ways of securing programing:

Commission—covering all production costs and holding all global distribution rights;

Co-production—splitting the production budget with outside producers and allowing the latter to sell the front- and back-end rights to other non-Discovery territories;

Acquisition—Discovery's various international territories cherry-pick the show and pay only an agreed-upon license fee. (Freeman, 2004: B4)

The scale of Discovery's global corporate network has allowed for the internalization of co-production as regional networks co-produce with each other. Internal global co-production gives Discovery the opportunity to substantially increase the funding for programs and series, according John Hendricks, Discovery's founder:

When we launched in 1985, we could barely afford an average programming budget of $7,000 per hour. In many markets around the world today, if you really look at the economics of running a channel, the budgets would be similar, perhaps in the range $7,000–$10,000 an hour. Discovery's self-syndicated system of operating which gives us all of our international units contributing to the [overall cost of a programme] which in the US means we can recover $400,000 per hour on a production, add in another $400,000 from our international division, and that's $800,000 per hour of production value that we can put on screen. But one of our much smaller markets might only be contributing $5,000–$10,000 of that, yet getting the higher value on screen. (Hendricks quoted in Forrester, 2003a)

Discovery has an extensive presence in the various television markets, with offices in Copenhagen, Warsaw, London, Munich, Paris Madrid, Toronto, São Paulo, Buenos Aires, Mexico City, New Delhi, Singapore, Beijing, Shanghai, Taipei, and Tokyo, in addition to its world headquarters in Silver Springs (US) and other US offices in Miami, Chicago, Los Angeles, and New York. What characterizes 'the globalization of large cultural enterprises' is their global network of 'subsidiaries and branch offices' linking 'urban clusters of cultural production' (Krätke, 2003: 607). Discovery's operations exemplify a more general development where global media firms often establish themselves in 'production centres of the global cultural industry, in particular in Los Angeles, New York, Paris, London, Munich, and Berlin' (Krätke, 2003: 612).

The internally co-produced programs circulate within the global Discovery television network. This production arrangement makes it easier for Discovery to keep the worldwide rights for the programs, and this in turn makes the flow of programs across the world more efficient. The internal co-production approach also gives Discovery increased control over the production and content of television programs (Senior executive (2), DNE, interview with author, London, 12 May, 2004).

While a Discovery program may be produced by a television producer based in London, the activities in developing and financing the program therefore extends globally within the company. Discovery's globalization of production has introduced new job functions and titles, such as 're-versioning specialist' and 'global commissioning editor'. The former oversees 'language customization of programming'. According to a job advert for this position for Discovery Latin America/Iberia, the responsibility includes 'audio and editorial quality control of all translated, dubbed and /or subtitled programming', as well as 'monitor editorial content and inappropriate cross-cultural words, gestures or symbols in regional productions.' Among the further requirements are 'hands-on experience and in-depth knowledge of social and cultural sensitivities in Brazil' (Discovery, 2004a). In a similar way, one may observe how the global and the local interact in the Discovery system when producing on-air spots for global programing. Previously, the broadcaster had to ship video tapes 'to remote offices upon demand' taking up to a week for feedback from overseas staff causing production delays. When producing the on-air promotional spots for the Discovery Channel program series *Extreme Engineering*, McKelvy at Discovery explains that the broadcaster decided to 'Re-use the promotional spots, created in the United States, on our international networks' by distributing them online (McKelvy quoted in McKelvy and DeLuca, 2003). The spots were placed on servers in London, Miami, Singapore, and India, and 'At each site, the marketing teams could quickly review the spots online and then localize them for their own markets' (McKelvy quoted in McKelvy and DeLuca, 2003).

EUROPEAN MEDIA REGULATIONS AND LOOPHOLES

The global television program format is a program form highly adapted to a globalizing television industry, and also has the ability to circumvent European media regulations. One of its key characteristics is its ability to be customized for a specific territory. The traditional co-production practice involves two or more partners that create a program that ideally includes various content elements with appeal in each partner's television territory. The partners may create slightly different versions for each territory, including language adaptations. In contrast, the same television format can be specifically adapted for many different territories across the globe. Formats such as the British factual formats *Changing Rooms* (Endemol Entertainment, UK) and *Who Do You Think You Are* (Wall to Wall, UK) are usually developed by a broadcaster or a producer in one country and then licensed to broadcasters (Moran, 1998: 25–26). The television industry report, *Rights of Passage-British Television in The*

Global Market points out that formats are attractive as they: 'enable the creation of domestic programs which tend to appeal more to domestic audiences' (Television Research Partnership, et al.: 2005). Another reason for the popularity of television formats among broadcasters is that they can exploit a loophole in the EU Commission's Directive, *Television Without Frontiers*. A format adapted to a national territory contributes to the national and European production quotas. Waisbord claims that this has become 'part of business strategies to bypass local programming quotas' (Waisbord, 2004: 363). The *Big Brother* factual format 'may well be the easiest way to fulfill these kinds of policy targets, although this was hardly the original intended outcome' (Syvertsen, 2003: 162). Discovery draws attention to how European media regulations, such as the quota policy, may prevent the distribution of programing that is produced across national borders. In response to the EU Commission's public consultation regarding the *Television Without Frontiers* Directive's policy on a European programing quota that requires broadcasters to transmit a majority of European works 'where practicable', Discovery argues:

> We also urge the Commission to be wary of the notion that such quotas should be measured on a value basis, as the methodology against which this could be measured would need to be capable of reflecting an extraordinary degree of complexity. In Discovery's case, our content is sourced from a mixture of fully funded commissions, co-productions and acquisitions. In the case of our co-productions, these are often undertaken in partnership with Discovery's sister operations around the world along with third parties and can take several years, in the case of research or exploration based material, to come to screen. The burden placed on both broadcasters and regulators to quantify and report upon such a measurement of investment would be onerous. (Discovery letter to the EU Commission, 2003)

Although the quota system may restrict the free flow of programs within Europe, there is a co-production loophole in the *Television Without Frontiers* Directive undermining this part of the regulations. The loose definition of 'European works' is considered an additional loophole in the *Television Without Frontiers* Directive. The Directive states that programs co-produced in a non-European country but 'made mainly with authors and workers who reside in Europe' qualifies as 'European works' (European Commission, 1989). Venturelli describes this as 'an open-door for large scale multinational-content monopolies to enter the European market.' It is possible to omit the 'cultural quota' by cooperating with European program producers on a contractual work-for-hire basis. These consequences were not anticipated by the European policy makers (Venturelli, 1998: 204–205).

GLOBALIZATION OF FILM AND TELEVISION LABOUR

The drive to reduce production costs and increase profit has intensified the movement of production on a global scale. The multinationals have pioneered the practice of switching production sites in search for the most lucrative production locations (see Held and McGrew, 2007).

Cities, countries, and regions have responded by introducing financial incentives to attract production. This development has been criticized for leading to the lowering of wages and job insecurity, especially within manufacturing industries (see Held and McGrew, 2007). A similar development is taking place within the film and television industry. The term 'runaway production' describes the process in which various stages of the production of both films and television programs are moved to new locations to lower costs (Miller, et al., 2005: 137). The proportion of Hollywood productions shot overseas increased from 7 to 27 the last decade. Eighty-one per cent of these productions were shot in Canada (Miller, et al., 2005: 137). Hollywood films are outsourced to Canada, Australia, or Romania, but usually 'conceived and financed' by film studios in Southern California (Verrier, 2005). Highly developed production skills, language, foreign exchange rates, and business links are crucial in attracting these productions (Miller, et al., 2005: 137). Canada and other countries have introduced tax credits as an incentive for film and television production. In 2005, *LA Times* reported that Ontario offered 18 per cent tax credit on labour, and in Toronto producers would only be 'charged 78 cents for every Canadian dollar spent on city services' (Verrier, 2005). Peter Leitch, Chair of the Motion Picture Production Industry Association of British Columbia, explains: 'We know we have to be globally competitive . . . It's not that easy. Without the tax credits, we'd be struggling right now, big time' (Leitch quoted in Verrier, 2005). Discovery programs produced by Canadian producers have benefited from the tax credit and financial arrangements in Canada. Programs have received tax credit from The Government of Ontario/Ontario Film & Television Tax Credit and Quebec Film and Television Tax Credit, and interim financing from the National Bank of Canada TV & Motion Group.

The three key practices associated with the globalization of film and television production are: global and cross-national co-production, the harnessing of loopholes in the EU's *Television Without Frontiers* Directive, and the globalization of film and television labour. The next part of the chapter explores how the major global partnership between BBC Worldwide and Discovery has adopted some of these practices, and also considers the wider consequences of this collaboration.

A MARRIAGE OF CONVENIENCE?—
THE BBC AND DISCOVERY

In 1998, BBC Worldwide and Discovery formed the most extensive formal factual television agreement in international television history. The two media organizations both wished to grow outside their home territories for commercial reasons, and sought a partner that could support the expansion. The Discovery Networks US's 11 channels had entered over 60 million American homes by the early 1990s, and started expanding overseas in the mid-1990s. However, the consolidation at home and the planned expansion required large quantities of factual programing. Discovery US was now in a financial position to intensify investment in programing production. Across the Atlantic, BBC's commercial arm, BBC Worldwide, was given permission to expand into international markets under a 1996 Charter (Steemers, 2004: 84). The aim was to increase the profit of BBC Worldwide to help fund the BBC organization. BBC Worldwide had ambitious plans: 'Over time, BBC Worldwide's aim is to develop a world-class portfolio of programme brands that rivals those of Disney or Time Warner' (BBC Worldwide, 1998). BBC's commercial arm argued that an American partner was crucial to help realize the bold plan: 'We (BBC Worldwide) were looking for a partner internationally . . . Which ever way you look at the world market, the US is absolutely dominant in programing. So unless you make progress there, the rest of it doesn't add up' (Emery, Former Managing Director, BBC Worldwide, interview with author, London, 16 May 2003). BBC Worldwide chose Discovery as its long-term factual television partner. There was a strong belief that the emerging global cable and satellite television enterprise would contribute significantly to fulfill BBC's goals. Dick Emery, former Managing Director of BBC Worldwide, recalls:

> Basically, the BBC brought the volume of the content and Discovery brought the cash and the international expertise that the BBC had really no experience in developing channels around the world. Let's say in India or the Far East, Discovery had people on the ground in the local markets. They had infrastructure to do it. So, adding another channel or two wasn't a big deal. They had people on the ground to do it. To try to set up the infrastructure and the commercial expertise the BBC didn't have was almost an impossibility. So, BBC got a share in the channels that were launching and got sale of programing to these channels, which helped it to work, and what Discovery got was secured content in the US, which differentiated them in the competition. (Emery, Former Managing Director, BBC Worldwide, interview with author, London, 16 May 2003)

The partnership was organized in three parts:

- Joint-Venture Programming (JVP): The co-production of television programming:
- Joint-Venture Networks (JVN): The development of television channels
- The US distribution and marketing of the television channel BBC America

Discovery invested $290m in creating new joint-venture television channels (JVN), such as Animal Planet and People+Arts in South America. Discovery was to further invest $100 million to market and distribute BBC America. The joint-venture programing (JVP) replaced BBC Worldwide's program sales offices in New York. Although the deal was made between BBC Worldwide and Discovery, it indirectly involved parts of the BBC organization involved in programing production. The 50/50 owned JVP functioned as a centre for the partnership. Discovery's television channels Discovery Channel, The Learning Channel (TLC), Animal Planet, and the Travel Channel, and the JVN would have a guaranteed 'first-look' at all the BBC Production's ideas for factual programing from the BBC departments included in the deal. In return, BBC Production received a minimum of $175 million over five years for direct commissions or co-production of factual programing (Beavis, 1998; Deans, 1998: 22; BBC Worldwide, 1999). Furthermore, the BBC was not liable for any possible losses from the BBC Worldwide/Discovery deal, and received 50 per cent of the profits from the partnerships (BBC, 2004b). The partnership has run for over a decade, with the two media organizations becoming intertwined in several ways.

INTERTWINING 1: COMPANIONS AND COMPETITORS

The partnership exemplifies a more general development of large enterprises and organizations sharing power and knowledge to expand internationally (Castells, 2000). In the media industry, conglomerates also compete and cooperate as a way of reducing risks (Croteau and Hoynes, 2006: 141). Dick Emery, former Managing Director of BBC Worldwide reflects on this paradox:

> I saw us as almost direct competitors to Discovery. (. . .) The idea that we would end up working together seemed to me to be rather bizarre. But, the more we talked and the more they talked about their vision of a digital world, and consumer choice and more streams of programing, it was clear that they had a very clear vision of where they were going, and they needed content and they recognized that the BBC had more of the content that they needed. (. . .) So, we very quickly got to a common understanding. (Emery, Former Managing Director, BBC Worldwide, interview with author, London, 16 May 2003)

BBC executives justified the deal by arguing that the amount of funding provided by Discovery would be a principal means of fulfilling the BBC Governors' demand for an increase in the revenues. The deal would raise BBC Worldwide's earnings for the BBC from 5 to 15 per cent over the next 10 years (Deans, 1998: 24). In the US, the cable operator Tele-Communications, Inc. (TCI) could offer the BBC distribution for BBC America from Liberty Media, and Discovery would market the channel in the US (Guider, 1997). McElvouge argues that Discovery's main owner (TCI) had, in the US, 'forced a number of channels off its cable systems so they can carry Discovery's latest channel, Animal Planet' (McElvouge, 1997: 14). The partnership also marked a change in the power relations between Discovery and the BBC. Discovery US, had for a long time, been dependent on BBC selling them programing. Now the two organizations had become major industry allies, and the BBC would guarantee programing for the US cable and satellite broadcaster. As pointed out earlier, the collaboration also gave Discovery global co-branding opportunities with the BBC, not least in former colonial countries familiar with the British public broadcaster (McElvouge, 1998a: 40).

INTERTWINING 2: COLLABORATION AND CONTROL

Since 1998, Discovery's funding has trickled through parts of the BBC organization either through co-production or direct commissions. The Discovery channels in the US had, in return, a 'first look' at the ideas for factual programing from the departments covered by the agreement seeking US co-production money (Deans, 1998: 22). These BBC departments were:

- London-based BBC Production science, documentaries and history and features and events departments are included in the factual deal.
- The Natural History Unit (NHU) and features department in Bristol,
- Network production in Birmingham,
- Entertainment and features and religion in Manchester.
  (Deans, 1998: 22)

Discovery practically controlled BBC's US co-production activity through the 'first look' principle. Only the ideas and program proposals rejected by Discovery were to be presented by the JVP to other potential US co-producers, such as the cable channel A&E or the public service broadcaster PBS (Reguly, 1997). However, BBC executives claimed that the $175 million guaranteed by Discovery represented 40 per cent more funding than what the BBC at the time received from the US co-production partners. This was an important reason for entering into the exclusive long-term partnership (Dawtrey, 1998). The American PBS had been a significant co-production partner for the BBC's factual program production (Tunstall, 1993: 42).

However, since 1997, the collaboration between the two has been reduced (Steemers, 2004: 125). The two used to collaborate in the making of programs for their science documentary strands *Horizon* (BBC) and *Nova* (PBS). The British terrestrial television channel Channel 4 has taken over much of BBC's role as PBS's factual television program co-production partner (Keighron, 2002: 15).

The BBC/Discovery partnership was extended for another 10 years in 2002 (BBC, 2002a). The partners would continue the development of television channels and the distribution of BBC America. Discovery would invest a further $35 million to $40 million each year on programing until 2012 (Moss, 2002). From 1998 to 2004, Discovery had invested over $226m in BBC programs (BBC, 2004b). The size of Discovery's funding is significant also in comparison with the BBC organization's total annual budget for 2005 of £351 million for the factual and learning genre (BBC, 2005). The intensified co-production collaboration between the BBC and Discovery is further documented in the BBC Worldwide International Sales Catalogues (*see* Table 4.1).

The first column of Table 4.1 shows the number of program productions offered in each factual programing category annually. The numbers in brackets show programs co-produced by the BBC and the Discovery-owned television channels, such as Discovery Channel, TLC, The Science Channel, Travel Channel, Discovery Health Channel, Discovery Wings, or for the joint-venture channel Animal Planet. Some of these productions have additional international co-production partners. The figures show the extensive range of factual television genres included in the BBC/Discovery collaboration. BBC- and Discovery-owned television channels, or the joint venture Animal Planet, co-produce nearly one-third—462 of 1509—of all factual television productions presented in BBC Worldwide Program Sales Catalogues. The number of BBC/Discovery co-productions is highest in the factual program sub-genres Natural History (156 out of 309), Science (117 out of 268), and Wildlife (61 out of 71). The sub-genres listed are Discovery's core program categories. Discovery has hardly any involvement in the News and Current Affairs category, and takes only part in 8 out of 213 programs within this sub-genre. The BBC and the American PBS have only produced 25 of the programs featured. The factual program productions featured in the BBC Worldwide International Sales Catalogues that are not co-produced with Discovery are mainly financed by BBC alone, and some with funding from international co-producer partners.

The close relation between BBC and Discovery reflects the historically strong Anglo-American relationship in international television co-production. British documentary producers have 'bigger problems with Europe than we do with America' according to André Singer at West Park Pictures—the London-based factual television production company (Singer, Creative Director, West Park Pictures, UK, interview with author, London, 16 June, 2004). A common language and a 'common cultural game,

Table 4.1   Number of BBC and Discovery Co-Productions Presented in BBC
Worldwide Program Sales: 2002–2006*

Year/	2002**	2003	2004	2005	2006**
Factual genres:					
Natural History	40(20)	66(30)	73(46)	84(40)	46(20)
Wildlife	15(13)	29(25)	25(21)	2(2)	—
Documentaries General	32(8)	62(6)	—	—	—
History General	25(14)	59(27)	43(15)	31(12)	22(7)
History Strand– Timewatch	7(0)	16(0)	22(1)	22(9)	12(7)
Science, incl. Horizon Strand	27(13)	60(29)	64(29)	73(30)	44(16)
News and Current Affairs	34(2)	54(3)	30(1)	65(0)	30(2)
Religion	—	—	7(3)	12(4)	—
Leisure, Lifestyle, and Society	17(4)	34(6)	94(8)	90(1)	49(1)
Total	197(74)	380(126)	348(111)	381(98)	203(53)

Notes:
*Program series are counted as one production.
**Data is based on one of the two annual BBC Worldwide International
Sales Catalogues for 2002 and 2006.
(Source: BBC Worldwide, 2002; 2003a; 2004; 2005a; 2006)

that has been played for so long makes it easier for us in America,' André
Singer points out (Singer, Creative Director, West Park Pictures, UK, interview with author, London, 16 June, 2004). The relationship is further
documented in the television industry report *Rights of Passage—British
Television in The Global Market*, 2005. Although television co-production funding, in general, 'remains relatively small in comparison to overall
network expenditure on programing in the UK,' the report claims that it
is increasingly important in 'higher production budgets/values for top-end
programs and series in offsetting the risks associated with those budgets'
(Television Research Partnership, et al., 2005: 19). The UK producers rely
heavily on North American partners as providers of funding for the general co-production for television programing. In 2003, 93.1 per cent of UK
TV co-production finance came from North American partners. Partners
from continental Europe represents 4.3 per cent of funding and 'the rest
of the world' only 2.6 per cent of the total funding. The US cable television channel A&E and the public broadcaster PBS are considered as the

main co-production partners for UK broadcasters in this report (Television Research Partnership, et al., 2005: 19).

The BBC has, indirectly, become involved in the competition between Discovery and its global factual television channel competitor, National Geographic Channel. The partnership agreement prevents BBC from co-producing and working with National Geographic, according to Stuart Carter, Managing Director of the UK-based factual television production company, Pioneer Productions:

> It's all about stopping a lot of high-quality factual programming going into the American marketplace on something other than a Discovery channel. So, it's a strategic cost it has to bear whether it likes it or not. That's a very smart business move because if Nat Geo gets hold of that BBC content it will just steamroll Discovery flat. (Carter quoted in Keighron, 2002: 15)

BBC and National Geographic Channel co-produced only 12 of the programme productions featured in the BBC Worlds Sales Catalogues 2002–2006.

INTERTWINING 3: BBC WORLDWIDE/DISCOVERY CO-PRODUCING: WHO DECIDES?

The announcement of the deal sparked debate in the press and among producers and BBC executives. Some were concerned about possible editorial conflicts pointing to the power Discovery would have as they funded substantial parts of the production costs. Others were confident that the BBC would be in charge. *The Economist* reported on 'discontented BBC producers concerned about the editorial output and also concerned about the effect that Discovery's editorial input will have on BBC programmes' (*The Economist*, 1998: 63). *The Economist* also addressed the possible clashes in production policy and the way the two broadcasters defined their audience. The magazine claimed that Discovery divided its demographic audience group into 'info-actives,' 'info lites' and 'info-practicals', and split each audience subgroup into tribes such as 'machos', 'escapists', and 'boys' toys': 'This ethos will sit uncomfortably with the inclusive high-mindedness that lies deep in the soul of the BBC' (*The Economist*, 1998: 63). However, Ron Neal, Chief Executive of BBC Production, defended the agreement by pointing out that the contract between the partners stated: 'Co-production programmes shall be made by and under the direct supervision and control of the BBC, on behalf of BBC Worldwide, and final artistic and editorial control shall be vested in the BBC at all times' (Neil quoted in Deans, 1998: 24).

Georgina Born's BBC ethnography *Uncertain Vision* (2004), gives an indication of the potential for disagreement between BBC and Discovery. The following passage describes a BBC Rights Agency meeting in 1997. The Rights Agency was formed to deal with possible problems arising from BBC's increased involvement in commercial activities, such as tackling disputes between BBC departments over rights and help co-ordinate 'external trading' such as co-production:

> The discussion shifts to factual co-productions, which necessarily involve the 'JVP' or joint-venture partnership, the bulk deal to co-produce factual and documentary programmes by the BBC and Discovery. The JVP is almost finalised but not signed, yet Discovery are already invoking it in various questionable ways. They discuss *Rhythm of Life*, a series commissioned by Music and Arts and made by an indie, which means it lies outside the JVP. But Discovery are claiming that it does come under the agreement and have thrown their considerable weight around, making increasingly unreasonable editorial demands. The collective view is to go back to Discovery and agree to some of the changes requested, as long as Discovery proceeds on the basis of the original deal, including rapid payment. Jonathan, from a legal perspective, adds that he's very concerned they clarify with Discovery now that normal co-production deals allow for consultation but do not give Discovery final editorial clearance. They must hold out for this principle or a dangerous precedent might be set; after this story every one solemnly agree.
> (. . .)
> They turn to *Under the Sun*, the ethnographic film strand, also part of the JVP. Oliver reports that the controller of BBC2 wants to change the remit: it must become 'glossier, lighter'. The archetype for the new feel is a film called *Painted Babies*, and the strand editor is keen on this direction. But Paul reports that on a film currently being edited, *Kung Fu Monks*, Discovery are pressing for more violence, 'for kicks and blows every ten seconds!" There is cynical laughter.
> (. . .)
> As we close, the Music and Arts commercial manager bursts out, as though incapable of repressing any longer an unexpressed truth, that they all know how difficult—how incredibly picky and fussy—Discovery are editorially. It will lead to major problems in future on the JVP. 'Just imagine what would happen if Discovery had got to grips editorially with *Rhythm of Life* . . . ', he poses rhetorically, implying that if they had it would be horrifying, beyond the pale. (Born, 2004: 171–172)

However, in response to the possible disagreement between the partners, Glenwyn Benson, BBC's joint Head of Factual and learning, argues: 'If Discovery wants a slightly different version, we make it—we do reversions. But you never see anything on the BBC which isn't the way we'd want to make it' (Benson quoted in Keighron, 2002, 15). Four years into the BBC

Worldwide/Discovery partnership, the British based factual television producer André Singer argued:

> Certainly there's been a change in the kind of products. Crudely, one can label a product that comes from Discovery, in terms of style and quality, as different to what comes from the BBC and I think those two boundaries have certainly drawn closer to each other over the years. (It is hard to say) whether it's because we're in a global market and audiences are pressuring broadcasters indirectly for that kind of product, or whether its because of the direct involvement of Discovery within the BBC, but there's certainly been a shift in product. (Singer quoted in Keighron, 2002: 15)

The tendency for the boundaries between Discovery and the BBC to draw closer is most noticeable in the partners' global factual brands. These mega productions represent the introduction of the Hollywood blockbuster logic to the factual genre.

INTERTWINING 4: THE BLOCKBUSTER LOGIC AND GLOBAL FACTUAL BRANDS

The natural history television series *Life on Earth* (1979) helped secure the BBC's international reputation for impressive factual programing (Scott and White, 2003: 320). However, a different kind of spectacular factual programing emerged in the mid-1990s. The arrival of BBC and Discovery co-produced global factual brands signaled the introduction of the blockbuster logic to the genre. These branded media productions are distributed in as many media forms as possible for both public and commercial purposes. Traditionally, feature films are a driving force in this process (Murray, 2005: 416).

High–budget television productions spearhead the distribution of branded factual media content in various media forms. Formulas and sequels are central in this strategy as 'a few global hits that can be marketed across different media outlets as opposed to many small projects with lower profit margins' (Fürsich, 2003: 135). BBC Worldwide and Discovery are able to repeatedly raise the majority of funding and provide the resources needed for realizing such mega projects. These factual media brands serve the interests of both the BBC and Discovery in several ways.

In 1999, *Walking with Dinosaurs* was launched by the partners and the German television channel ProSieben. The blockbuster film, *Jurassic Park* (1993), and the sequel, *The Lost World* (1997), were important 'cultural reference point(s)' for most television viewers (Scott and White, 2003: 320). *Walking with Dinosaurs* was rapidly developed into a string of *Walking with . . .* media brands (*see* Table 4.2).

The *Walking with . . .* brand has generated over £43 million in total since the launch in 1999. The television programs have been turned into books, magazines, DVDs and CD. Book sales for *Walking with Dinosaurs* reached 1.5 million copies by 2003 (BBC Worldwide, 2003b). This approach is also evident in the more conventional natural history television series *Blue Planet* and *Planet Earth* (BBC and Discovery co-productions). *Blue Planet* is reported to have cost a total of £7 million. The series was turned into a best-selling non-fiction book, a CD soundtrack and the international motion picture *Deep Blue* (BBC, 2004a; Cottle, 2003: 176). The series was sold to 150 territories worldwide and generated £5 million. The sales of a *Blue Planet* DVD version generated £10m and the book sold for £3.5 million. The series *Planet Earth* is an attempt to repeat the success of the natural history series *Blue Planet*. The 11-part series *Planet Earth* costs £1 million an hour to produce. The series is financed by licence fees from the BBC's domestic channels, BBC Worldwide, Discovery and NHK and was completed in 2006 (Winslow, 2004). Discovery holds the rights for North America, NHK has the rights in Japan, and BBC Worldwide the rights for the rest of the world (Robinson, 2006). *Planet Earth* is also being turned into $15 million feature length film (BBC Worldwide, 2005c). BBC Worldwide believes the rights for the *Planet Earth* brand will increase as new digital distribution forms, such as mobile phone and search engines, will create more demand for content (Robinson, 2006). By 2008, the BBC has sold 2 million DVDs of *Planet Earth*, and the Discovery version has sold 600,000 DVD copies (Levin, 2008a).

Frozen Planet is the next major factual television co-production involving the partners. The eight-part program series about the wildlife and human populations in Antarctica and the Arctic is estimated to have a budget of $16 million. In addition to BBC and Discovery Channel, and Discovery Channel Canada, the European broadcasters ZDF (Germany), Antena 3 (Spain), and Skai (Greece) are co-production partners (Levin, 2008a; Moss, 2008).

These practices have a direct parallel to the Hollywood film industry: 'although producers will attempt to maximize streaming of most content packages, and may well pre-select content proposals on the basis of streamability, only a handful of content properties will achieve the status of cross-platform phenomenon' (Murray, 2005: 431). The nature and function of

Table 4.2   The Walking With . . . Factual Brand

Walking with Dinosaurs (1999)
The Making of Walking with Dinosaurs (1999)
Walking with Beasts (2001)
The Science of Walking with Beasts (2001)
Walking with Cavemen (2003)
Walking with Spacemen (2004)
Walking with Monsters (2005)

(Source: Meza, 2003; BBC Worldwide, 2005b)

the *Walking with . . .* branded television programs resemble Disney/Pixar animation films such as *Monsters, Inc.* (1998), *Finding Nemo* (2003), *The Incredibles* (2004) and *Cars* (2006). These are global financially successful animation films that also promote other related media products, as well as merchandising such as toys, videos, and clothing (Artz, 2005: 76). In The Walt Disney Company's Annual Report, the belief in these films is specifically expressed: 'Disney believes that the creation of high quality feature animation is a key driver of success across many of its businesses and provides content useful across a variety of traditional and new platforms throughout the world' (Disney, 2006: 87).

The logic behind the *Planet Earth* brand has similarities, as pointed out by Mark Young, BBC Worldwide's Managing Director: 'A higher proportion of profits are made by a smaller number of programmes . . . *Planet Earth* will be among the top 10 programmes we've sold' (Young quoted in Robinson, 2006). The central role of costly film and television productions, and the attempt to create and direct a flow of media content and related products, exemplify the phenomenon Murray describes as 'media branding':

> Content has come to be conceptualized in a disembodied, almost Platonic, form: any media brand which successfully gains consumer loyalty can be translated across formats to create a raft of interrelated products, which then work in aggregate to drive further consumer awareness of the media brand. Given the dominance of film divisions within global media conglomerates, the content package driving this process is frequently a feature film. (Murray, 2005: 417)

In the US, the Disney Channel was, at first, not considered a serious competitor by the other cable television channels. However, from the middle of the 1990s, the television channel introduced Disney feature films. Films such as *Toy Story* (Pixar/Disney), *The Lion King*, and *Pochahontas* contributed to Disney Channels increased ability to draw both a young and grown up television audience from other competing television channels (Kalagian, 2007: 149).

The factual blockbuster television programs provide 'strategic programming' for both the BBC and Discovery. They deliver large audiences for free-TV channels and drive 'consumer uptake' for pay-TV (Humphreys and Lang, 1998:13). The productions are heavily promoted and attract large audiences, press, and attention, and have become important in creating an image and associations among audiences for both the BBC and Discovery. The *Walking with Dinosaurs* series had an audience of 40 million people in the US. The production is rated as the second most watched BBC TV program in 1999 (BBC Worldwide, 2003b). The global brands also transcend international borders and may reach an audience not familiar with factual television programing (Steemers, 2004: 164). *Walking with Dinosaurs* was licensed to around 90 territories, *Walking with Beasts* to over 50 territories and *Walking with Cavemen* to over 30 territories (BBC Worldwide, 2003b). The genre-crossing docu-drama *Pompeii: The Last Day* (BBC/Discovery) attracted 10 million viewers, and *Colosseum—Rome's Arena of Death* (BBC/The Learning Channel, TLC) was watched by 8.8 million when broadcast on BBC1 in the UK (Brown, 2003). *Supervolcano* was co-produced by the BBC; Discovery; ProSieben, the German television channel; Mediaset in Italy; and NHK, the Japanese public service broadcaster. The docu-drama achieved ratings over average on terrestrial television channels both in the UK (BBC1) and in Belgium (RTL-TVI) (TBI, 2005).

The average viewing figure in the UK for the factual series *Planet Earth* was higher than for *Blue Planet* with 8.5 million, compared to 6.7 million (Robinson, 2006). The BBC believes that the natural history programs such as *Blue Planet* may help promote the 'public service value' of the BBC, explains Keith Scholey, Head of the BBC's Natural History Unit:

> We need to be distinct, we need to be public service, and we need to claw in large audiences. And the BBC gets rewarded in all sorts of ways for productions like Blue Planet which is important in audiences terms but is very, very important in terms of overall BBC public perception terms; that we are there to provide and to inform, educate and entertain. And so there is a lot of support to carry that on. (Scholey quoted in Cottle, 2004: 90)

This view is reflected in the Table 4.3. The programs featured are the 'most memorable factual programmes in 2003' in the UK according to a survey. The survey was included in the 'Review of the BBC's Royal Charter: BBC response to the Department of Culture, Media and Sports consultation'.

However, four of the seven programs credited to either BBC One or BBC Two are actually high budget BBC/Discovery co-productions (*see* Table 4.3, in bold). BBC promotes these programs as 'BBC productions' while Discovery US refers to them as 'Discovery productions': 'We claim it as the BBC *Blue Planet* and vice versa in the States, but this is all part of friendly banter and rivalry,' according to Rupert Gavin, Chief Executive of BBC Worldwide (Gavin quoted in Snoddy, 2002: 20).

The process of the globalization of production has both forced and facilitated increased movement and activity within the film and television industry. The production practices of global and cross-national co-production of television programing, the increased possibility for the harnessing of loopholes in European media regulation and the globalization of film and television labour have become part of this industry. Discovery has rapidly adapted to a globalizing media industry and adopted some of these practices. The enterprise does not own production facilities and operates as a global television publisher that co-produces, commissions, and acquires programing from external producers and broadcasters. The

Table 4.3 The Ten Most Memorable Factual Programs, 2003

Ranking	Channel	Program	Factual Sub-Genre
1	ITV1	*Michael Jackson Tonight Special*	Documentary
2	BBC One	**Pompeii – The Last Day**	Science/History
3	BBC One	**The Life Of Mammals**	Natural History
4	BBC Two	*The Day Britain Stopped*	History
5	BBC One	**Colosseum: Rome's Arena of Death**	History
6	BBC Two	*The Victoria Cross: For Valour*	History
7	BBC Two	*When Michael Portillo Became A Single Mum*	Documentary
8	BBC Two	**Seven Wonders of the Industrial World**	History
9	C4	*Wife Swap*	Documentary
10	C4	*Royal Deaths and Diseases*	History

(Source: BBC, 2004b)

global scale of the enterprise has allowed for the internalization of co-production practices.

Discovery's regional television networks pool their financial resources to commission costly television programing to be distributed throughout its global television network. The practice gives the broadcaster increased control over the content and form of programing suited for the enterprise's brand. Discovery is also able to benefit from the financial incentives provided by Canadian institutions to attract television productions. The BBC Worldwide and Discovery partnership is a spectacular example of the consequences of deregulation, the importance of economies of scale and the outcome of the liberalization of cross-border activity within the media industry. BBC Worldwide and the BBC have adapted to the new political and economic conditions and expanded internationally by adopting practices traditionally associated with large commercial media companies. However, together BBC Worldwide and the public BBC organization are extremely resourceful and competitive, compared to other public-service broadcasters. It is difficult to imagine another European public-service broadcaster capable of repeating BBC's response to globalization. However, the BBC and Discovery collaboration signifies how the global integration of the media industry is challenging the traditional borders between private and public media. The global factual brands represent a media product that serves both public and private increasingly merging interests of high ratings, branding possibilities, and profit. However, these factual productions have also achieved unprecedented audience ratings around the world, reaching a wider television audience for the genre.

5   Discovery's Localization Strategies

When American satellite television channels first expanded into Europe, there was a belief in 'corporate circles' that cultural differences were diminishing and a global culture was emerging, and that English was seen as the coming universal language even in Europe (Chalaby, 2005b: 53). Although global broadcasters like MTV thought that the channel's content had a universal appeal, by the mid-1990s, managers at MTV, for example, realized the need to adjust to more local conditions in Europe (Chalaby, 2002: 195). This chapter explores the dynamics of localization within the television landscape. It investigates how Discovery's televisual culture approaches localization not only in Europe, but also in Latin America, and parts of Asia.

IMPERATIVES FOR LOCALIZATION

The media industry in Europe operates in a region consisting of many countries, numerous national and local languages, and a rich cultural diversity. The region represents a site for the exploration of the imperatives for localization of media content and outlets. When the satellite television phenomenon emerged in the early 1980s in Europe, it was considered by some to be a danger to public-service broadcasters, as well as to the presence of national programing on European television channels (Collins, 2002: 9). The public-service initiated Eurikon and Europa satellite television channels were launched in the mid-1980s by a group of members of the European Broadcasting Union. Eurikon and Europa, and later Eurosport and Euronews, represented a significant response by public broadcasters to the rise of commercial satellite television. These services were also considered by some as a way of fostering a cross-national European culture and 'public sphere' (Collins, 1998: 9). However, proponents of these initiatives were to be disappointed. The idea of a 'pan-European' television service was difficult to realize in practice:

> pan-European television proved to be less successful in fostering and expressing a collective European identity and culture than European

unionists wished. European viewers' responses to the pan-European public service channels of the early 1980s suggests that European television viewers' tastes and interests (their cultures) were so dissimilar as to make the term 'European culture' nonsensical. (Collins, 1998: 31)

The cultural and linguistic diversity of the European television audience also proved to be problematic for the early commercial pan-European operators. Both SuperChannel and Sky Channel experienced major difficulties in producing large enough advertising revenues, and according to Collins, Super Channel's programing strategy failed:

> There was insufficient communality of taste in the potential audience for SuperChannel to attract significant audiences in different national markets for a common programme stream (what was most liked in one location was not most liked in others). Nor was the 'best of British' programming strategy successful in attracting and retaining minorities in different locations that aggregated together would constitute a viable audience. (Collins, 1990a: 65)

Although SuperChannel claimed to 'recognize the distinctive nature of a transnational audience', there was a belief that music and sports programing had a general appeal to the European television audience. Again, the idea of catering for a cross-national European audience, proved to be wishful thinking:

> audience research was to show that few programmes approached a 'universal appeal' and that on the contrary there was little in Super-Channel's repertoire of programmes that appealed widely to distinct European audiences. Rather, audiences in different countries valued different programmes and there was no shared West European public taste addressed in SuperChannel's 'best of British' programme mix. (Collins, 1990a: 66)

These early experiences suggest that, in comparison to satellite television channels, terrestrial channels are in a more favourable position. They already have a presence in the market and are familiar to the television audience, and have a financial advantage (Collins, 1990b: 107). Several of the early pan-European satellite television channels eventually closed down, as they were unable to attract either enough viewers or advertising revenue to justify their existence. However, the pan-European Eurosport and Euronews channels originally set up by public-service bodies continued to exist (Collins, 1998).

US-based cable and satellite television channels also launched European versions in the 1980s and 1990s: Discovery Channel launched in Europe in 1989 and, as pointed out previously, it was (initially) a small operation.

The channel launched into a British television landscape where both the BBC and Channel 4 already provided documentaries. Some claimed that Discovery Networks Europe had yet to make an impact by the mid-1990s (Kilborn and Izod, 1997). However, this began to change in the first decade of the twenty-first century: while many European initiated pan-European television channels had to close, several of the American television channel initiatives such as Discovery consolidated their European presence. The financial resources of Discovery US and its American owners, together with Discovery's marketing efforts and ability to harness the communication infrastructure, resulted in a major pan-European position. The ratings are small compared to national European terrestrial channels, but Discovery has a major pan-European distribution. In 2006, Discovery Networks Europe EMEA's (Europe, Middle East and Africa), 12 Discovery television channel brands reach 173 million cumulative subscribers in 104 countries with programing available in 22 languages (Discovery, 2006b). As the numbers of television channels in Europe exploded, the numbers of thematic documentary channels followed (*see* Table 5.1).

What is characteristic of the growth of the thematic genre channels is that a small number of international groups control the majority of channels in these genres. Furthermore, much of the growth in channels is not due to the emergence of new channel operators, but to the 'on-going launch of local-language versions of global branded channels such as Fox Kids, MTV, and Discovery' (*Screen Digest*, 2003b).

In 2003, of the 81 thematic documentary channels in Europe, *Screen Digest* reported that 25 of them belong to Discovery Networks Europe's operations (*Screen Digest*, 2003b). Discovery had a share of over 30 per cent of the thematic documentary channels in Europe and a growth in subscribers across the region. Parallel to this development, Discovery has continued to launch country specific channels. Despite Discovery's extensive expansion, Guy Bisson, senior analyst at *Screen Digest* points out that this does not signal the emergence of distribution monopolies of factual television:

> I don't think monopoly is the right word. I don't think that is what we are seeing at all. I mean, certainly Discovery is not the only provider of documentary channels by any means. (. . .) Just the fact that documentary is mainstay program content on national terrestrial channels as well (. . .) prevents effectively a monopoly anyway. And, even if Discovery was the only one, which it isn't, we've also got National Geographic and we've got some independent operators as well. (Bisson, Senior analyst, *Screen Digest*, interview with author, 24 September, 2004)

The national terrestrial television channels are still large providers of factual television programing. The total number of hours of 'documentary programming' on the Nordic and UK national broadcasters (both commercial and public service television channels) supports Bisson's view (*see*

Table 5.1   European Growth of Channels by Genre: Documentary Channels

Year	No. of channels:
1990	2
1991	2
1992	2
1993	4
1994	4
1995	7
1996	17
1997	27
1998	47
1999	64
2000	69
2001	73
2002	81
2003	81
2004	—
2005	108
2006	139

(Source: EAO, 2005; *Screen Digest*, 2003b; *Screen Digest*, 2005 quoted in Thussu, 2006: 118)

Table 5.2). Although the Danish and Swedish public service broadcasters' television channels DR1 and DR2, and SVT1, have reduced the number of hours of factual programing, there is still a significant presence of this programing genre on all the Nordic national terrestrial channels.

While the BBC has seen a reduction in its factual television output, its television channels continue to be the main British national outlets for factual programing. During the first part of the 2000s, BBC's television channels distributed thousands of hours of television programing in the category 'factual and learning' (*see* Table 5.3).

In contrast to pan-European broadcasters, national public and commercial broadcasters in, for example, Northern Europe focuses on reaching their own national territories. Discovery Networks Europe claims to have become a major factual television outlet for the European audience, but how does the broadcaster engage with a European audience characterized by a variety of national and local tastes, and cultural and linguistic diversity? MTV was forced to change their original 'One Planet—One Music'

Table 5.2   Documentary Pogramming (Hours) on Public-service Channels in Europe, 2002–2004

		Hours per Year		
Country	Channels	2002	2003	2004
Denmark	DR1	794	1179	756
	DR2	—	1179	431
	TV2	—	237	239
	TV2 Zulu	—	276	254
	TV2 Charlie	—	—	77
Finland	YLE TV1	1106	1178	1201
	YLE TV2	436	482	419
	MTV3	—	—	2
Norway	NRK1	488	601	644
	NRK2	359	359	334
Sweden	SVT1	334	220	183
UK	Channel4	283	289	210

Notes:
1) Documentary programming consists of diverse categories such as 'information' and 'Arts, Humanities and Science'
2) No data from the following channel: Norway, TV2
(Source: : Table adapted from EAO, 2005)

strategy. This is explained, to a large degree, by the arrival of local music broadcasters and the increased competition for audience and advertising revenue (Roe and De Meyer, 2001). However, as Joyce Taylor, former Managing Director of Discovery Networks Europe, recalls, when Discovery Channel launched in Europe, it was first confronted by the differences between Europe and the US:

Table 5.3   Hours of Factual and Learning on BBC Television Channels

		Hours per Year	
Country	Channels	2002/2003	2003/2004
UK	BBC One	1686	1432
	BBC Two	1293	1020
	BBC Choice	876	774
	BBC Three/BBC Four	522	769

(Source: BBC, 2004c)

The US didn't have a documentary tradition, whereas Europe has a huge documentary tradition, so we felt that you can't take these very American documentaries and ship them into Europe, because they just wouldn't fit with the culture. It was just like everyone was going: (. . .) "(T)his is so American" and all the references were American. (. . .) We had to find suppliers who were much more European than American. (Joyce Taylor, former Managing Director, DNE, interview with author, London, 18 June, 2003)

The development of Discovery's European branch proved to be a complicated task for several reasons. Discovery faced competition from national broadcasters in Europe, and Discovery's European operations could not distribute British factual television program that had played a key role in developing Discovery US's presence:

(O)ne of my frustrations was that it was hard . . . it seemed to me . . . to get the Americans who where running the company to understand that, in Europe, it was a very different kettle of fish, that the air waves were awash with documentary television of the very finest quality tailored specifically to national audiences. And, Discovery's output of second-hand programing, which it mostly was, either bought from local terrestrial channels or imported from other countries (. . .) at pretty low cost, was not as exciting to European audiences as the similar sort of thing was to the US audience. The other thing is, of course, that the US audience got the cream of BBC and Channel 4 programs because Discovery (US) went out and bought them all up. But, of course, we in Europe couldn't access those programs. (Comer-Calder, former Senior VP and General Manager, DNE, interview with author, 4 October, 2004)

Another challenge for Discovery was that the small subscriber base in Europe limited the possibility for the company's European branch to invest in new programing. However, in contrast to MTV, Discovery Networks Europe claims to have recognized the cultural differences *within* Europe when it launched to a modest group of 120 000 subscribers in Northern Europe in 1989:

(W)hen VIVA (a local German music television channel set up in 1993) started in Germany, it (VIVA) was much more competitive because it was much more targeted to (the) marked . . . MTV went though a hugely difficult time trying to survive, so what they had to do was create MTV Italy, etc., . . . whereas Discovery had always, kind of from the start, realized that a "one size fits all" doesn't work; cultures are different. (Joyce Taylor, former Managing Director, DNE, interview with author, London, 18 June, 2003)

VIVA started broadcasting in December 1993. By 1997, it reached 22 million homes in Germany, Austria, and Switzerland becoming more popular than MTV-Europe in its home territories. The VIVA Video Jockeys spoke German and the channel practiced a policy of 40 per cent German music (Roe and De Meyer, 2000: 149). However, despite VIVA's attempt to compete with MTV through increased localization, the channel did not succeed. Viacom, the owner of MTV, decided to buy VIVA Media, which included VIVA and VIVA Plus channels in Germany, the Netherlands, Poland and Switzerland. Together with the television channels MTV and MTV Pop, the acquisition of the two VIVA television channels led to a consolidation of MTV's presence as the main music television operator in Germany (Clark, 2004).

Although the majority of global media firms have become conscious of the significance of local culture, the actual degree of localization varies. Competition from other media outlets and television channels in a region, the size of the television market and the actual costs of producing local programing content, all influence the level of localization. Localization is a key part of Discovery's worldwide expansion strategy, although the extent of it varies from region to region.

At the time of Discovery's launch in India, the amount of programming from India was very limited. Rahul Johri, senior Vice President, General Manager, Discovery India, recalls: 'When we started, we had very little India content' (Johri quoted in *Indiantelevision*, 2008). Since its launch in 1995, Discovery Networks India has gradually localized—or 'Indianised'—its channel offerings, according to Deepak Shourie, Managing Director, Discovery Networks India:

> The first step taken towards Indianising the channel was taken in 1998 with the introduction of a parallel Hindi feed. The aim was to attract national viewership, encompassing the mini-metros and small towns. The next significant step was taken in 2001 when the Indian programming team was empowered to buy and acquire content independently for India. For the first time ever, the programmes were scheduled by the Indian programming team. (Shourie quoted in Pinto, 2005)

Since then, Discovery has introduced a one-hour weekly program segment on Discovery Channel called Discovery India Series that included programs such as *Pandit Ravi Shankar: Between Two Worlds, Life of Buddha, Men of Our Time—Mahatma Gandhi*.

Discovery's program localization within the US also includes the targeting of the Spanish speaking part of the American television audience. Discovery Networks US Hispanic Group is a division of Discovery Communication and broadcasts the television channel, Discovery en Español. The channel's programing consists of television programing content for the Spanish-speaking audiences, with content centered on Latin America and the US. In 2007–2008, Discovery increased the number of hours 'produced specifically for

Spanish-speaking audiences' in the US. The channel offered programs such as the documentary *Objetivo: El Northe*, about the immigration debate; *Viviendo en Las Sombras*, a program on the life of illegal immigrants in the US; *Relatos Con Sabor*, about traditional food recipes; and *Espaciao Vital*, on beauty treatments (Discovery, 2007c).

In an attempt to move closer to the Chinese market, Discovery and the Olympic sponsor Visa initiated and sponsored six Chinese filmmakers to produce five-minute program segments about six cities that have previously hosted the former Olympics. These short programs were broadcast on the Discovery Travel and Living programing block in China (*Indiantelevision*, 2007).

Although Discovery point out that they recognized the cultural differences both *between* Europe and the US and *within* Europe, at first it only catered for local differences within European through subtitling and dubbing:

> Well, it (Discovery) recognized it, but could only do a limited customization. The first customization you do is put the language on. From the beginning, it was a percentage that was languaged, and that built up to a 100 per cent. (Joyce Taylor, former Managing Director, DNE, interview with author, London, 18 June, 2003)

From a program content point of view, the localization was also complex:

> I think the idea really was (. . .) that factual television, in itself, is not very culturally specific, that these were universal stories of . . . either about nature, or science or history, or human endeavor, and therefore touched (. . .) universal interests, and therefore would be universally appealing. I just think that, again, because the resources were so small for tailoring the programing to local taste, we really just had to charge ahead and put out the signal and then find nice things to say about that, why, you know, why it made sense, but actually it was purely driven by commercial needs. (Comer-Calder, former Senior VP and General Manager, DNE, interview with author, 4 October, 2004)

Technological shortcomings and the lack of a large enough and measurable audience also limited the early pan-European television channels (Chalaby, 2005b: 48). Trade magazine *Television Business International* questioned the narrowcasters' and niche channels' possibility for success in Europe: 'If U.S. niche channels find it hard surviving in a universe of over 200 million households, what chance for the viability of narrowcasting elsewhere?' (Flynn, 1992: 32). The ideal television niche audience was one that cuts across Europe's national boundaries, according to Joyce Taylor, the operations manager for United Artists Entertainment and Head of Discovery Europe. However, as early as in 1992, Taylor pointed out that Discovery's factual television programing needed sub-titles, which was not acceptable in Germany and France, and, furthermore, this solution would weaken the economies of scale that a pan-European niche television operator could exploit (Flynn, 1992: 32). The increase in households with access to cable and satellite gradually created a feasible commercial market. From 1991 to 2001, the number of homes connected to cable and satellite increased from 25.1 million to 107 million (Chalaby, 2005b: 49–50). The arrival of digital satellite distribution made it increasingly possible to introduce program opt-outs, local advertising and local on-air presentation into the feeds. As with magazine publishing, thematic channels could increasingly operate with regional versions (Brown, 1998). From 1996, although Discovery Networks Europe operated through localized channels, until 2000, it tended to focus on creating a schedule to target the British television market and audience, as it was in this territory that ratings figures existed (Senior executive (2), DNE, interview with author, 30 July, 2003).

The UK broadcast industry was dramatically transformed with the growth of the digital multi-channel market. A key driving force in the digital environment was further localization as the competition for audience toughened. An important stage in Discovery's localization in Europe was to split the service. On 31 January 2000, Discovery Networks Europe was divided into Discovery Networks Europe UK and Discovery Networks EMEA programme feeds (Europe, Middle East, & Africa) (Tobin, 1999). The spilt was necessary to increase the possibilities for catering for Europe outside the UK, according to Marian Williams at Discovery Networks Europe:

> When we first split the schedule it was more to do with taste and lifestyle, and a valid criticism was that we were too Anglo-focussed, both UK and USA in content. It was true, and we were hugely self-critical looking very closely how we built our primetime schedule, although being a bit more relaxed—as we had to be—elsewhere in the schedule. We gave primetime a much more Continental feel and flavour, concentrating on History and upbeat observational material. (Williams quoted in European Television Guild, 2003)

The two feeds shared the program catalogue, but the two schedules were targeting the television audience of two countries: the UK and the Netherlands. So, despite a range of localized channels in Europe, until the mid-2002, Discovery Networks Europe still targeted only two European countries: the UK and the Netherlands (Discovery Germany being a separate business, not part of DNE). In October 2002, the feed structures and program schedules were changed yet again. Although DNE provided language customization and local promos and interstitials for each local channel, Discovery decided to split the one European feed into five feeds: Nordic, Benelux (Belgium, Netherlands, and Luxembourg), Central and Eastern Europe, Italy, and one feed for Africa, Middle East, and Turkey. The localization increased, but each region was led by the rating figures available in one country: Netherlands, in the region consisting of Belgium, the Netherlands, and Luxembourg;

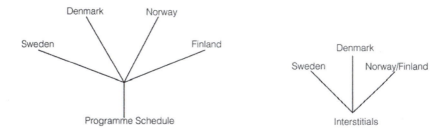

Figure 5.1 Discovery networks Europe regional structure: the Nordic region

Denmark for the Nordic region; and Poland for the Central Eastern Europe region (Senior executive (2), DNE, interview with author, 30 July, 2003).

Each region has a separate program feed, so each country within the same region will have the same schedule (*see* Figure 5.1). The interstitials (the bit between the programs) are more customized for each country than the program content.

Although the program localization was limited, by 2003 Discovery had developed an extensive localization operation in Europe in 21 languages, either dubbed or subtitled (*see* Table 5.4.).

As global channels adapt to local or national linguistic preferences, they are also faced with Europe's differences in lifestyle and television-viewing patterns. The further south in Europe, the later the television primetime. While peak-viewing time in Scandinavia is at 7 pm, in France it is at 8 pm, and in Spain 10 pm (Chalaby, 2005b: 55).

One way to address both local and European levels is through themes of common interest. A program on Venice would be very popular in Italy, but it would also achieve ratings elsewhere. Similarly, a program about the Vatican would be popular in Catholic countries such as Poland and Italy, but it would attract audiences in the rest of Europe not so familiar with the Vatican (Senior executive, (2) DNE, interview with author, July 30, 2003). The production of the global series *Extreme Engineering*, aired in 2003, may serve as an example of how Discovery Networks Europe deals with the relation between the global and the local or national. Through Discovery's 'buy-in' round—the internal co-production procedure—programing produced anywhere 'within the Discovery world is also put forward to the larger group to see whether they are interested in taking and investing in it, with an opportunity to steer local elements into that story,' according to John Begert, Vice President of Content and Marketing, Discovery Networks Europe. DNE decided to invest in the Discovery US-initiated, 13-part series, and two of the episodes focused on Holland's barriers to the sea and the tunnels under the Alps between Austria and Italy. The programs were marketed and 'were picked up by the local press' and 'as a result those particular episodes were the highest rated episodes of the

Table 5.4   All Feeds—Discovery Europe Networks

Country	Subscribers	Language	Dub/Subtitling
UK			
UK	10,258,690	English	—
Ireland	481,455	English	—
Total	**10,740,145**		
Nordic			
Sweden	937,464	Swedish	Subtitled
Denmark	1,206,832	Danish	Subtitled
Norway	604,531	Norwegian	Subtitled
Finland	35,490	Finnish	Subtitled
Iceland	16,125	English	—
Total	**2,800,442**		
Benelux			
Holland	5,732,812	Dutch	Subtitled
Belgium	160,000	Dutch	Subtitled
Total	**5,883,812**		
Germany			
Germany	1,902,885	German	Dubbed
Total	**1,902,885**		
Middle East, Africa, Turkey and Israel (MEATI)			
Turkey	1,362,500	Turkish	Dubbed
South Africa	924,939	English	Subtitled
Israel	400,000	Hebrew	Subtitled
Middle East	163,333	Arabic	Dubbed
Total	**2,850,772**		
Iberia			
Spain/Portugal	2,236,319	Spanish, Portuguese	Dubbed
Total	**2,236,319**		
Central & European Europe			
Romania	2,228,327	Romanian	Subtitled
Hungary	992,869	Hungarian	Dubbed
Russia	1,013,218	Russian	Dubbed

(continued)

Table 5.4 *Continued*

Czech Republic	385,769	Slovak/Czech	Dubbed
Bulgaria	340,254	Bulgarian	Subtitled
Slovenia	237,152	Slovenian	Subtitled
Lithuania	243,494	Russian	Dubbed
Slovakia	162,879	Slovak/Czech	Dubbed
Latvia	132,631	—	—
Greece DTH	137,816	Greek	Subtitled
Ukraine	177,536	Russian	Dubbed
Kazakhstan	76,207	Russian	Dubbed
Estonia	49,302	Russian	Dubbed
Croatia	196,018	Russian	Dubbed

(Source: Discovery Mediapack, 2003a)

series in those countries' (Begert quoted in c21media, 2004b). Although a regional network may say 'no' to participating in the production presented in the global 'buy in' round, it creates a dilemma for a regional network, according to André Singer, Creative Director at the London-based factual television production company West Park Pictures. Singer also has previous experience of working at Discovery:

> If you are sitting running a channel in Europe (. . .) and say 'no' to most of these projects that come from Silver Springs (Discovery's previous headquarters in the US), you have to find other projects for your regions, and that means the money you can afford will give you a lower value, in production value terms, because you cannot afford that kind of project otherwise. So, (the commissioning editor for Discovery Networks Europe) is always having to try to balance between having to version what is sent from Discovery headquarters with high production values, and then make it valuable to the Poles or the Czechs; or saying 'no' to all of that and spending what little money the commissioning editor has available on cheaper projects which the Poles would feel is much more Polish, and that's very difficult balancing. (Singer, Creative Director, West Park Pictures, UK, interview with author, London, 16 June, 2004.)

This indicates a possibility for tension between the European and the US networks. Greg Ricca, President and CEO of Discovery Networks International, underlines the extensive power of Discovery US networks in relation to the national Discovery Channels around the world when asked about the amount of programing produced or commissioned locally by Discovery Channel:

> There isn't a rule that can be applied here, but certainly we've increased the amount of US network product on Discovery Channel, and we will definitely increase it on the other networks, as well. Upwards of 60 percent or 70 percent of the budget is focused on major product that is produced in the U.S. I think it's really key, though, that we talk about this in the right terms. A vast part of the programming that is made for the U.S. networks is developed and produced outside of the U.S. The locales are global, a lot of the production companies and producers are from all around the world—the content is global even though it's centrally done. We'll certainly continue to develop programming in our regional operations, and that programming will still be critical, because it's very important [for the individual brands]. Certainly there are programs, even in the factual context, that aren't going to work everywhere. And there is programming the US develops that the international networks are not going to be interested in. But we are finding that our ability to offer high-impact programming is what distinguishes us from smaller local players. We can't be indigenous in every market we are in. If we had a hundred channels internationally that we were trying to develop programming for, we couldn't come near the great quality and the impact that we can have by partnering with our US channels. (Ricca quoted in Carugati, 2007)

This further underlines the importance of 'high production value' of programing in Discovery's global television networks, in contrast to locally less costly programing.

Discovery Networks Europe emphasizes how it addresses the European diversity of language and cultural preferences. In comparison with MTV, Discovery did subtitle or dub their output from an early stage. However, pursuing a strategy of localization creates a dilemma for the broadcaster. Increased competition in the television market demands localization, but localization of television programing depends on financial feasibility. The smaller the market is, the less advanced the localization. To create programing, Discovery Networks Europe needs to take into account the demand for local programing and programing with 'European resonance' (Senior executive (2), DNE, interview with author, July 30, 2003).

Both the series *Hot Art,* on art crime, and *Industrial Revelations: Europe,* commissioned by Discovery Networks Europe, exemplify how the network attempts to combine a certain universal appeal and local elements. The theme of art crime is a universal theme that crosses borders. Although the program series *Hot Art* aimed to have a universal appeal across Europe, Discovery wanted to tie in elements of localization in the series for it to appeal in specific countries. One way is to include stories from Holland and Sweden that would create interest in those countries.

In 2003, Discovery UK commissioned the 10-part series, *Industrial Revelations,* about the industrial revolution, for the UK market with the English presenter Mark Williams. The series was successful in the UK, and Discovery Networks Europe decided to do a European version of the series. A dilemma was which presenter to include in the European series for it to have European appeal. The UK version of *Industrial Revelations* series had a British presenter, and the European version ended up with a Dutch presenter speaking English (Senior executive (1), DNE, interview with author, London, 12 May, 2004).

The factual television series *Extreme Engineering, Hot Art,* and *Industrial Revelations* all show how Discovery Networks Europe attempted to localize programing. By inserting national or local elements within a global and pan-European program framework, these series aimed to have both a global and pan-European audience, while at the same time have national and local appeal. The next section investigates the localization process in closer detail by exploring segments of content from two European television markets: Norway and the UK.

COMPARATIVE PERSPECTIVES: DISCOVERY CHANNEL UK AND DISCOVERY CHANNEL NORWAY

A content analysis of a random week's sample of Discovery Channel UK and Discovery Channel Norway television feeds gives an opportunity to explore aspects of how Discovery addresses a small European television market and its main European market in terms of language and program themes.

In 2006, between 30 January and 5 February (seven days), the content on Discovery Channel Norway and Discovery Channel UK was recorded between 20.00 and 23.00. The content was split into catagories such as 'Program', 'Commercial advertising', 'Program promos', and the group 'Other', consisting of channel promotion trailers and graphic links between programs and advertising (see Tables 5.5 and 5.6).

The schedule between 20.00 to 23.00 is the prime time programing segment, and it is in this part of the schedule one is most likely to find localized content. The content analysis is only able to capture a small part of Discovery Channel's programing offer in Europe. However, although the content analysis only gives an indication of the characteristics of the channel's distributed programing and localization efforts, the majority of the programing analysed are part of long running series or formats, some over several seasons. This gives an estimate of the quantity of this type of programing. Also, these series are distributed across Europe and in the US, as well as in most of the regional Discovery Channel networks worldwide. The content analysis also allows for the closer examination of aspects of globalization of production and distribution by tracing the location of programs, and location of production companies and financial production arrangements.

Table 5.5 Discovery Channel UK: Percentage of Content in Categories (%)

	30 Jan.	31 Jan.	1 Feb	2 Feb	3 Feb	4 Feb	5 Feb	Average:
Program:	77.5	77.2	77.9	76.2	75.8	77.6	77.5	77.1
Commercial Advertising	17.1	18.3	15.6	17.8	17.1	17.2	17.8	17.3
Program Promos:	2.3	2.5	2.6	3.6	3.5	2.9	4.4	3.1
Other (3-sec. Channel Idents* and Graphic Links)	3.1	2.0	3.9	2.4	3.6	2.3	0.3	2.5

*Channel idents are short promotion trailers for the Discovery Channel

It is also important to note that Discovery Networks Europe shares the same programing.

PROGRAMING, LANGUAGE AND ADVERTISING

Together, Tables 5.5 and 5.6 show how Discovery Channel UK has nearly three times as much advertising content as Discovery Channel Norway: a daily average of 17.3 per cent, compared with 6.1 per cent. However,

Table 5.6 Discovery Channel Norway: Percentage of Content in Categories (%)

	30 Jan.	31 Jan.	1 Feb	2 Feb	3 Feb	4 Feb	5 Feb	Average:
Program:	84.4	83.8	83.1	84.2	83.6	85.6	83.7	84.1
(Of Which Discovery Channel Short Films)	—	—	—	—	—	—	—	(5.9)
Commercial Advertising	5	8.3	6.1	7.1	6.4	4.4	5.7	6.1
Program Promos	2	2.2	0.8	2	1.1	0	1.7	1.4
Discovery/Unesco Films:	2.7	1.7	4.4	3.8	4.4	2.8	6	3.7
Together TV:	5.1	3.3	3.8	1.7	3.7	5.7	1.1	3.5
Other (3-sec. Channel Idents* and Graphic Links)	3.1	2.0	3.9	2.4	3.6	2.3	0.3	2.5

*Channel idents are short promotion trailers for the Discovery Channel

the lower level of advertising in Norway is made up for by three segments of content not present on the UK channel. The *Discovery Channel Short Films* (5.9 per cent) are Discovery property and have the form of documentaries, which are included in the programing category. The second segment is short films on *Endangered Languages* produced by Discovery Communications, Inc. and UNESCO (3.7 per cent), and the third segment is *Together TV* (3.5 per cent) produced by Christian Aid in partnership with the Irish aid agency, Trocaire, and supported by the European Union's Development Education Fund.

Analysing the language used in programing shows the dominance of the English language (*see* Table 5.7). Although there may be the occasional person talking his or her native language in programs, the English language is the dominant among interviewees and all voice-over is in the language. Furthermore, all program promos are in English. However, all programing on the Norwegian channel is subtitled in Norwegian. Contrary to other European countries Norwegian television channels do not have a tradition of dubbing programs and, instead, non-Norwegian programing is subtitled. The *Discovery Channel Short Films* represent the language variety of Europe to a larger degree, although they represent a small proportion of the total program segment analysed. The protagonists in these films speak their own languages such as Swedish, Spanish, Dutch, and German, and are subtitled in English. The Norwegian localization of content is more predominant in the advertising. All advertising on the Norwegian channel has a Norwegian voice-over, actors, or text.

On Discovery Channel Norway, *Discovery Channel Short Films* (5.9 percent) are in European languages: Italian, Swedish, German, Dutch, and Spanish, all with English subtitles. The persons in the program *Building the Winter Games* speak Italian, French, and English, without dubbing, but with English voice-over.

Also, programing about technical and engineering issues dominate on both channels. However, the *Discovery Channel Short Films* on aviation make up seven of the programs in the technical and engineering category on the Norwegian Channel. So, the time taken up by this category is larger

Table 5.7 Main Language of Programing (Weekly Average %)

	Discovery Norway	Discovery UK
Protagonists: English Language	86.7	100
Protagonists: Non-English Language	13.3	—
Protagonists: Norwegian Language	—	—
English voiceover	100	100
Norwegian subtitles	94.1	—
English subtitles	5.9	—

on the UK channel. Programs with hosts testing how things work have a higher proportion on the Norwegian channel than the UK channel. This is also because the series *MythBusters* is broadcast every day on the Norwegian channel. Table 5.8 shows the proliferation of programs on technical, engineering, and science. The hosted programs such as *MythBusters* are also preoccupied with measuring, weighting, and practical testing, although in a 'quasi-scientific' way.

Discovery's schedule consists of a variety of factual sub-genres, and the mixing of them. There are 15 programs in the traditional documentary format on the Norwegian channel and 9 on the UK channel. The format is characterized by its voice-over led narrative, interviews, and reconstructions. On the Norwegian channel, there are 11 programs within the docu-soap/reality TV format; and there are 12 on the UK channel. These programs follow a group of people doing a job or hosts supervising other people who are doing a task. What is important to note is if one excludes the seven Discovery short film segments on the Norwegian channel, the two schedules are remarkably similar.

Table 5.8   Total Number of Programs Broadcast in Thematic Categories: (The Daily Broadcast of Discovery Channel Short Films Counts as One Program)

Discovery Channel Norway	
Medical sciences	1
Technical/Engineering	15
Hosts testing how things work	7
Crime investigation	3
Emergency/Rescue	1
Celebrities	1
Examing a phenomenon	—
Total number of programs	28

Discovery Channel UK:	
Medical sciences	1
Technical/Engineering	14
Hosts testing how things work	1
Crime investigation	3
Emergency/Rescue	1
Celebrities	—
Examining a phenomenon	1
Total number of programs	21

Table 5.9   Ofcom, Factual Television Genre Definitions

Main Genre	Sub-Genre	Definition
FACTUAL	Consumer Affairs	Programs providing consumer advice (on consumer, health, education, financial, or other matters) or warnings on trading standards for consumers
	Factual Entertainment	Including reality shows, human interest stories, and other similar factual material.
	Hobbies and Leisure	Including gardening, homes, DIY, travel, cookery, and other leisure pursuits.
	Serious Factual	Documentaries covering, for example, science and medical issues, nature and wildlife, history, and other topics.
	Special Events	All special events (excluding sports events), such as coverage of parliamentary proceedings, party conferences, royal events.

(Source: Ofcom, 2004)

Discovery Networks Europe is transmitted from London and receives the broadcast licence from the British body for regulation and competition in the media and communications industries, Ofcom. Ofcom divides the factual television program genre in the following sub-genres (*see* Table 5.9)

How does the Discovery Channel programing analysed here relate to the Ofcom categories? The programing does not fit into the categories Special Events, Hobbies and Leisure, Consumer Affairs, but corresponds within the Factual Entertainment and Serious Factual definitions. Serious Factual is defined according to the following topics: 'science, medical issues, nature and wildlife, history and other topics'. *Face Lift* (about facial transplanting) and *Changing Sexes* are the only programs dealing with medical issues in a scientific way. There are no programs on history. As established in Table 5.8, the majority of the programs are characterized by its technical and engineering focus. Although one may place these themes within the Serious Factual category, these programs deal with topics and issues in a certain way. The program *Changing Sexes* is an exception exploring the changing of sex in terms of medical science, social acceptance, and the experience of four individuals. However, in general, the programs seem to have a limited critical focus. Although the programs may explore controversial issues, these are limited to, for example, UFO's: 'More UFO's are reported by people in Scotland than in any other country . . . But what is the truth: have aliens invaded Scotland?' (*The World's Strangest UFO Stories*, introduction, Discovery Channel UK, 5 February, 2006)

In *The Worlds Strangest UFO Stories,* the existence of UFOs is explored and authorities are questioned about possible cover-ups of military activity. However, Discovery's programing both in Norway and in the UK is characterized by a technical and engineering viewpoint. The voice-over in the introduction to the program *The Greatest Ever: Bombers* on Discovery Channel Norway gives an example of this viewpoint: 'Coming up on *The Greatest Ever*: the world ultimate bombers. We'll get up close and personal with the latest high-tech terminator. And go flying in a World War 2 classic. Also on the list: dive-bombers, torpedo bombers, and jet-attack bombers. And you'll hear what its like to drop the biggest bomb of all' (*The Greatest Ever: Bombers*, Discovery Channel Norway, 1 February, 2006). The building or demolition of constructions is another frequent theme. *Building the Winter Games* is about the preparation for the Winter Olympics in Turin, Italy. We follow engineers and designers involved in the 'coolest construction projects'. In *Mega Builders*, we follow two engineers from New Zealand and Canada in the construction of a holiday resort island in Dubai:

> It's a 21st century wonder. Giant palm trees are taking shape off the coast of Dubai. When completed these will be the biggest manmade islands the world has ever seen . . . It's an unprecedented challenge with more than a share of engineering marvels . . . They are using the world's biggest cutted dredges ... and enough rock to circle the globe three times . . . Two mega builders are overseeing the construction of an island city for 100,000 thousand people. (*Mega Builders*, introduction, Discovery Channel UK, 3 February, 2006)

Although the program describes the major engineering task of building the island, the point of view means that you will, for example, not learn about Dubai's one million immigrant labourers that earn around $4 a day. According to Human Rights Watch, workers may spend most of their earnings to pay interest on a $3,000 loan they have taken up to get work permit (Fortune, 2006: 29). Other programs are about destroying buildings or moving large constructions. In *The Blasters,* explosive experts demolish buildings and constructions, and in *Monster Move*, railroads are moved in New Mexico and Nebraska, US. Although technical and engineering issues are vital for human life and civilization, these programs present a view of the world in which there is limited space for critical reflection.

The focus on the technical is further emphasized in the docu-soap/reality TV programs *American Chopper, Rides*, and *The Garage* that make up a large part of the Norwegian and UK broadcast. The series *American Chopper* is based on the Teutel family running Orange County Choppers in the US. We follow the daily life at the garage where motorcycles are built. In the program *Rides*, we follow a caravan of car enthusiasts crossing the US. *The Garage* is about British expatriates working in a car garage in Marbella, Spain. These programs fit more easily in Ofcoms' definition of

Factual Entertainment, defined as 'Including reality shows, human interest stories and other similar Factual material' (Ofcom, 2004). *FBI Files, Forensic Detectives, Psychic Witness,* and *On the Run* are programs on crime investigation mainly in the US. These programs have a significant presence on both channels. The format consists of interviews with investigators and witnesses, and relies heavily on reconstructions of events. In the introduction to an *FBI Files* program (starting at the end of the recorded period) a US voice-over sets the tone of the show:

> In Beirut, armed extremists seize a plane to make a political statement. They terrorise the crew and passengers including two US citizens. As attacks increase against Americans abroad FBI and CIA undertake a daring operation to arrest the hijacker and to send a powerful message to terrorists everywhere. (*FBI Files*, introduction, Discovery Channel UK, 31 January, 2006)

These programs focus on the crime committed, how the crimes where solved, and the technicalities of the process. There is no contextualization of the crime in terms of social and political explanations. It is in the two segments—consisting of short films—*Endangered Languages* produced by Discovery and Unesco and *Together TV*, both on Discovery Channel Norway, that social and cultural issues are addressed. In *Endangered Languages*, groups of people or a tribe in different parts of the world talk about their cultural traditions and role of their local endangered language. In *Together TV*, we meet a Zambian woman volunteering in the local community working with HIV/AIDS and TB victims, an Israeli mother who has lost her son and now works in a Palestinian/Israeli group for peace, and—in stark contrast to *The Greatest Ever: Bomber*—an African artist in Mozambique creating art out of weapons. However, these two are only shown on Discovery Channel Norway and represent an average of 7.2 per cent of the analysed content in comparison to ordinary programs of 84.1 per cent. These segments are not broadcast on the UK channel. Discovery Channel UK carries nearly three times as much advertising content as the Norwegian, although the amount of programing time is similar for the Norwegian and UK channel. One may, therefore, ask if the *Endangered Languages* and *Together TV* segments will be reduced if advertising increases on the Norwegian channel.

The English language dominates the two channels. And, when examining the main location of programs on both channels the UK and US dominance is clear. On the UK channel, apart from two programs, the majority of the programs—10 out of 14—are filmed on location in the US or have significant segments from US or UK locations. On Discovery Channel Norway, 13 out of 16 programs (including the Discovery Channel Short Film segment) are filmed at similar locations. Although it is difficult to know the nationality of the persons participating, the vast majority have a UK or North American accent on both channels. Furthermore, although some of the program locations may be outside the UK and US, the protagonists are from English-speaking countries, such as in *Face Race* (North American accent), *The Blasters* (UK/ North American accent), *Mega Builders* (New Zealand/Canada), and *The Garage* (UK expatriates). The protagonists in *Europe's Richest People* are Uri Geller, matador Enrique Ponce, singer Engelbert Humperdink, and bike racer Carl Fogharty. The program *Europe's Richest People* is filmed in the UK and Spain. All speak English except for the Spanish Enrique Ponce, who is filmed on location in Spain and is dubbed in English. The program *Face Race* is mainly filmed in the US, with a short segment from India about a transplant operation. The interviewees are dubbed in English. This further reflects the importance of the US and UK television market for Discovery.   .

The practices of transnational co-production, and arrangements associated with the globalization of television production labour, are employed in producing Discovery's programing (Appendix II provides an overview of the names and head office locations of the production companies, and some of the financial production contributions or arrangements). Of the total of 26 distinct programs broadcast on Discovery Channel Norway and Discovery Channel UK, ten are made by companies with a head office in the US, five by UK companies, five from Canada and one in Italy, and one is co-produced by a Canadian- and a UK-based production company. Of these, one of the programs is co-produced by Discovery/Channel 5 (UK broadcaster)/UK production company, another is an UK/Canadian co-production between Discovery Networks Europe/Five (UK channel)/ Discovery Channel. A third program is co-produced by Discovery Canada/Ztele (Canadian broadcaster)/Canadian production company, and a fourth by Discovery/Canal D (Canadian broadcaster)/Canadian production company. As discussed previously, programs produced by or co-produced with a European producer can make the program qualify as a 'European production' according to the European Commission's *Television Without Frontiers* Directive. However, Discovery's US-based formats (i.e., *American Chopper, MythBusters*) are not formats that are localized with national European participants, such as *Big Brother*. Furthermore, we see how Canadian producers and broadcasters have a substantial involvement as producer or co-producer. The financial contributions and arrangements of 6 of the 26 programs are produced with the support or funding from the Canadian national or regional authorities. To compete globally, Canada has introduced incentives to attract production. Discovery benefits from these arrangements by involving Canadian partners or producers. Program production receives tax credit, interim finance, and financial participation from Canadian authorities. Although the UK has traditionally been a centre for television production—and especially factual television—we see how Canada is positioning itself to compete for global television production.

This chapter has examined how Discovery's globalizing televisual culture operates to respond to the cultural and linguistic diversity of Europe.

In each European region, local production caters for the ratings-led country's audience, yet smaller European countries, like Norway, get only language subtitling and, so far, no local/national production at all. Discovery Channel UK has a UK voice-over in most of the programs; all promos are in UK voice with accent, and the advertising has either UK voice-over and/or UK actors. All programing on Discovery Channel Norway is subtitled in Norwegian and advertising is in Norwegian. Other European languages do have a presence—although small compared to English. However, although most of the programing is in English, it is important to note that the Norwegian population has a high proficiency in English. In general, Discovery Networks Europe's interstitials are more localized than the actual programing. Discovery also localizes global series productions by including local stories. This approach is also used on a European level. A program may appeal specifically to one or two countries, but is also believed to have interest for the whole European region. This shows a variety of ways that Discovery's televisual culture is incorporating the local in an international or global framework. However, when examining the programing closely, we notice that North America and the UK dominate the two channels in program content and production arrangements.

6   Global Resonance
Television Programing for the World

Discovery and other pan-European and global television and media out-lets consciously incorporate different forms of localization—although to a varying degree—in their effort to expand throughout the world. Media content and brands are produced, shaped, and adjusted to increase their proximity to national and local conditions, and to thereby strengthen the overall appeal of the cross-national and global media outlets. Despite the implementation of localization initiatives, aspects of the 'global' and 'universal' have a significant presence in Discovery's televisual culture, and within television program genres that are distributed cross-nationally. The ideal program has a national appeal, while at the same time appeals to segments of the European or global television audience. This chapter explores the characteristics of 'global programing' and the global television market, and shows how Discovery connects to these characteristics as the enterprise attempts to create content with 'global resonance'.

GLOBAL PROGRAMING: FICTION, ANIMATION, AND FACTUAL TELEVISION

The US dominates international and global sales of television program-ing. The country has an over 70 per cent share of the global television program sales market, followed by the UK with 10 per cent, Canada with 4 per cent, and France representing 3.5 per cent of the global sales of tele-vision programing (Television Research Partnership, et al., 2005: 3). The market for television programing is further split into different genres. The sales of drama represents 37 per cent of the market, and films represent around 23 per cent of the total trade of programs. The rest of the market share is split between programing for children (13 per cent), light enter-tainment (13 per cent), factual programing (8 per cent), and television movies (6 per cent; DCMS, 1998: 42). However, why are some television program genres distributed globally more than others? To understand this, we need to first examine some of the central dynamics of the global television programing market.

Developments in the European television landscape provide an insight into why fiction has been heavily imported to the region. The US export of fiction television programing and films increased parallel to the proliferation of commercial television channels in Western Europe throughout the 1980s. The imported programing was cheaper to buy for these new channels than domestically produced programing. However, domestic programing has had a growing presence especially in prime-time on broadcasters throughout Europe. This shift is amongst others due to the development of stronger domestic production communities (Iosifidis, et al., 2005). Also, 'as markets have matured, mainstream channels have sought to raise their profile and ratings with domestically produced drama or entertainment formats in peak time' (Steemers, 2004: 150).

However, although American fiction features less in prime-time on Western European television channels, it still forms the largest part of the acquired fiction programing among television channels. The imported US fiction genre is still cheaper than domestic production and continues to perform financially for the television channels also outside prime-time (Iosifidis, et al., 2005: 138). Furthermore, the US's capability to finance program series increases the possibility for sales overseas, as they can be scheduled on television networks throughout the week (Steemers, 2004: 43). Another underlying economic factor that helps explain the American dominance of the exports of television programing is Hollywood's ability to sell the bulk of television programing on the back of films. If television distributors or channels want to buy the most sought-after feature films, they may have to buy television programing that they not necessarily are interested in from the Hollywood studio or distributor. Throughout the 1990s 'output deals' became more and more common. These deals involve a contractual agreement over several years between Hollywood studios and buyers to take all programing produced over a particular period of time, as well as older programing (Havens, 2006: 29).

Although fiction is the most exported genre, television programing for children represents a significant part of the global program market. Within this genre, animation programing travels particularly well across borders, as it is very visual and less dependent on language or culture. The genre can be easily localized to different territories and television markets by dubbing animation characters, as pointed out by Artz: 'Raised by the apes, Tarzan speaks German, the Powhatan Pocahontas may not know her own language, but she speaks fluent French and Italian.' The costs of distribution of animation television programs are low, and the possibility for reaching cross-national television audiences is high (Artz, 2005: 80). However, animation television programing is expensive to produce, and broadcasters in Western Europe often have to acquire or pre-buy animation series (Iosifidis, et al., 2005: 144).

The US has the dominant position within the global television programing market for children's programing, with an 85 per cent share, followed by the UK's 8 per cent share (DCMS, 1998). In 2001, a selection of television channels and broadcasters across the world spent an average of 67.1 per cent of their children's programing budget on animation programs. Nearly 80 per cent of this budget was spent on the acquisition of programing, and the rest on production and co-production of programing. Animation television programing was mainly bought from the US, but also from Canada, France, Germany, Spain, and Japan (Informa, 2002).

Disney's collaboration with—and later acquisition of—the animation-film producer Pixar shows how central the animation genre is for the global media conglomerate. The two companies have produced computer-animated films such as *A Bug's Life* (1998); *Monsters, Inc.* (1998); *Finding Nemo* (2003); *The Incredibles* (2004); and *Cars* (2006). These films are distributed throughout the world in a range of media content forms including television (Disney, 2006: 87; Pixar, 2007).

Although the US heavily dominates the export of all genres, its position within the factual television genre is significantly weaker. The US has a market share of 37 per cent, and is followed by the UK, with a share of 18 per cent of the export market (*see* Table 6.1).

The UK's position within this genre is amongst others explained by its production capacity and lengthy experience and expertise (DCMS, 1998: 41).

There are several explanations for the factual television genres' position in the global television market, and its ability to cross borders. First, the increase in the global sales of both animation and the factual television genre is due to the growth of thematic cable and satellite television channels, and the two genres are 'seen as uniquely suited for global trade because replacing the speech of animated characters or voice-over narrators causes less of a disturbance for viewers than dubbing or subtitling live actors' (Havens, 2006: 44). Second, while the majority of factual television is produced for local distribution, certain forms of factual television

Table 6.1　Market Share by Genre (%)

Exporter/Genre	US	UK	France	Australia	Canada	Germany	Italy	Japan
Drama	72	8	1	4	2	4	1	0
Factual	37	18	1	4	3	1	0	1
Film	63	12	6	1	1	2	4	0
Light Enter.	60	4	0	3	5	0	1	6
Kids	85	8	2	1	0	0	0	0
TV Movies	01	6	1	1	3	1	1	0

(Source: DCMS, 1998: 41)

programs have more potential for cross-national distribution than others: 'Ageless "uncontroversial" programmes dealing with natural history, wildlife and science are in most demand internationally' (Iosifidis, et al., 2005: 142). And, third, in contrast to television fiction, it is difficult to identify which country some of these programs are made in, and this makes them more attractive internationally (Iosifidis, et al., 2005: 143). The emergence of factual television program formats signalled the arrival of a program form with increased abilities to cross national borders, and be sold across the world. Although the adaptation of global television formats is far more complex than traditional subtitling or dubbing in national languages, the formats are attractive for broadcasters and producers as they are considered as national domestic programs, and at the same time are popular among the national television audiences: '(they) fuel local and in-house production and contribute to domestic production quotas' (Television Research Partnership, et al., 2005). This means that both cultural and financial factors influence the attractiveness of the various television genres within the global television program market. Buyers and television channel executives will consider the appeal and costs of a possible imported program in comparison to the appeal and costs of a program produced domestically (Havens, 2006: 44).

The US and the UK are the largest exporters of factual television in the world, and the two countries are also the two largest domestic television markets. This dominance has an impact on the production and content of factual television programs to be distributed globally also within Discovery's televisual culture. Cross-national co-production within parts of the factual television genre gives insight into the position of the two exporters. According the documentary television producer, Steven Seidenberg, to succeed in securing international co-production deals for factual programing on themes such as history, religion, or archaeology, the stories needs to have universal interest. The history programs that will be internationally funded are the ones about World War II 'because everybody all around the world is interested in World War II.' A program about British kings and queens will have an appeal in several countries: 'but then if you want to do Nordic kings and queens or German chancellors, (they) won't go anywhere; you can't get international funding,'

> So, history is only useful if it is universal. Christianity you can do. You can do programs about the life and times of Jesus, the Real Moses, the subject that crosses the boundary between universal world archaeology. Tutankhamun isn't an "Egyptian" subject. Tutankhamun appeals to everyone. Egyptology is of universal interest. But if I want to do the archaeology of the Maya or the Inca in South America the market immediately contracts. There are huge parts of the world that don't know

about South American kingdoms and don't care to know about South American kingdoms. No one in Asia would buy a program about the Maya or the Inca. If I want to do one about the archaeology of Japan it's dead. I can't get that program off the ground to save my life. (Seidenberg, documentary television producer, interview with author, London, 14 July, 2003)

As a consequence, programs about Tutankhamun and the Ancient Egypt will continue to be produced: 'Year after year there will be more programs churned out, each with a new angle.' Seidenberg's company (at the time of the interview, Café Productions) has produced several programs on Tutankhamun: 'There is an insatiable appetite globally for programs about Tutankhamun' (Seidenberg, documentary television producer, interview with author, London, 14 July, 2003).

However, how is the term 'universal' interest defined, and by whom? A suggested explanation is that certain themes dominate because they have been popularized through the Western—and to a large extent English-speaking—media in the last 50 years. Stuart Carter points out how certain topics have become popular across the world:

You can write a list of the 100 best things. Very few of them will be Nordic; very few of them will be French; a disproportionate amount of them will be from the English–speaking world, but you do get these things like the pyramids from the ancient world. You can't really blame television for that. It's the way that society has grown up with books, authors, magazines, over the last 50 years, that at least some topics have just become very, very popular, and have sparked people's imagination. (Carter, Managing Director of Pioneer Productions, UK, interview with author, London, 23 March, 2004)

The popularity of the Loch Ness monster can also be understood in a similar way:

That has, again, a disproportionate importance. (. . .) We are just about to make another Loch Ness monster program. Now it's a crazy, stupid thing, but it is fun. (. . .) It is an investigation into human nature actually, human belief. And, of course there are monsters and stuff from all over the world, from China, Asia, and thinking about monsters is nothing new. (. . .) But, why is this one so important? Again, it's because it's in an English speaking nation. So the Americans can understand it. Now, if we have one that's in Mongolia, (. . .) now, it might be interesting, but it's not as easy to understand as (the) one that is in Scotland. (Carter, Managing Director of Pioneer Productions, UK, interview with author, London, 23 March, 2004)

The Loch Ness monster is a theme: 'that the American market can understand, (. . .) probably most of the European, (and) the British market, so the whole thing does get distorted certainly first to the West, and then secondly to the English part of the West. That's true in every bit of modern culture at the moment on the mass media, feature films, books, (and) television' (Carter, Managing Director of Pioneer Productions, UK, interview with author, London, 23 March, 2004). To what extent does this discussion translate into Discovery's programing?

Discovery's *Global Specials* programs (*see* Table 6.2) are all made for distribution throughout Discovery's worldwide television networks. It is important to note how several of these programs connect with the previous discussion on universality and Western skew or 'distortion' within parts of international factual television: themes featured in these *Global Specials* include Ancient Egypt and Greece, large cities in the West, world conflicts reported by Western journalists, World War II, and the Olympics:

Table 6.2 List of Discovery's *Global Specials* for 2004

Global Specials—Quarter One

Thunder Races 2—New series
Each week, three teams are pitted against each other in a race to build a souped-up mega banger that they will race over a dastardly obstacle course. The teams are made up of three enthusiastic punters: One is a professional mechanic, the second an enthusiastic Discovery viewer with design skills, and the third a stunt driver. The teams have one day and £1,500 to find a suitable second-hand vehicle and soup it up!

Living With Tigers
Two Bengal tiger cubs, Ron and Julie, born in a Cincinnati zoo, have spent the last 3 years being taught how to hunt and live wild in South Africa. They are the forerunners of an audacious plan to help save the world's population of wild tigers.

We Built this City
How some of the world's great cities were created—New York, London, and Paris. This is popular history, mixed with fascinating cgi technology, to create a fresh and living take on the past of three of the world's most famous cities.

Reporters at War
In war, truth is always the first casualty. This series will bring out the untold stories behind the most iconic moments, sound bites, and images of the great conflicts of the past 150 years. Centre-stage will be the big-name reporters themselves, telling it like it was (and is): the likes of Kate Adie, John Pilger, Walter Cronkite, and Martin Bell.

(continued)

Table 6.2   continued

Global Specials—Quarter Two

Queen Mary 2
Carnival Cruise Lines has built an ocean superliner as an addition to their
QE-2, the only other superliner in operation today. QM-2 will be the
heaviest floating thing ever put on the water, and Discovery goes behind the
scenes of the construction, launch, and first voyage of this amazing vessel.

Lost Temple to the Gods
In 20 B.C., the Egyptian city of Heracleion was a pleasure ground, a
veritable Las Vegas of the ancient world. But after a long decline, the city
eventually mysteriously disappeared beneath the sea. Now, archaeological
discoveries piece together an historical jigsaw puzzle that explains how this
area evolved to gain such notoriety in the ancient world.

Greatest Military Clashes
In every military clash, opposing sides have raced to develop technologically superior equipment that will give them the edge and ultimately win
them the battle. This series will take these iconic machines and tell the
fascinating narrative of their development from design to battlefield.

Seven Wonders of Ancient—Greece, Rome, and Egypt
From the team that created the BAFTA nominated Seven Wonders of the
Ancient World, this three-part series uses the very latest computer technology, from its award-winning special effects unit, to bring the elaborate
building feats of ancient Greece, Rome, and Egypt to life. With the world's
leading architects, archaeologists, and historians, we uncover the revolu-
tionary technology and architectural genius behind their construction, and
reveal-little known insights into the legends and mysteries that surround
them.

D-Day in Colour
Special D-Day program containing colour footage of the events leading up
to D-Day 60 years ago.

Global Specials—Quarter Three

Rivals—New series
Rivalries between the rich and powerful have always captured the public
imagination. This brand new five-part series uncovering the secrets behind
the most notorious celebrity clashes of the past decades. From Lennon and
McCartney, to Prost and Sena, this is a fascinating insight into some of the
most influential figures of our time—and their not so savoury feuds.

Olympics 2004
A celebration of all things Olympian, including 'Beastly Games'—the story
of how the Romans transported thousands of wild animals from every
corner of their Empire to feed the blood-thirsty sensationalism of 'to the
death' animal fights in Rome—and 'Ancient Greek Olympics'—the real
story of the ancient games.

(continued)

Table 6.2   continued

Animal Face Off—New series
Many of nature's deadliest confrontations are never seen or recorded; and some of the planet's mightiest beasts are destined never to meet: until now. For the first time ever, this series explores the most intriguing and, as yet, unanswered question in natural history: what happens when two animal gladiators, each king of its own domain, come face to face, to lock horns in mortal combat.

MythBusters
Hosted by two experts, one a sceptic and the other a true believer, Myth-Busters sets out to examine three myths every hour and tries to validate urban myths by whatever means necessary! Humorous, entertaining, and accessible science, including a test to see if the story of the woman held fast to an airline toilet seat by air pressure is really true!

Greatest Military Clashes
In every military clash, opposing sides have raced to develop technologically superior equipment that will give them the edge and ultimately win them the battle. This series will take these iconic machines and tell the fascinating narrative of their development from design to battlefield.

Global Specials—Quarter Four

Zero Hour—New series
A look at the most crucial hour of the most catastrophic events in recent history. From Chernobyl and the Lima Siege to the tragic events of 911, we've used archive footage and eyewitness accounts to recreate the scenes and establish exactly what happened and why.

Becoming Alexander
One of the hottest stars in Hollywood, Colin Farrell, will start preparing to play Alexander the Great under the watchful eye of one of Hollywood's legendary directors, Oliver Stone. In Becoming Alexander, the viewer will follow Farrell as he immerses himself in the life of the megalomaniac philosopher-king, 'becoming' the man of dark legend.

Ultimate Cars
In each episode of Ultimate Cars, we celebrate a different machine: from sports cars to convertibles, from Italy's glamorous supercars to the power machines of Japan. These will be the world's ultimate cars, but which will win the 'Ultimate Car' top spot?

Dangerman
A thrilling new adventure featuring 'Dangerman' Geoff Mackley. Geoff, an accomplished television cameraman, has already visited many of the world's hot spots, from active volcanoes to war zones, from hurricanes to the Himalayas. He is engaging and great at communicating his adventures, describing his techniques and equipment and the excitement of the danger with clarity and enthusiasm. In this new series, we will follow Geoff as he travels the world taking on some of the hardest challenges known to man.

(continued)

Table 6.2   continued

Madrid—Diameter of a Bomb
On 11 March 2004, 14 bombs exploded in Madrid. They would not only kill 200 people and injure a thousand more, whilst causing chaos and mayhem, they would, after a few hours of confusion, send a chilling message. Al Qaeda or its heirs were back in town, and they meant business. Three days later, the bombs and the terrorists succeeded in doing what no other terrorist movement has ever accomplished in such a short time: they took a political party out of the game and out of government.

Although the *Global Specials* television programs circulate worldwide, the themes and topics of many of these programs centre on the Western part of the world. This skew is further observed in other parts of Discovery's televisual culture. The regional Discovery networks co-produce with each other, and this internal co-production model allows the company to produce expensive programing for distribution throughout Discovery's global network. However, the US is the region that often contributes the largest part of the total programing budget when the regional Discovery networks co-produce. Furthermore, the US's strong position within the global television network is also evident on Discovery Channel UK and Discovery Channel Norway. This focus represents a certain aspect of homogenization within the programing. However, documentary television producer Steven Seidenberg suggests that this is changing as Discovery expands globally:

> So, yes, there is a homogenisation; if you take the Discovery US dollar, you do things the Discovery US way, and you do subjects that works for the Discovery US, and if it doesn't work for the US, you're not going to get their money. That's all true, and those are all compromises, but what that's also doing is that it is stimulating the local demand for more production. And so, for example, Discovery initially starts out in new territories . . . Discovery Asia starts out by flooding Discovery Asia with the best of the programs from Discovery US, TLC, and wherever else, and they shove those programs out, and what happens is they build the audience, but then the audience says, "But tell us stuff that is closer to home!": And I couldn't get an archaeology program off the ground about Stonehenge for Discovery Asia, because they don't care. They're not going to be interested when they've never hear of it. It's too remote. But there is an ancient temple complex in India, that I've never hear of, but they've heard of because its kind of on their door step, and they're saying, "Give us a program about that." And that's exactly what happens; Discovery Asia saves its money to do local programs of local interest. And the point is that now the budgets are small, because the numbers of viewers are small, but as the numbers of viewers go up, Discovery Asia is going to be the main player. It's not going to be

Discovery United States; Discovery Asia is going to have more money. Maybe it will take 20 years, but it will become a hugely powerful engine driving documentary production. (Seidenberg, documentary television producer, interview with author, London, 14 July, 2003)

This development has been observed on Discovery Channel UK. The television programing is much more UK-specific, compared to Discovery Channel Norway. Still, both channels seem to be dominated by US programing, and the consequence for Discovery Channel Norway is that it may never grow large enough to financially justify large amounts of Norwegian specific programing.

Discovery US's strong position seems to be further underlined by the importance of producing programs of 'high production value'—programs that are—and look—expensive. These programs also distinguish Discovery from other local television outlets. André Singer, Creative Director of West Park Pictures, elaborates on the US position in Discovery's global networks in relation to regional networks:

My view (. . .) is that production values have become too important for global television now to abandon and I think that occasionally you want something that is: "This is Polish" or "This is Czech", but more often than not viewers actually prefer something that looks good but feels as though there is something local involved. And, that's a matter partly of language, inserting it (. . .) how you schedule it. And, I think the global brand is probably becoming more and more important, not less. Everybody who runs a regional (Discovery) Network wants it to be the other way around, because it is their channel, and they want for their people. (T)hey don't want to accept control from Washington or wherever it's coming from. But, in reality that control is going to rule, and I don't think they can switch it back. It (regional Discovery Networks) will never be big enough and they will never, never have enough finance. And, also, perhaps even more important, if you are a viewer in Poland or if you are in Prague or wherever and you have your list of channels and one says "Discovery" you're expecting a product now—from Discovery—of a certain value, of a certain content and a certain style, and if you don't get that, the brand starts weakening and you just choose one of the others. So, the only way you sustain that is by providing people what they expect to get from that brand and that's going to come from the international market, not from the local market. (Singer, Creative Director, West Park Pictures, UK, interview with author, London, 16 June, 2004)

Although the US and UK, and possibly Asia in the future, represent television markets big enough to justify substantial programing investment, the currently strong Anglo-American position in Discovery's televisual culture mirrors the power relations seen in the trade of film and television pro-graming, which, to a large degree, is dominated by the two countries.

THE SPECTACULAR AS GLOBAL INFOTAINMENT

There is a tendency for the content on both Discovery Channel Norway and Discovery Channel UK to apply the spectacular as a focal point. The spec-tacular is embodied in parts of the programs, in the program titles, and in program promos: the greatest bomber planes or helicopters (*The Greatest Ever*, series); biggest, tallest, heaviest, buildings, or constructions (*Monster Move, The Blasters, Mega Builders*, all series); richest people (*Europe's Richest*); deadliest job (*Deadliest Catch*, series); dirtiest job (*Dirty Jobs*, series); strangest UFOs (*Worlds Strangest UFO Stories*, mini-series); dra-matic medical operations (*Changing Sexes, Face Race*, both single pro-grams); crime and emergency (*FBI Files, Trauma, Forensic Detectives*, all series); or global event (*Building the Winter Games*).

Although the content analysis of the two Discovery Channels is only able to capture a sample of Discovery Channel's programing, several of the featured programs are part of long-running series, some over several seasons. Most of these series are distributed across Europe and in the US, and throughout the regional Discovery Channel networks worldwide. The element of the spec-tacular is also present in a large part of the *Global Specials*, these include: the world's greatest cities (*We Built This City*); rivalry between the rich and famous (*Rivals*, series); Queen Mary 2—the heaviest floating thing (*Queen Mary 2*); and the most catastrophic events ever (*Zero Hour*, series), as well as the *Greatest Military Clashes* (series) and *Olympics 2004—A Celebration of all Things Olympian*. The *Global Specials* programs are produced specifi-cally for global distribution throughout the Discovery Channel. Chris points out that Discovery's programing is characteristised by elements of 'spectacle and sensationalism' (Chris, 2007: 152). Furthermore, the spectacular located within Discovery's televisual culture also has a certain resonance with Kell-ner's critical writings on the concept of 'media spectacle'. 'Media spectacle' is a 'phenomena of contemporary society and culture', and television is often a 'medium of spectacular programmes' in various forms (Kellner, 2003: 6).

The spectacular has a central role in Discovery Channel's programing, and this feature also plays a part in enabling the media outlet to reach a wider global television audience. A large share of the funding provided by Discovery, as part of the BBC/DCI co-production agreement, goes toward high-budget factual programs characterized by dramatic narratives and spectacular visuals. These globally distributed factual programs have been given slots on some European channels that have not traditionally had a fac-tual program offer, and thereby have reached audiences not used to this genre (Steemers, 2004). Programs such as *Walking with Dinosaurs, Supervolcano, Pompeii*, and the much celebrated and widely distributed natural history series *Blue Planet* and *Planet Earth* have all attracted millions of viewers around the world, and sometimes achieved over the average audience share when broadcast on national television channels. The worldwide appeal of the television programs of the *Walking With . . .* brand may also, to a certain extent, be ascribed to the animation genres' general ability to cross borders and appeal to a diverse audience.

The two series *Blue Planet* and *Planet Earth* have provided rare insights into life on earth and the complexity of the natural world. However, although these major global program brands may reach an audience not familiar with factual programing, such programing is rare, due to the enormous resources involved (Steemers, 2004: 164). Including the major global factual brands, the BBC Worldwide Sales Catalogues indicate that between 2002 and 2006 the BBC/DCI deal has resulted in around 500 factual television programs and series. The majority of these programs are documentaries and series popularizing science, wildlife, natural history, history, archaeology, and civilization. These are less costly than the major global factual brands, but often have a substantial budget, and are distributed globally by BBC Worldwide. What is important to note is that many of the factual programs coming out of the BBC/DCI alliance belong to the group of programs often referred to in Europe as a 'BBC documentary' and in the US as a 'Discovery program'. In the early phase of the BBC/DCI partnership, BBC representatives expressed unease with Discovery's emphasis on aspects of the spectacular (Born, 2004: 171–173). Discovery's reported approach to popularization may be explained by the tougher competition Discovery faced in the American media market, but also that Discovery targets an American audience not used to the documentary in the same way as BBC's viewers.

POLITICALLY NEUTRAL OR NON-POLITICAL?

Although, as established in the previous section, the US market plays a role in influencing Discovery's programing, it may prove more fruitful to examine the relationship between Discovery's global presence and its global programing. This involves pursuing Discovery founder John Hendricks' claim that 'Discovery is unique in that our content tends to be government-friendly' (Hendricks quoted in Thal-Larsen, 2003: 8). Mette Hoffmann Meyer, Chief Executive for co-productions and Documentaries at TV2 Denmark, points out how Discovery's global presence influences the programing content:

> Well, a channel like Discovery are [sic] trying to satisfy a worldwide audience. This is not really interesting for the viewers, as we all have our different backgrounds. So a film that can be shown in China, Denmark, Africa, South America will have to (be) very simplified to satisfy political and cultural sensitivities, as well as the level/direction of knowledge differs from country to country. When Discovery introduce

a film about the pyramids in the states—they start out by explaining where Egypt is . . . (It) does not work in Denmark. Also they often want to meet interest from different Discovery partners and must have case stories from typical US, Canada, and UK, etc. This is then (a) corporate decision and not what is best for the film. (Hoffmann Meyer, Chief Executive for Co-productions and Documentaries, TV2 Denmark, e-mail interview with author, 20 January, 2006)

Tue Steen Müller, Managing Director of the European Documentary Network, reflects on the 'globalness' of Discovery's programing:

> The philosophy behind Discovery is also that it is a bit like, and I am quoting from a meeting I was at attending in Berlin a couple of years ago: 'It's a global family'. They look upon themselves as a kind of United Nations, so they are not national and for that reason, like the UN, they are not dealing with—and not expressing opinions. They don't have strong points of views on political issues or historical issues, because the programs have to travel to all kinds of regions, so when they are doing something on Kursk (Russian submarine), they are not saying, like many printed news media are doing, they are not blaming, for instance, the lack of security from the Russian authorities. They are playing the story in a different way. (. . .) I am just characterizing now, don't take it as an evaluation. (Steen Müller, Managing Director, European Documentary Network, interview with author, June 21, 2003)

Also, the scholar Fürsich argues in a similar vein, pointing out that 'This programming logic means that for nonfiction television to be globally successful it cannot be overly critical. Criticizing political issues in different countries or the impact of globalization itself may be considered too risky because media and policy decisions are often strongly interrelated' (Fürsich, 2003: 144). However, Jonathan Hewes, Deputy Chief Executive and Head of International Production of Wall to Wall, UK, elaborates on the issue, explaining that factual programing does not necessarily have these qualities:

> I think that there is a big chunk of the factual programing that it doesn't matter. It is not there to be edgy or controversial. It is there to be interesting, great stories beautifully told, or well dramatised. (. . .) We've done series about dinosaurs, and ancient Egyptians, construction, and the fact that they are not edgy is kind of 'neither here nor there'. They just do something else, and are absolutely valid in doing that. And, that's Discovery's purpose in life. (. . .) Discovery's business proposition makes lots of sense if they're trying to be global. (Hewes, Deputy Chief Executive and Head of International Production, UK, interview with author, London, 23 March, 2004)

In Chris' view, Discovery's international networks 'have largely avoided current political matters and historical subjects irreducible to curiosities or long-resolved dramatic conflicts, although noteworthy exceptions are sprinkled throughout its schedule, especially in regard to the environment and some health-related coverage' (Chris, 2002: 22). This attempt to 'sprinkle' such programing in its schedule may be reflected in the employment of former news anchor Ted Koppel at the American national television terrestrial channel ABC. Koppel joined Discovery in 2006, to produce factual programing. According to *The Washington Post*, when Koppel was shown a Discovery-produced documentary from China, he commented: 'It's exquisitely shot, it's beautiful, but it isn't going to ruffle any feathers in Beijing,' and added, 'What if we were to do a real documentary in China in which its legal system and human rights record is questioned?' (Koppel quoted in Kurtz, 2006) However, two years later, in November 2008, news agency Reuters reported that Ted Koppel and Discovery were parting company.

After joining Discovery in 2006, Koppel and his production team created 15 hours of factual programing, including a series about China and a documentary on Iran (Gough, 2008). According to trade magazine *Broadcasting & Cable*, President and General Manager of Discovery Channel, John Ford, commented on the parting by saying that: 'We want timeless programming that has shelf life, and also programming that can go global'. Ford elaborated, 'Given that, it is not as great a fit as one might have thought before. Anything Ted Koppel does is topical, but it is from an American journalist's point of view. The core of Discovery is continuing along that timeless and global route. There is just less and less of an interest in things that have a short shelf life' (Ford quoted in Weprin, 2008).

From the discussion of the characteristics of the global television programing market, it is evident that the US dominates within all television genres, although the UK has a significant share of the export of factual television programing These countries are, themselves, major television markets and, although they export factual programing, this programing may, first of all, target these countries. Furthermore, within parts of the global factual television genre, certain themes are believed to have worldwide universal appeal or 'global resonance', such as archaeology and history, in the form of Ancient Egypt, Greece, World War II, and the Olympics. These themes have a significant presence among the *Global Specials* television programs distributed by Discovery's television channels worldwide. In general, the characteristics of this global programing, such as 'timelessness', give it the ability to travel across cultural and political borders. This ability should also be seen as a response to the globalization of factual television in terms of the increased cross-border distribution. However, there are exceptions within Discovery's televisual culture, for example through Koppel's programs, as possible sensitive political, social, or cultural content are represented by the 'sprinkling' of such programing (Chris, 2002: 22).

7 Negotiating the Global and the National Through Televisual Culture

Discovery's televisual culture consists of a number of components that all play a role to enable its televisual culture to operate in an increasingly global media landscape, and to steer between the global, regional, and national to create platforms at all levels for its factual television and new media output. This chapter shows how these operations and negotiations can be expressed in terms of the theoretical concepts of cultural homogenization, cultural hybridization, and cultural heterogenization. These concepts co-exist in several dimensions and on different levels within Discovery's globalizing televisual culture. This chapter explores the presence of these three dimensions within Discovery's televisual culture in general, but focuses, in particular, on Discovery Channel.

A starting point is to assess the extent of the 'globalness' of Discovery's televisual culture. Are there any fundamental geographical asymmetries within Discovery's televisual culture that may influence these negotiations? Discovery Channel and other Discovery-owned television channels are part of a group of channels described as 'global channels' (McMurria, 2004: 39), having a 'global reach' (Chalaby, 2005a: 7). Discovery Communications refers to itself as the 'leading global real-world media and entertainment company' (Discovery, 2006a). This 'globalness' of Discovery needs first to be scrutinized, and it may be measured according the three factors: a) the access to Discovery, b) the actual viewership, and c) the media content.

Discovery's television channel brands reach over 1.5 billion cumulative subscribers (i.e., one home with the television channels Discovery Channel and Discovery Civilization counts as two cumulative subscribers) in over 170 countries and territories and 35 languages. Outside the US, Discovery Networks International television networks reach 877 million cumulative subscribers (Discovery, 2008b).

When examining the numbers of subscribers, a skew in global distribution emerges. Discovery Networks US is the market with the highest number of cumulative subscribers, compared to the other Discovery Networks International regions. Although Discovery emphasizes its international growth, the US television market still makes up the largest block of subscribers. In a global context, one should note that, although the US is Discovery's main television market, it is still only one country out of the 170 countries in which the television networks have a presence. However, the size of the US market is reflected in the split between the US and international networks' revenues: annually from 2001 to 2005, approximately three-quarters of total revenues came from the US and only a quarter from all other countries (DHC, 2006; Freeman, 2004). Such a difference between US and international revenue is also found in the largest media conglomerates such as News Corporation, Viacom, and AOL Time Warner (Sparks, 2005: 22). Discovery's total revenues are much lower than the aforementioned global conglomerates, but the proportion of its international revenue to total revenues are among the highest. These territorial differences in Discovery's revenue streams are key to understanding its global activities. There is a strong US presence and, to a certain extent, UK presence on several levels in the programing content analysed. In terms of location, protagonists, themes, and language, the US, and secondly the UK, have a dominating position in Discovery Channel's programing distributed in the UK and Norway. Although having 1.5 billion cumulative viewers—which is an enormous potential audience—the fact is that the Discovery Channel and its tier of sister-channels each have a very small number of actual viewers, compared to terrestrial national channels in European countries. On the other hand, Discovery Channel does have global presence that few cross-national television operations—and none of the national terrestrial channels—can compete with.

DISCOVERY AND HOMOGENIZATION OF GLOBAL TELEVISUAL CULTURE

Dimensions of cultural homogenization and standardization have a presence in Discovery's television and media content, as well as branding. The original US network model of television channels based around the Discovery logo and name has been replicated across the globe. Discovery Networks International's global television network is split into Discovery-branded regional networks, and the use of the Discovery name and logo extends to branding activities outside the traditional television networks, such as the new media outlets Discovery Mobile, Discovery Digital, Discovery Global Education Partnership, the European Discovery Campus initiative, as well as the Discovery Education division. Through the synergy of logos and trademarks, media content, cross-promotion and brand extensions, Discovery attempts to create a global homogenized brand. Aspects of cultural homogeneity also extend to the media content distributed. The branding and marketing is given priority when Discovery is launching new television channels throughout the world. The programing is often taken from the existing Discovery programing library, and localized in terms of language for the new outlet. These new channels are gradually introducing regional, and sometimes national, specific programing.

The program offerings analysed from Discovery Channels in the UK and in Norway gives an insight into this. Discovery Channel Norway broadcast no Norwegian or Nordic-specific programing. The program sample suggests a strong North American presence, mainly represented by the US (and to some extent by the UK) on the Discovery Channel Norway and Discovery Channel UK, both in terms of program content and production arrangements. This indicates a certain 'asymmetry' within Discovery's televisual culture (Kraidy, 2005). Furthermore, Discovery's televisual culture serves as an example of the general strong position that the US and UK hold in a globalizing televisual culture. There is also a notion of certain homogeneity in Discovery's television content. There is a strong themed focus on factual topics such as science, civilization, engineering, and medical issues. In addition, there is a tendency in the analysed programing to have a limited critical point-of-view and representation of the world.

THE 'REAL WORLD' AND INFOTAINMENT

Discovery describes itself as a 'global real world company', and have used the factual television categories 'documentary' and 'factual entertainment' when referring to its television programing and media content (Discovery, 20006a; Comer-Calder, former General Manager, DNE, interview with author, telephone, 4 October, 2004). Discovery Channel's programing comprises the traditional documentary and other factual television formats.

Although the mixing of television genres has been an ongoing process through television history, it has become increasingly challenging to define 'television documentary'. However, it is possible to locate 'documentary' by examining how media institutions define the word, how the real world is represented, and also the historical functions of 'documentary'. One may define 'documentary' by simply saying that: 'Documentaries are what the organizations and institutions that produce them make.' (Nichols, 2001: 22) According to Nichols, such an 'institutional framework' means that: 'If John Grierson calls Night Mail a documentary or if the Discovery Channel calls a program a documentary, then these items come labeled as documentary before any work on the part of the viewer or critic begins' (Nichols, 2001: 22).

Although they may be criticized, television producers and broadcasters are free to call a television production 'documentary'. Similarly, Corner points to the 'fluid' meaning of the term 'documentary'. 'Documentary' is difficult to pinpoint and define because the very understanding of 'documentary' 'is always dependent on the broader context of the kinds of audio-visual documentation currently in circulation' (Corner, 2001: 125). For example, compared to Grierson in the 1920s, today's documentary creators are working under very different conditions and expectations. However, although the meaning of 'documentary' may change and vary as the media landscape transforms, Corner points out that a general characteristic of the factual form 'is an interest in using images and sounds to provide an exposition or argument about the real world' (Corner, 2001: 125).

Does a 'documentary', or the other factual forms of programing produced and distributed by the Discovery Channel, have specific qualities and a certain representation of the 'real world'? A large part of Discovery Channel's programs fit into the British media regulator Ofcom's category of 'Serious Factual' categories (which includes the category 'documentary'). However, the analysis of segments of Discovery Channel's television programing indicates that Discovery Channel's approach to the 'real world' is, to a large degree, characterized by a certain worldview. It is the mechanic, explorer, engineer, or scientist who present or describe the 'real world'. This brings us closer to an understanding of Discovery Channel's 'institutional framework'. There is no doubt that Discovery Channel's programs cover themes of importance, such as scientific progress, engineering, mechanical solutions, medical breakthroughs, and also the wonders of the natural world, but there is a notion of a limited treatment of the 'real world'. As with several other narrowcasting-themed television channels, such a themed scope of television program serves to define Discovery's main global television channel, the Discovery Channel.

From a branding and marketing perspective, this approach contributes to a clearer understanding among stakeholders of what Discovery Channel is. As discussed in previous chapters, the cultivating of defined brands is increasingly prioritized among global media enterprises and their media outlets. Such branding strategies are also applied to Discovery's other television channels, Discovery Health, Discovery Kids, and Discovery Sci-Fi. The programing analysed on Discovery Channel represents a flow of core themes presented in a specific way. Part of the logic behind DCI/BBC's global brands and the *Watch With the World* programs, is to create an idea of the Discovery brand to stakeholders—on a global scale, and serve as global vehicles for cross-media content. This is of importance in differentiating Discovery from other media outlets, just as it is important for other outlets to differentiate themselves. This consistency in the television program content relates to Discovery Channel's capability of building and consolidating its brand identity. The strength of the brand depends on its ability to differentiate, and also to maintain, a certain perception of Discovery among its audience and other stakeholders, and the programing supports this process.

Since its launch in 1985, Discovery Channel has pioneered the branding of factual television channels, and has shown a remarkable capability to expand its brand globally. The focus of the programing is a key reason for its ability to create and consolidate a global presence. The programing and brand building process is intertwined and shows how Discovery Channel is working to maintain itself in terms of its 'identity' and brand. The process serves to define and communicate an understanding of the experience and programs that one may expect from the Discovery Channel. However, such a strong focus in terms of program content, the global distribution of programing, and the carefully defined brand parameters leads to the leaving out of certain topics in the program content, and also poses limits to the way themes are covered and approached.

There is an indication that the main television channel of the 'leading global real world company' has a defined, but limited, engagement with social, cultural, and political aspects of the 'real world'. It may seem as if Discovery Channel leaves to other broadcasters to provide for this type of content. This brings us to the historical role of the documentary. Corner emphasizes the historical function of the documentary as a 'journalistic enquiry and exposition' and as 'radical interrogation and alternative perspective' (Corner, 2002: 259). The content analysis points to how Discovery Channel programing does give priority to these issues. The inquiries and examination centres around its core themes and point of view: Do UFOs exist in Scotland? Why is there a problem with the ice in the Olympic ice rink in Turin? What are the complexities involved in sex change operations or in face transplants? How can a motorbike be fixed? How do the engineers in Dubai deal with the sea when building an island resort? However, in most cases the scope of inquiry does not extend to outside the scientific or technical point of view. One should note that the programs *Changing Sexes* and *Face Race*, and the sponsored *Endangered Languages* and *TogetherTV* segments, all go further in their presentation of the real world by addressing the world in a wider sense. *Face Race* and *Changing Sexes* address the social experiences of the patients, as well as the reflections by psychologists and medical doctors. The people featured in the *Endangered Languages* and *TogetherTV* are addressing the social and cultural issues that are, only to a limited degree, present in Discovery Channel Norway and Discovery Channel UK's ordinary programing.

The *Global Specials* include the programs *Madrid—Diameter of a Bomb*, about the terrorist bombing in Madrid on 11 March, 2004; and the series *Reporters at War*, which covers 'the great conflicts of the past 150 years', featuring internationally known correspondents including Kate Adie, John Pilger, Walter Cronkite, and Martin Bell. However, the quantity of such programing seems to be limited. It is also important to keep in mind that the *Global Specials* programs are created in such a form that they may cross national cultural borders unhindered. This influences the treatment and 'journalistic inquiry' of these potentially political and socially sensitive topics. The different approaches to a similar theme may be further exemplified by how one of the sponsored *TogetherTV* short films shown on Discovery Channel Norway, as part of the interstitials, deals with the violence caused by arms in Africa, yet the ordinary Discovery Channel program *The Greatest Ever: Bombers* has a technical point of view preoccupied with the efficiency, speed, and accuracy of military bomber planes.

The tendency for a range of Discovery's programing to include the 'spectacular' as an infotainment device in a variety of forms influences the content of programing. The theoretical discourse of 'infotainment' has focused on television news and current affairs. Growing commercial pressures and competition within the television industry are seen as key explanations for an increase in the use of entertainment within these genres, at the cost of challenging in-depth coverage and serious treatment of themes globally (Blumler, 1999: 241–242; Thussu, 2006; 2007). One of the functions of the documentary presented by Corner explicitly connects the factual genre to the 'infotainment' debate. The lightness in which the way themes are covered has become more important internationally with the arrival of popular factual entertainment. This is used strategically to raise the commercial appeal and increase the competitiveness of the documentary (Corner, 2002: 260, 262).

However, some have also applauded this development. Elements associated with 'infotainment' encourage news and current affairs to be presented in such a way that it reaches a larger audience (Brants, 1998: 332). Parallel to the rapid growth of factual categories such as factual entertainment, reality TV, and docu-soap, the 'infotainment' debate has increasingly come to include the factual television genre. In terms of the factual genre, Brunsdon emphasizes that the popular factual television form, 'lifestyle programs', plays an important role as it 'represents a greater attention paid to the stuff of everyday lives and a broader definition of what "cultural broadcasting" might consist of' (Brunsdon, 2004: 88–89). One may appeal to audiences by presenting the 'real' and 'social and political issues . . . through the experience of being entertained' and that the documentary may benefit from these qualities associated with popular factual programing forms (Roscoe, 2003 quoted in Hill, 2005: 171). Brunsdon develops her argument by pointing out that; 'It is not the presence of lifestyle, an easy and visible target, but the increasing absence of other programing to which we should be attentive' (Brunsdon, 2004: 89).

This duality is present in parts of Discovery's televisual culture. Discovery Channel has had great success in the popularization of themes such as history, civilization, science, and engineering for television. There are suggestions that their programs represented a 'fresh' visual form and a treatment of themes that made them more 'popular' and accessible, compared to traditional approaches to scientific topics on terrestrial television channels in the UK and parts of Europe at the end of the 1980s and the early 1990s. The 'factual entertainment' label emerged in the early 1990s within the organization. The content analysis provides insight into Discovery Channel's approach to popularization. There is a tendency for the content on both Discovery Channel Norway and Discovery Channel UK to apply the spectacular as a focal point. The spectacular is embodied in a large part of the programs, in the program titles, and in program promos. This limits the themes of the programing. However, such infotainment devices also enable Discovery to reach a wider global television audience.

Furthermore, in contrast to the traditional documentary form, which often feature officially recognized experts or scientists, the docu-soaps and reality TV formats have been welcomed for providing a space for 'ordinary' people's lives. The series *American Chopper* that is distributed in prime time on Discovery Channel in most global regions, and *The Garage* and *Southern Chopper*, all mix the docu-soap and reality TV formats. These programs do have the quality of portraying everyday life of people previously rarely represented in factual television. However, one should note that the main characters in these series are either North American or British engineers or mechanics, and the focus of the programs is on technical issues. Although the programs describe the work, frustrations, and friendship of 'ordinary' people, both the docu-soap and reality TV formats and themes correspond to Discovery Channel's institutional framework and remain within the brand definition.

The content analysis shows that there was no programing from Norway on Discovery Channel Norway in the week analysed, and the vast majority of programing was related to the US or UK. Smaller television territories, it appears, are given less priority in the global network. Although Discovery is emphasizing its commitment for further global expansion and increased international revenue, the company's operations do seem to bear out the critique that Anglo-American global news channels are embedded in their national market. Discovery is a rapidly growing global media company, and the Discovery Channel is fronting its television operations and branding efforts. Schlesinger calls for the monitoring of transnational broadcast news television as the global competition for hegemony increases and for its possible influence on national independence and identities (Schlesinger, 2001). Discovery takes part in this escalating transnational media competition. However, although Discovery may be branding itself as having a certain public service ethos, the media enterprise is not taking over from national public broadcasters in decline on a global scale (Fürsich, 2003: 146). While Discovery has a wide pan-European distribution, its impact is limited, compared to the audience shares of national broadcasters in Europe. The themed focus of Discovery Channel's programing and its policy of targeting an audience segment create limitations. From such perspective, Discovery's televisual culture resonates with Sparks' argument that 'global media', such as commercial transnational television channels, provide less access and possibilities for involvement compared to the prevailing national public-service broadcasters (Sparks, 1998: 120). Although Discovery Channel does have its limits, a celebration of the state-bounded media may fail to capture aspects of its historical role within a national territory. The national was defended within the cultural imperialism paradigm, but may have had just as dominant a role as the global (Rantanen, 2005a: 75). The BBC and other European national public broadcasters have gradually come to address the diversity of the national population. At the same time, transnational satellite and cable broadcasters such as Zee TV and

Al-Jazeera have rapidly emerged as providers of services to cross-national viewers whose idea of national identity are more multifaceted than often traditionally conceived. CNN was a pioneer in creating an 'extra societal expansion of political information' on a global level (Volkmer, 1999: 106). Discovery's pioneering global distribution may be considered as such an expansion of factual television. As such, Discovery Channel plays a similar role for certain factual information on a global and European level.

However, there is a limitation in Discovery's televisual culture and in the sample Discovery Channel programing in terms of themes and approaches to political and socio-cultural perspectives. One should recognize that although Discovery Channel targets a segmented audience, this represents an attempt to reach a wider audience than the predominantly English pan-European press outlets such as the *Financial Times* or *The Economist*. These have been criticized for narrowly catering for an international business and political elite (Habermas, 2001). Discovery Networks Europe addresses a cross-national audience through language localization in 21 languages. Few pan-European television networks, and no national European national broadcasters or pan-European newspapers or magazines, can compare with this effort. On the other hand, despite being a pan-European television network, the content analysis points to a lack of inclusion of European life outside the UK and a strongly themed, but limited, reflection of life in Europe. In this sense, the channel's programing has certain characteristics of homogenization that limits its portrayal of the 'real world'.

One way of thinking about aspects of Discovery's televisual culture is Ritzer's theory of *McDonaldization*. The theory emphasizes how the underlying principles of the fast-food restaurant are increasingly being applied in various sectors and societies worldwide, although with varying intensity in sectors. The principles efficiency, calculability, predictability and control are at the centre of McDonalds' global expansion (Ritzer, 2004: 12–15). A similar theoretical connection has been made in relation to television formats as a form of McTelevision (Waisbord, 2004: 378), and Discovery demonstrates certain aspects of an integrated global television system. The notion of homogenization and standardization has a presence in the Discovery Channel's program content analysed, and also its global branding activities have to a certain degree resonance with Ritzer's theories. The calculability is found in television channels' preoccupation with ratings. Especially, niche channels attempt to calculate the success of programs within the chosen demographic group (Ritzer, 2004: 75). There is also a presence of the principle of control. Discovery executes control as a producer and publisher of television programs over the production process and products, the use and protection of trademark logos globally, and the approach to the local, as the European Discovery Channel directors are involved in 'managing local expression of global brands' (Discovery, 2004b). The logic is also seen in the long running *American Chopper* and *MythBusters* series, and also within the blockbuster logic of the *Walking With* . . . sequels. This also relates to the predictability principle when targeting the audience through differentiating the Discovery brand and programing. Discovery Channel targets a male audience segments on a global scale, interested in technical issues and popular science, and the same logic is applied as new Discovery channels are rolled out, targeting different cross-border audience segments such as Discovery Kids (children) and Discovery Health.

DISCOVERY AND HYBRIDIZATION OF
GLOBAL TELEVISUAL CULTURE

There are various aspects of the process of cultural hybridization located in Discovery's televisual culture. The content analysis gives insight into the general transformations that have taken place within the factual television genre. Discovery Channel's program offerings reflect the variety of traditional and hybrid television program forms now existing. The genre mixing is a form of cultural hybridity that has influenced Discovery's televisual culture, but Discovery has also initiated changes within the factual genre. There is a large presence of traditional documentary formats characterized by voice-over narration, interviews, footage, and reconstructions (examples include: *Changing Sexes, Europe's Richest, FBI Files, The World's Strangest UFO Stories, The Greatest Ever: Bombers,* and *The Greatest Ever: Helicopters*). However, a large part of the programing has explicit hybrid features. The mixing of docu-soap and reality TV is evident in programs where we follow people at work (*The Blasters, Mega Builders, Monster Move, Dirty Jobs,* and *Deadliest Catch*), hosts supervising people doing a task or experiment (*Brainiac*), or hosts that are the presenters and main characters doing a task or experiment (*MythBusters, American Chopper,* and *Southern Chopper*). Most of these hybrid formats are distributed throughout Discovery Channel's global network.

The BBC/Discovery alliance's introduction of the high budget genre-crossing blockbuster docu-drama, mixing science, dramatization, and computer graphics, marked a new form of hybrid programing. The *Walking With...* series uses both science and reconstruction of prehistoric life using computer animation. The two-part program *Supervolcano*, first shown in 2005 on BBC, follows a group of researchers in the build-up to and after an imagined volcano eruption in the Yellowstone National Park in America. These docu-dramas were not part of the week's programing analysed. However, it is clear by examining Discovery's programing schedule that it has embraced the changes taking place within the factual genre, and also initiated a new form of global program category.

A further dimension of cultural hybridity is found in Discovery's televisual culture use of national culture within globally distributed television productions. National territorial culture and stories are inserted strategically in Discovery's televisual culture at various levels. Discovery's televisual culture is incorporating the regional or national in its infrastructure and programing. First, on the level of infrastructure, the global Discovery logo and name is accompanied by the name of a specific region, and then broken down to national country names. On one level, this points to how 'managing local expression of global brands' is part of Discovery Channel's approach to branding in Europe (Discovery, 2004b). Second, on a programing level, a similar logic is applied. The major 13-part series *Extreme Engineering*, aired in 2003, was broadcast throughout Discovery Channel's global network, but stories from various countries and territories were consciously included. This mixing was done in the hope that the national cultural specific elements would increase the appeal of the entire series. Through the global 'buy-in' round, regional Discovery networks can co-produce costly series or single programs and incorporate regional-specific angles and cultural elements. Stories from Holland, Austria, and Italy were embedded in *Extreme Engineering*. On a pan-European level, the series *Hot Art*, on art crime, and *Industrial Revelations: Europe*, distributed on the Discovery Channel, incorporate national specific program elements in a theme believed to have a pan-European appeal.

A similar approach to localizing pan-European programing is done by attempting to appeal specifically to one or two countries, but also the whole European region. The program *Building the Winter Games* fits into this category, as it has special interest in Italy and provides original localized programing for the newly launched Discovery Channel Italy (2003), and is thought to have interest in other regions. The pan-European *Building the Winter Games, Hot Art, Industrial Revelations,* and the global series *Extreme Engineering* all show how Discovery applies the strategy of glocalization or 'global localization' on several levels by bringing the 'macroscopic' aspects of life together with 'the microscopic' (Robertson, 1992: 173). Discovery Channel consciously embeds the 'microscopic' in the form of national and local cultural elements within a 'macroscopic' regionally or globally themed framework. This leads us to the television formats where both the notion of hybridization of genre and national territorial culture content are at work.

Discovery has developed factual formats in the form of the docu-soap/ reality TV series *American Chopper, Southern Chopper,* and *The Garage,* or as formats series where hosts are doing experiments, for example, *Myth-Busters*. In contrast to factual formats such as Endemol's *Who Wants to be a Millionaire?* or BBC's *The Weakest Link*, these formats are 'closed'. Although Discovery Channel broadcasts Discovery's own formats globally, they are not 'open' for the insertion of national participants, which is considered as key to its local audience appeal. Instead, the glocalization is represented by national language subtitles.

The US, UK, and Canada have a significant role in the examined parts of Discovery's televisual culture in terms of the geographical location and territorial culture portrayed in programing. Although Discovery is spreading its production around the globe, production companies with head offices in the US and UK produced 15 out of the 26 programs examined in the study. Only four of the 26 programs are co-produced externally. These co-productions are produced by Discovery and Western production companies or broadcasters based in the UK or Canada. However, the US has also a central role in Discovery's internal co-production activity between the Discovery regions. The Discovery US region may invest 50 per cent of the total program costs, and the smaller international Discovery regions make lesser contributions (Forrester, 2003a). When examining the programing closely, we notice that North America, represented by US and Canada, and the UK dominate the two channels in program content and production arrangements. On Discovery Channel UK, 10 out of the 14 programs are filmed on location in the US or have substantial segments from a US or UK location. Thirteen out of the sixteen programs on Discovery Channel Norway have a similar US and UK skew in content.

The concept of hybridity may, in theory, seem like an open-ended process of mixing cultural codes, language, and genre conventions. However, an examination of the conditions under which some of the dimensions of hybridity takes place within Discovery Channel's televisual cultural helps to locate aspects of power. Discovery Channel's form of hybrid glocalization serves as a device to connect the global with the local or national. Discovery Channel's inserting of national cultural elements and codes and an Anglo-American skew in programing exemplifies the certain presence of 'asymmetry in culture, place, descent' inscribed in its televisual culture (Nederveen Pieterse, 1995: 57). The content analysis points to how power is reconfigured in cultural hybridity and inscribed within Discovery Channel's televisual culture. The English language dominates the two channels, and when examining the main location of programs on both channels, the US and UK's strong positions are strengthened. On the UK channel, the majority of programs is filmed in the US or has significant segments from a location in the US or the UK. The vast majority of people featured in the programing on both the UK and Norwegian channel have a UK or North American accent. Non-English speakers are dubbed in English. As an example the traditional documentary, *Face Race* does have a segment from India, but the main part is filmed in the US.

DISCOVERY AND HETEROGENIZATION OF GLOBAL TELEVISUAL CULTURE

Discovery's televisual culture both embodies and applies cultural homogenization and cultural hybridization. To what extent is the third dimension—cultural heterogenization—present in this televisual culture? Cultural heterogenization relates to aspects of cultural hybridity and glocalization by providing a connection between the global and the national or local. However, cultural heterogenization is found on other levels, as well. The dimension has a strong presence in the form of the priority the US is given within Discovery's televisual culture, but also how national and local preferences developed over time outside the US serve as a limit to Discovery's expansion.

MTV and other US-originated, pan-European networks have attempted to adapt to a culturally and linguistically fragmented Europe. The discussion in the previous section highlighted Discovery's attempt to glocalize their programing content. The content analysis also showed how Discovery Networks Europe localizes through national languages. Discovery Channel UK has UK voice-over and English speaking participants in the majority of programing content, all promos are in British voices, and the advertising has either British voice-over and/or UK actors. There are no Norwegian speaking participants in the week's Discovery Channel Norway's programing, but all programing on Discovery Channel Norway is subtitled in Norwegian and the majority of advertising has a Norwegian voice over and/or Norwegian-speaking actors. These strategies attempt to address the same difficulties posed by the linguistic differences experienced by the early satellite television operators in Europe (Collins, 1990b, 1998). However, the interstitials are more localized than the programing on Discovery Channel Norway. The content analysis can only give an indication of the two channels program schedule, but it suggests that the UK and US national are given considerable priority in terms of the location of filming, the people participating, and the language spoken. This makes sense in financial terms, as the US is the biggest market in Discovery Channel's global television network, and the UK is its main European television market. This is also an indication of the significance of mediated territorial culture—and thereby cultural heterogenization—represented by the US and UK. What emerges does have resonance with the findings of the analysis that reports a decrease in factual international programing on Britain's four largest terrestrial channels, but also a change in the form of such programing. The study suggests that there is a tendency for factual international programing to consist of 'Brits abroad', Brits on adventures and travel programes, or reality game shows, in contrast to the 'realities of life for non-British people' (*Third World and Environment Broadcasting Project*, 2003). There are some similarities between this development and characteristics of Discovery Channel's programs. There is a tendency for some of Discovery Channel's programing to include North American or British people at home or abroad. The docu-soap/reality TV series *The Garage*, about British expatriates running a car garage in Marbella in Spain, is a good example of such programing. Overall, the segment of analysed programing indicates that Discovery Channel's programing distributed in the UK and Norway has a skew, culturally and linguistically, toward its main markets the US and UK. This gives a further indication of the strength of the national territorial specificities of the US and the UK within Discovery's televisual culture. On the other hand, for smaller European territories such as Norway, the UK and US-focused programing represent factual international programing with non-Norwegian participants.

How does the presence of cultural heterogenization compare with arguments for the processes of 'deterritorialization' in today's society? Discovery Channel does have a weaker attachment to national territory and culture. Although the US and UK market is given priority, there is an attempt to appeal to a cross-national audience segment both in themes and through its scientific and technical representation of the world. There is a trans-border flow of factual programing that no traditional national broadcaster can rival. Although Chalaby makes an explicit link between deterritorialization and 'transborder' television, and Morley and Robins argue that globalization of electronic media challenges the conventional connection between the territorial and the social, there are indications that cultural heterogenization or, in Nederveen Pieterse's words, 'cultural differentialism', represented by national cultural preferences and languages, pose a limit to Discovery's appeal and reach (Chalaby, 2003: 462; Nederveen Pieterse, 2004: 55–57; Morley and Robins; 1995: 132). Of course, the various Discovery television channels only represent a part of the total of transborder television flow, but the findings presented suggest that these channels, alone, represent a limited deterritorial force. Discovery Channel has developed a complex language localization strategy, but has very small overall ratings in the UK, Germany, France, and the Nordic countries. However, Discovery's television channels do not compete for a national audience like national broadcasters, but target a cross-national audience segment.

Recent developments in global media and communications have renewed the theoretical discourse on deterritorialization and individualization. The plethora of new digital media distribution forms and personal communications systems is thought to play a significant role in increasing cross-border communication, individualism and deterritorialization. Discovery is rapidly expanding into digital media, offering distribution through mobile telephony, broadband, and the Internet. It is worth noting that Discovery applies a similar national language and branding localization strategy in its corporate Web site portals on the Internet, as in its television services.

The forces of cultural homogenization, cultural hybridity, and cultural heterogenization penetrate Discovery's televisual culture, and are also consciously incorporated by Discovery in a variety of ways and at different levels. Although Discovery may seem to 'blanket the world', it is important to note the nature of it's 'globalness'. The US television and media market comprises the largest subscriber block and the majority of the revenues and is, therefore, given priority in terms of programing within Discovery's televisual culture. Also, although Discovery has an enormous global cumulative subscriber base, its channels have a small reach, compared to terrestrial national channels in Europe.

8   The Duality of Globalization in Discovery

There is no single theoretical definition of the concept of globalization that reaches consensus across disciplines. Even within specific disciplines, such as social sciences, it is difficult to find a theoretical understanding to agree upon (Sparks, 2005). This represents a challenge when studying globalization. The approach taken by this book has been to first establish the existing inter-disciplinary agreement of the centrality of a cross-national media and communication infrastructure, and how this development facilitates increased global interconnectedness (Rantanen, 2005a: 8). The key aim has been to use Discovery's televisual culture as a 'test bed' to give insight into the extensiveness and intensity of the possible increased worldwide connectedness, and then to identify some of the consequences and outcomes of this process. This concluding chapter first assesses the possible double role that Discovery's televisual culture plays in its relationship with the general globalization of televisual culture. This will lead into the development of a theoretical model of the Discovery televisual culture's engagement with globalization.

Discovery's televisual culture plays a double role in relation to globalization of televisual culture in the following way: on the one hand, Discovery's televisual culture has benefited from and harnessed the processes facilitating the increased global connectedness. The main owner of Discovery, Liberty Media, has had a role in the development of the global media communications infrastructure. Discovery Channel and its tier of sister-channels and new media outlets are harnessing the increased possibilities for distribution of media content and conducting branding activities throughout this infrastructure. Discovery's corporate activity is organized in national and regional nodes forming the global media network. Discovery is benefiting from the globalization of production through globalization of labour and transnational co-production of programing. Discovery's engagement with globalization of labour, especially in Canada, corresponds to the general description of globalized industries as enterprises search the globe for favorable trading and production environments, to lower costs and increase efficiency. Discovery co-produces television programs with external partners across world. By co-producing with European partners, the programing may qualify as a European production and count towards the EU's program quota. But Discovery has also incorporated the co-production process internally in its global network, as regional networks co-produce with each other. This gives the media enterprise an increased degree of control over the production and form of media content.

On the other hand, Discovery and its television networks have played a role in the globalization of televisual culture, and certain aspects of the development of the factual television genre. Discovery Channel introduced the narrowcasting of factual programing, first in the US and then throughout the world, to specific audience segments. The media enterprise has also had a pioneering role in the popularization of specific factual topics and factual television genres. Since the end of the 1980s, Discovery Channel has become one of the major global providers of popularized science, natural history, history, exploration, and civilization, within the factual television genre. In recent years, its pioneering role is also evident in Discovery Channel's introduction of some of these themes to the docu-soap and realty TV formats, and the distribution of these programs globally. Since the late 1990s, DCI has. together with the BBC, introduced a blockbuster logic to the factual television genre through the creation of global factual brands. This represents a major change in factual television as the threshold for participation in the financially most lucrative segment of factual programing is raised. Only a few broadcasters, fronted by Discovery and the BBC, can afford to invest in these high-budget productions and major branding and marketing activities and reap the majority of profits and branding advantage. Last, Discovery has influence in the global televisual culture through its engagement with the globalization of labour and, thereby, contributes to the justification of these production practices.

STANDARDIZE TO GLOBALIZE AND STANDARDIZE TO LOCALIZE

The contextualization of the central theoretical discourses of globalization of televisual culture—cultural homogenization and standardization, cultural hybridization and cultural heterogenization—show how these theoretical concepts all contribute to an understanding of Discovery's televisual culture. This confirms the complexity of the globalization phenomenon and partly explains the difficulty in reaching a consensus regarding a definition of the term 'globalization'. However, it is possible to draw out certain theoretical commonalities that will help in reaching a theoretical synthesis of parts of Discovery's televisual culture.

This book identifies a number of aspects of standardization in Discovery's global televisual culture—although of varying intensity and forms. Focusing on Discovery Channel's programing, it is possible to argue that, on one level, the channel's televisual culture may be theoretically explained by a combination of the seemingly contradicting processes of *standardize to globalize* and *standardize to localize*. This involves the attempt to connect and unite aspects of the global with the local in its programing to reach a global and local audience. To develop this argument, we return to the founder of Discovery, Inc., John Hendricks', statement in the opening of the book. The statement was made over ten years ago, as Discovery was rapidly increasing its international and global presence:

> (A) principle is to think globally and to act locally. The new technologies give us the chance to span the world and tie it together in ways never before imagined. The goal is not to export one culture in an effort to dominate and denigrate others. It is to showcase a mosaic of influences—to venerate the best of many cultures in hopes of forming a truly global culture. (Hendricks, 1999)

In what way does the exploration of the various components of Discovery's televisual culture, together with the theoretical analysis, provide an insight into what Discovery considers as 'the best' and 'global culture'? One must assume that 'the best' and 'global culture' are chosen according to the Discovery Channel's program policy and its targeted audience. Although Discovery Channel is a major global provider of factual information, the programs' account of the real world has a defined focus. This also includes a notion of 'government-friendliness' (Hendricks quoted in Thal-Larsen, 2003: 8), and a certain limit of critical portrayal of the real world in many programs. However, this gives the global television channel a crucial ability to cross cultural, political, and religious boundaries unhindered. There is a certain presence of entertainment in Discovery Channel's programing represented by the spectacular. This indicates that—on one level—'the best of many cultures in hopes of forming a truly global culture' involves the worldwide search for the spectacular in various forms and contexts, although within a certain scope of the real world. These themes and stories form parts of television programs or are woven into series distributed by Discovery Channel throughout the world. This brings us to Discovery Channel and its audience. The television channel attempts to target a global audience segment throughout 170 countries. The local in this context represents a segment of the national television audience. The Discovery Channel attempts to appeal to the preferences of a local *and* global audience through its form of factual television.

There is a tendency for the spectacular to serve as a connection between the local and the global, or the particular and the universal. This suggests that Discovery Channel's televisual culture embodies the dual process of 'particularization of the universal and the universalization of the particular' (Robertson, 1992: 177–178). Discovery Channel is attempting to harness this processes through a variety of inclusions of standardization in its televisual culture. Although languages are localized on a large scale and cultural heterogenization is a significant force to be addressed, it is still possible to understand Discovery Channel through Robertson's theoretical concepts. The particularization of the universal is linked to the search for '*global* fundamentals' and 'the 'real meaning' of the world'. Universalization of the particular is the 'global universality of the search for the particular for increasingly fine-grained modes of identity presentation.' The Olympic Games and Nobel prizes are examples of such 'particular-universal developments' (Robertson, 1992: 178–179). Discovery has incorporated this dual process on several levels. Some of Discovery's programing embodies this logic. The programs about the Vatican or Winter Olympics in Italy (*Building the Winter Games*) have particular interest in a few countries, while at the same time are thought to have appeal to a European or wider television audience. The *Watch With the World* events and several of the global factual brands are attempts to create programing about particular themes that have global/local appeal. Similarly, the *Global Specials* television program on the Olympics, also exemplify the 'particular-universal' process. On one level, Discovery Channel's programing strategy is characterized by its 'search for (global) fundamentals' presented as 'global culture' in the form of the spectacular in a range of forms and contexts (Robertson, 1992: 178, 180). This means that Discovery Channel's incorporation of the 'particular-universal' process, and the way the treatment of themes and the *spectacular* are applied to make the process work, can be contextualized as the concept of *standardize to globalize* and *standardize to localize*.

One may criticize this argument by referring to Discovery Channel's small audience ratings in Europe as an indication of the inadequacy of the model and the limit of the appeal of such 'global fundamentals'. Still, it is important to remember that the television channel is not trying to reach the world's television audience, but targeting a local/global audience segment. The argument resonates with parts of Roe and De Meyers conclusion in their study of MTV. Although MTV Europe had to retreat from its original standardized 'One World—One Music' concept, the global music television network uses new technology to distribute largely the same content in the form of Anglo-American music videos to the same group of people across the world and is a profitable enterprise. (Roe and De Meyer, 2001: 42)

Discovery contributes to the powerful media position of the United States and the substantial Anglo-American activity in the cross-national media system. Discovery is a giant provider of factual television, and there are US and UK influences on various levels within Discovery's globalizing televisual culture. Also, a majority of Discovery's global television networks and new media outlets are organized around a central idea and definition of broadcasting manifested in a common brand (Chalaby, 2005b: 56). The aspects of *McDonaldization* present in Discovery's televisual culture have, to a certain degree, resonated with business scholars description of 'the ultimate form of standardization' which emphasizes worldwide offering of identical products, distribution channels and sales and branding and promotion approaches (Mooij, 2005: 20). Although Discovery and

Discovery Channel's televisual culture incorporates standardization and to some extent cultural homogenization, the exploration of the various components do not support the traditional argument of media and cultural imperialism claimed by theorists fearing a totalizing cultural homogenization nor of global 'cultural convergence' (Nederveen Pieterse, 2004: 55–57). Discovery Channel and its sister channel's low ratings in Europe stand in stark contrast to the European Commission's anxiety of wall-to-wall Dallas (European Commission, 1984: 47), and the early fears of US cultural imperialism in a European context (Schiller, 1985, 11). However, the central role of the US and, to a certain extent, the UK in Discovery's televisual culture on several levels corresponds with the general agreement among media scholars (from both the traditional political economy and cultural studies schools) on the relevance of some parts of the media imperialism thesis. But, despite the presence of cultural homogenization and standardization in Discovery's televisual culture, there are limitations to the power of these forces, as the dimensions of cultural heterogenization and cultural hybridization are incorporated and influencing not just Discovery's but also a general globalizing televisual culture.

DISCOVERY AND PUBLIC KNOWLEDGE

Although Discovery Channel has pioneered the addressing of niche audiences and cross-border mediation, recent technological developments have facilitated increasing possibilities for reaching individuals, as well as unprecedented possibilities for individuals, themselves, to communicate across boundaries according to preferences and interests. The question is how Discovery will approach these new conditions. To what extent will the *standardize to globalize* and *standardize to localize* model be viable as the forces of cultural heterogenization or individualization may intensify? On the other hand, will these developments lead to increased deterritorialization or cultural convergence? At present, Discovery is rapidly expanding its content and brands into the new digital media forms, again relying on collaborations and alliances, this time with new media giants Google, YouTube, Amazon, and the iTunes media content store. Television content is streamed into personal digital distribution forms such as mobile telephony and the Internet, and cross-promoted on the different platforms.

This activity is relevant to more recent reflections on the theoretical discourse on media imperialism. The discourse should also include the US originated global communications enterprises' dominant role in the development of the global electronic infrastructure (Boyd-Barrett, 2006). Discovery Communications, Inc.'s main owner, Liberty Media, had a central role in building the US cable infrastructure, and is currently a major developer of the global electronic infrastructure, through Liberty Global, throughout 19 European countries, South America, and Asia. Sources point to how Discovery has benefited from having cable operators as owners. The cable operators that took control over Discovery in the 1980s played an important role in its US expansion by committing to include the Discovery television network in its distribution. In 1997, McElvouge reported that Discovery's main owner, the cable operator TCI, made room for the Animal Planet channel in the US, and *Variety* claimed that the Liberty Media-owned cable operator J:Com gave Discovery cable distribution in Japan and other Asian territories (Chris, 2002: 12; Freeman, 2004; McElvouge, 1997: 14).

Discovery Channel's programing provides information within the scope of science, civilization, natural history, engineering, technical, and mechanical themes. There is a tendency for a US and UK emphasis in Discovery Channels televisual culture on several levels. Although the US has a significant role in Discovery's global televisual culture, there is no indication that the media enterprise serves as a mouth-piece for US political interests, nor that its programing represents the global distribution of US propaganda. However, Discovery Channel does take a stand through its defined involvement with the world. Discovery's seemingly selective engagement represents a different cause for concern, but may also partly explain the limits of Discovery's *standardize to globalize* and *standardize to localize* approach to the real world.

The factual television genre has a significant presence not only on Discovery's television networks, but also on Nordic and European national public and commercial television channels. The genre, in its various forms, is proving popular among television audiences. Discovery is a major supplier of such programing globally, also through its relationship with the BBC. The two media organizations co-produce factual television programs that are sold and distributed internationally. Many of the BBC/Discovery productions draw very large audiences on national television channels. This production relationship has contributed to making natural history, architecture, science, history, and wildlife more accessible to a worldwide audience, and for people without formal education in these subjects or for people deprived of such programing. In this sense, Discovery has contributed in the development of a global space for nonfiction programing and played a role to raise the global awareness of the factual television genre.

The factual television genre has an important role in the global and national media landscapes. It has the potential to give representation to people's everyday life through new forms of factual television. Furthermore, in recent years the documentary genre has shown its capability to address important global issues and attract large audiences worldwide at the same time. The documentaries *Supersize Me* (2004), *Fahrenheit 9/11* (2004), and *Break the Addiction: An Inconvenient Truth* (2006) with former US Vice-President Al Gore, are examples of critical documentaries covering corporate and health related issues, international political issues, and environmental issues.

What is important to note is that these documentaries are critical, entertaining, and very profitable. They are shown in cinemas and on television throughout the world. Discovery Channel has also broadcast Al Gore's documentary. These documentaries show how the factual genre has the ability to combine elements of infotainment and a multifaceted representation of the world with commercial interests. This is a rare combination in media output produced for the global media market. In a world of global conflict and terrorism, the factual television genre is vital if we wish to achieve a more cosmopolitan society. Discovery offers important factual information on the world we live in, but the documentaries mentioned previously indicate how there may be room for a cross-national factual television or new media outlets that can provide a portrayal of the 'real world' in a wider sense.

Appendices

APPENDIX I

A Chronology of Discovery

1985

Discovery Channel is launched 17 June with 156,000 subscribers in the US. The first program telecast is *Iceberg Alley*.

1987

Russia: Live From the Inside is telecast, 66 hours of live TV from the USSR on Discovery Channel US.

1989

Discovery Channel launches in Europe to homes in the United Kingdom and Scandinavia. Discovery Channel launches its US educational initiative, *Assignment Discovery*, a one-hour weekday morning program for teachers' use in the classroom. Discovery Channel launches its first original program, *Ivory Wars*.

1991

The Learning Channel (TLC) is acquired by Discovery Communications.

1992

In April, Discovery telecasts *In the Company of Whales*, filmed in 15 countries and several oceans.

1993

Discovery Networks, International (DNI) begins to present 15 hours of programing a week to cable subscribers in Japan through Satellite Channels, Inc.

1994

Discovery launches in Asia in January, and in Latin America in February.

1995

Discovery Communications, Inc. launches Discovery Channel Store and Discovery Channel Online. Discovery Channel launches in India and Australia.

1996

Discovery Channel launches in Italy and in Brazil and a joint venture takes Discovery into Germany, Austria, and Switzerland. Animal Planet is launched in June. In December, Discovery Communications announces plans for five digital networks in the US—Discovery Science, Discovery Kids, Discovery Civilization, Discovery Home & Leisure, and Discovery Wings. Discovery acquires The Nature Company's 114 stores.

1997

The Travel Channel is acquired by Discovery Communications. Discovery Channel Global Education Partnership launches its first Learning Centre in South Africa.

1998

Discovery Communications forms a global joint venture with the BBC.

1999

In March, Discovery Communications premieres *Cleopatra's Palace: In Search of a Legend*. The *Watch With the World* initiative reaches 142 countries in 23 languages in prime time the same night across the world. In August, the Discovery Health Channel is launched in the US.

2000

The three-hour special *Walking With Dinosaurs* on Discovery Channel sets the all-time cable ratings record in the US.

2001

Discovery Channel becomes the world's most widely distributed television brand.

2002

In April, the New York Times Co. and Discovery Communications form a joint venture and launch the Discovery Times Channel in the US. In June, Discovery HD Theater, one of the first 24-hour, high-definition channels, is launched in the US. BBC Worldwide and Discovery Communications extend the global joint-venture with 10 years. Discovery Channel Germany becomes wholly owned subsidiary of Discovery Communications, Inc. The BBC/Discovery program production *Blue Planet: Seas of Life* premiers on Discovery Channel. Discovery and NBC partner to create a three-hour program block, Discovery Kids on NBC, on Saturdays in the US.

2003

The factual program format *Trading Spaces—100 Grand* becomes the highest-rated show in the history of TLC. Discovery launches FitTV in the US. Discovery and the British national terrestrial channel Channel4 sign a factual programing partnership. German ZDF Enterprises and Discovery Communications, Inc. extend co-production partnership.

2004

Discovery Communications reaches 1 billion cumulative subscribers around the world. Discovery Channel launches in France, completing its footprint in Western Europe. The Discovery Education division is created as a source for the next generation of video-based learning. Discovery launches international lifestyle network portfolio Discovery Lifestyle Networks, and announces plans to roll out Discovery HD Theater worldwide.

2005

The Discovery Channel celebrates its 20th anniversary. Discovery becomes title sponsor of cyclist Lance Armstrong and the Discovery Channel Pro Cycling Team. Discovery Wings Channel becomes the Military Channel.

2006

The Discovery Channel US is ranked the number one Media Brand in Overall Quality for the tenth consecutive year, according to the 2006 EquiTrend brand study by Harris Interactive. Discovery Communications launches its first broadband channels: Discovery Channel Beyond and Travel Channel Beyond. Broadband channels for TLC, Animal Planet, and Discovery Health Channel to be launched. Discovery Communications announces the availability of Discovery video content on Google Earth, Google's satellite imagery-based mapping product. Discovery Communications launches its first direct-to-consumer WAP portal in the UK, allowing consumers to access Discovery's content via WAP, mobile TV, and i-mode platforms across Europe. BBC World Ltd. announced a new long-term partnership agreement with Discovery Communications, to distribute the BBC World News channel in the US. Discovery acquires Petfinder.com, an online directory of adoptable pets.

2007

Discovery acquires the Web site www.howstuffworks.com and the 'eco-lifestyle' Web site www.TreeHugger.com. Discovery HD television network launches in Singapore, the 14th country including South Korea, Japan, Canada, Germany, Austria, Ireland, the UK, Poland, the Netherlands, Denmark, Sweden, Norway, and Finland.

2008

Planet Green, a '24-hour eco-lifestyle television network' is launched in the US to 50 million homes. Discovery Channel presents the annual *Shark Week* for the 20th time. Discovery and Oprah Winfrey announce a joint venture to create the television network OWN: The Oprah Winfrey Network. Discovery Networks Asia and publisher Reader's Digest Asia launches Discovery Channel Magazine in China, Hong Kong, Indonesia, Japan, Korea, Malaysia, the Philippines, Singapore, Taiwan, Thailand and Vietnam

(Sources: Discovery, 2006a; Discovery Mediapack, 2003b; Hall, 2005; Discovery 2008a)

APPENDIX II

Location and name of producer of programs on Discovery Channel Norway and Discovery Channel UK

Program	Production Company	Head Office of Production Company	Financial Contribution or Arrangements
American Chopper	Pilgrim Film and Television, Inc. for Discovery Channel	US	
The Blasters	Cineflix (Canada), Next Film Production, and Media Productions in association with Discovery Communications, Inc.	Canada	Produced with the interim financing of National Bank of Canada TV & Motion Group; Produced with the financial participation of The Canadian Film or Video Production Tax Credit; Quebec Film and Television Tax Credit Administered by Sodec; The Government of Ontario/ Ontario Film & Television Tax Credit.
Brainiac	Granada Production	UK	
Building the Winter Games	Stefilm for Discovery Networks Europe	Italy	Developed with the support of the Media program; Produced by Stefilm in Association with Agenzia Torino, Toroc
Changing Sexes	Film Garden Entertainment for Discovery	US	
Deadliest Catch	Original Productions for Discovery Channel	US	
Dirty Jobs	Dirty Jobs, Inc. for Discovery Channel	US	
Europe's Richest People	ITN, ITN Factual for Discovery Networks Europe	UK	

Face Race/ Human Face Transplant	Mentorn	UK	
FBI Files	New Dominion Pictures in association with Discovery Channel	US	
Forensic Detectives	New Dominion Pictures	US	
How's it made?	Maj	Canada	Produced with the financial participation of: The Canadian Film or Video Production Tax Credit and the Quebec Film & Television Tax Credit
Indian Larry	Original Productions, LLC for Discovery Communications, Inc. Produced in association with Discover Channel Canada and ZTele (Canadian television channel)		
Mega Builders	Barna-Alper Productions Produced for Discovery in association with Canal D (Canadian broadcaster)	Canada	With participation of the Canadian Television Fund and the assistance of the Ontario Film & Television Tax Credit
Monster Move	Windfall Films Produced for Five (UK) in association with TLC	UK	
Myth-Busters	Beyond Productions for Discovery Channel	US	
On the Run	n.a.	n.a.	
Psychic Witness	New Dominion Pictures	US	

Rides	Brentwood Comms. Intl. Inc. for The Discovery Channel	US	
Southern Chopper	n.a.	n.a.	
The Blasters	Cineflix, Next Film Production, and Media Productions in association with Discovery Communications, Inc.	Canada	Produced with the interim financing of National Bank of Canada TV & Motion Group; Produced with the financial participation of The Canadian Film or Video Production Tax Credit; Quebec Film and Television Tax Credit, Administered by Sodec; The Government of Ontario/Ontario Film & Television Tax Credit
The Garage	Endemol UK for Discovery Networks Europe	UK	
The Greatest Ever: Bombers/ Helicopters	Cineflix Produced in association With Discovery Networks Europe/ FIVE/Discovery Channel: A UK/ Canada co-production	UK/ Canada	Produced with interim financing from National Bank of Canada—TV and Motion Picture Group; Produced with the participation of Quebec Film and TV Tax Credit Administered by SODEC; The Canadian Film or Video Production Tax Credit; The Government of Ontario and The Ontario Film and Television Tax Credit
The Science Of Lance Armstrong	Rivet Entertainment, LLC for Discovery Channel	US	
The World's Strangest UFO Stories	Proper Television, Inc. (Canada) co-produced with Mentorn (UK)	Canada/UK	With the support of Canadian Television Fund (LFP)

Trauma	Produced by NYT Television for Discovery Channel	
Discovery short films	n.a.	n.a.

APPENDIX III

OVERVIEW OF TELEVISION CONTENT

Television Channels: Discovery Channel UK and Discovery Channel Norway
Time frame: 20.00–23.00
Dates: 30 January–5 February, 2006

DISCOVERY CHANNEL NORWAY, 20.00.00–23.00.00, 30 JANUARY, 2006

20.00.00–20.08.34	Program: *Myth Busters* (Segment 1)
20.08.34–20.08.36	Discovery Channel ident
20.08.36–20.09.01	Advertising: Gjensidige, insurance
20.09.01–20.09.10	Advertising: Fishermans Friend
20.09.10–20.09.12	Discovery Channel ident
20.09.12–20.09.42	Discovery program promo: *The Greates Ever*
20.09.42–20.09.45	Discovery Channel ident
20.09.45–20.27.34	Program: *Myth Busters* (Segment 2)
20.27.34–20.27.36	Discovery Channel ident
20.27.36–20.28.06	Advertising: Microsoft
20.28.06–20.28.36	Advertising: Citibank
20.28.36–20.28.40	Discovery Channel ident
20.28.40–20.29.40	Program: *Endagered Languages*
20.29.40–20.29.43	Discovery Channel ident
20.29.43–20.45.48	Program: *Myth Busters* (Segment 3)
20.45.48–20.45.51	Discovery Channel ident
20.45.51–20.46.16	Advertising: BMW, car
20.46.16–20.46.19	Discovery Channel ident
20.46.19–20.47.33	Program: *Together TV*
20.47.33–20.47.36	Discovery Channel ident
20.47.36–20.52.20	Program: *Myth Busters* (Segment 4)
20.52.20–20.52.23	Discovery Channel ident

20.52.23–20.52.32	Advertising: Fisherman's Friend
20.52.32–20.53.02	Advertising: Dell, computers
20.53.02–20.53.32	Advertising: Citibank
20.53.32–20.53.33	Discovery Channel ident
20.53.33–20.56.00	Program: *Together TV*
20.56.00–20.59.30	Program: *Discovery Channel Short Films*
20.59.30–21.00.00	Discovery program promo: *The Greates Ever*
21.00.00–21.00.14	Discovery Channel ident
21.00.14–21.08.09	Program: *Changing Sexes: Female to male* (Segment 1)
21.08.09–21.08.14	Discovery Channel ident
21.08.14–21.08.34	Advertising: BMW, car
21.08.34–21.08.36	Discovery Channel ident
21.08.36–21.09.08	Discovery program promo, *American Chopper*
21.09.08–21.09.14	Discovery Channel ident
21.09.14–21.26.36	Program: *Changing Sexes: Female to male* (Segment 2)
21.26.36–21.26.40	Discovery Channel ident
21.26.40–21.27.10	Advertising: GMmoney, loans
21.27.10–21.27.40	Advertising: Incredible India, India as travel destination
21.27.40–21.27.43	Discovery Channel ident
21.27.43–21.27.13	Discovery program promo: *Brainiac*
21.27.13–21.44.53	Program: *Changing Sexes: Female to Male* (Segment 3)
21.44.53–21.44.57	Discovery Channel ident
21.44.57–21.45.07	Advertising: Fisherman's Friend
21.45.07–21.46.22	Advertising: Microsoft
21.46.22–21.46.52	Advertising: BMW, car
21.46.52–21.46.53	Discovery Channel ident
21.46.53–21.48.39	Program: *Endangered Language*
21.38.39–21.48.42	Discovery Channel ident
21.48.42–21.53.42	Program: *Changing Sexes* (Segment 4)
21.53.42–21.53.47	Discovery Channel ident
21.53.47–21.54.07	Advertising: Gjensidige, insurance
21.54.07–21.54.10	Discovery Channel ident
21.54.10–21.56.05	Program: *Together TV*
21.56.05–21.59.30	Program: *Discovery Channel Short Films*
21.59.30–22.00.00	Discovery program promo: *Myth Busters*
22.00.00–22.00.15	Discovery Channel ident
22.00.15–22.06.45	Program: *Trauma: Life in the E.R.* (Segment 1)
22.06.45–22.06.48	Discovery Channel ident
22.06.48–22.07.08	Advertising: Munich, film
22.07.08–22.07.28	Advertising: Gjensidige, insurance
22.07.28–22.07.58	Advertising: GMmoney, loan
22.07.58–22.08.00	Discovery Channel ident
22.08.00–22.08.30	Discovery program promo: *American Chopper*

22.08.30–22.08.35	Discovery Channel ident
22.08.35–22.24.58	Program: *Trauma: Life in the E.R* (Segment 2)
22.24.58–22.25.00	Discovery Channel ident
22.25.00–22.25.27	Advertising: BMW, car
22.25.27–22.25.30	Discovery Channel ident
22.25.30–22.26.00	Discovery program promo: *The Greatest Ever*
22.26.00–22.26.03	Discovery Channel ident
22.26.03–22.44.36	Program: *Trauma: Life in the E.R.* (Segment 3)
22.44.36–22.44.38	Discovery Channel ident
22.44.38–22.45.08	Advertising: Dell, computers
22.45.08–22.45.38	Advertising: India incredible, India travel destination
22.45.38–22.45.41	Discovery Channel ident
22.45.41–22.48.11	Program: *Together TV*
22.48.11–22.48.14	Discovery Channel ident
22.48.14–22.53.40	Program: *Trauma: Life in the E.R.* (Segment 4)
22.53.40–22.53.44	Discovery Channel ident
22.53.44–22.53.54	Advertising: Fisherman's Friend
22.53.54–22.53.56	Discovery Channel ident
22.53.56–22.55.56	Program: *Endangered Languages*
22.55.56–22.59.37	Program: *Discovery Channel Short Film*

DISCOVERY CHANNEL NORWAY, 20.00.00–23.00.00, 31 JANUARY, 2006

20.00.00–20.07.29	Program: *Myth Busters* (Segment 1)
20.07.29–20.07.32	Discovery Channel ident
20.07.32–20.08.02	Advertising: Munich, film
20.08.02–20.08.22	Advertising: Gjensidige, insurance
20.08.22–20.08.52	Advertising: GEmoney
20.08.52–20.08.55	Discovery Channel ident
20.08.55–20.08.25	Discovery program promo: *The Greatest Ever*
20.08.25–20.08.28	Discovery Channel ident
20.08.28–20.27.26	Program: *Myth Busters* (Segment 2)
20.27.26–20.27.29	Discovery Channel ident
20.27.29–20.28.01	Advertising: Citibank, loans
20.28.01–20.28.24	Advertising: BMW, car
20.28.24–20.28.27	Discovery Channel ident
20.28.27–20.29.40	Program: *Together TV*
20.29.40–20.29.44	Discovery Channel ident
20.29.44–20.46.59	Program: *Myth Busters* (Segment 3)
20.46.59–20.47.02	Discovery Channel ident
20.47.02–20.47.12	Advertising: Fisherman's Friend
20.47.12–20.47.42	Advertising: Gjensidige, insurance
20.47.42–20.47.45	Discovery Channel ident

20.47.45–20.48.15	Discovery program promo: *Brainiac*
20.48.15–20.48.18	Discovery Channel ident
20.48.18–20.52.45	Program: *Myth Busters* (Segment 4)
20.52.45–20.52.48	Discovery Channel ident
20.52.48–20.53.13	Advertising: BMW, car
20.53.13–20.53.43	Advertising: GEmoney, loans
20.53.43–20.54.03	Advertising: Gjensidige, insurance
20.54.03–20.54.06	Discovery Channel ident
20.54.06–20.57.02	Program: *Together TV*
20.57.02–20.59.57	Program: *Discovery Channel Short Films*
20.59.57–21.00.12	Discovery intro ident
21.00.12–21.06.26	Program: *Building the Winter Games*, Episode 2 (Segment1)
21.06.26–21.06.30	Discovery program intro/ ident
21.06.30–21.07.00	Advertising: Citibank, loans
21.07.00–21.07.30	Advertising: Microsoft
21.07.30–21.07.33	Discovery Channel ident
21.07.33–21.08.03	Discovery program promo: *American Chopper*
21.08.03–21.08.06	Discovery Channel ident
21.08.06–21.25.17	Program: *Building the Winter Games* (Segment 2)
21.25.17–21.25.19	Discovery Channel ident
21.25.19–21.25.49	Advertising: India Incredible, travel destination
21.25.49–21.25.52	Discovery Channel ident
21.25.52–21.26.22	Discovery program promo: *Brainiac*
21.26.22–21.26.25	Discovery Channel ident
21.26.25–21.43.35	Program: *Building the Winter Games* (Segment 3)
21.43.35–21.43.38	Discovery Channel ident
21.43.38–21.43.48	Advertising: Fisherman's Friend
21.43.48–21.44.18	Advertising: Dell, computers
21.44.18–21.44.43	Advertising: BMW, car
21.44.43–21.45.13	Advertising: Citibank
21.45.13–21.45.33	Advertising: Gjensidige, insurance
21.45.33–21.46.06	Discovery program promo: *The Greatest Ever*
21.46.06–21.46.09	Discovery Channel ident
21.46.09–21.52.28	Program: *Building the Winter Games* (Segment 3)
21.52.28–21.52.38	Advertising: Sponsored by pokerroom.com
21.52.38–21.52.40	Discovery Channel ident
21.52.40–21.53.05	Advertising: KIA, car
21.53.05–21.53.08	Discovery Channel ident
21.53.08–21.56.08	Program: *Endangered Languages*
21.56.08–21.59.33	Program: *Discovery Channel Short Films*
21.59.33–21.59.48	Discovery Channel intro ident
21.59.48–21.59.58	Advertising: Sponsored by pokerrooms.com
21.59.58–22.05.59	Program: *Deadliest Catch* (Segment 1)
22.05.59–22.06.09	Advertising: Sponsored by pokerrooms.com

22.06.09–22.06.12	Discovery Channel ident
22.06.12–22.06.42	Advertising: Citibank, loans
22.06.42–22.07.02	Advertising: Gjensidige, insurance
22.07.02–22.07.04	Discovery Channel ident
22.07.05–22.07.34	Discovery program promo: *Brainiac*
22.07.34–22.07.37	Discovery Channel ident
22.07.37–22.07.42	Advertising: Sponsored by pokerrooms.com
22.07.42–22.24.45	Program: *Deadliest Catch* (Segment 2)
22.24.45–22.24.55	Advertising: Sponsored by pokerroom.com
22.24.55–22.24.58	Discovery Channel ident
22.24.58–22.25.28	Advertising: Dell
22.25.28–22.25.53	Advertising: BMW
22.25.53–22.26.23	Advertising: GE money
22.26.23–22.26.26	Discovery Channel ident
22.26.26–22.26.56	Discovery program promo: *Myth Busters*
22.26.56–22.26.59	Discovery Channel ident
22.26.59–22.27.04	Advertising: Sponsored by pokerrooms.com
22.27.04–22.43.34	Program: *Deadliest Catch* (Segment 3)
22.43.34–22.43.39	Advertising: Sponsored by pokerrooms.com
22.43.39–22.43.42	Discovery Channel ident
22.43.42–22.43.52	Advertising: Fisherman's Friend
22.43.52–22.44.22	Advertising: Citibank
22.44.22–22.44.42	Advertising: Gjensidige, insurance
22.44.42–22.45.12	Advertising: Incredible India, India travel destination
22.45.12–22.45.15	Discovery Channel ident
22.45.15–22.45.45	Discovery program promo *The Greatest Ever*
22.45.45–22.45.48	Discovery Channel ident
22.45.48–22.45.53	Advertising: Sponsored by pokerroom.com
22.45.53–22.53.17	Program: *Deadliest Catch* (Segment 4)
22.53.17–22.53.26	Advertising: Sponsored by pokerroom.com
22.53.26–22.53.29	Discovery Channel ident
22.53.29–22.53.44	Advertising: Microsoft
22.53.44–22.54.09	Advertising: BMW, car
22.54.09–22.54.12	Discovery Channel ident
22.54.12–22.56.07	Program: *Together TV*
22.56.07–22.59.48	Program: *Discovery Channel Short Film*
22.59.48–23.00.02	Discovery Channel ident

DISCOVERY CHANNEL NORWAY, 20.00.00–23.00.00, 1 FEBRUARY, 2006

20.00.00–20.08.32	Program: *Myth Busters* (Segment 1)
20.08.32–20.08.35	Discovery Channel ident

20.08.35–20.09.05	Advertising: GEmoney
20.09.05–20.09.15	Advertising: Fisherman's Friend
20.09.15–20.09.18	Discovery Channel ident
20.09.18–20.09.48	Discovery program promo: *American Chopper*
20.09.48–20.09.51	Discovery Channel ident
20.09.51–20.27.35	Program: *Myth Busters* (Segment 2)
20.27.35–20.27.38	Discovery Channel ident
20.27.38–20.27.58	Advertising: Munich, film, Universal
20.27.58–20.28.28	Advertising: Dell, computers
20.28.28–20.28.53	Advertising: BMW, car
20.28.53–20.28.56	Discovery Channel ident
20.28.56–20.30.10	Program: *Together TV*
20.30.10–20.30.13	Discovery Channel ident
20.30.13–20.46.41	Program: *Myth Busters* (Segment 3)
20.46.41–20.46.44	Discovery Channel ident
20.46.44–20.47.09	Advertising: KIA, car
20.47.09–20.47.12	Discovery Channel ident
20.47.12–20.48.12	Program: *Endangered Languages*
20.48.12–20.48.14	Discovery Channel ident
20.48.14–20.52.37	Program: *Myth Busters* (Segment 4)
20.52.37–20.52.38	Discovery Channel ident
20.52.38–20.53.08	Advertising: GEmoney
20.53.08–20.53.38	Advertising: Netcom, mobile telephony
20.53.38–20.54.08	Advertising: Dell, computer
20.54.08–20.54.11	Discovery Channel ident
20.54.11–20.56.07	Program: *Together TV*
20.56.07–20.59.48	Program: *Discovery Channel Short Film*
20.59.48–21.00.02	Discovery intro ident
21.00.02–21.07.32	Program: *Europe's richest people* (Segment 1)
21.07.32–21.07.35	Discovery Channel ident
21.07.35–21.08.00	Advertising: KIA, car
21.08.00–21.08.03	Discovery Channel ident
21.08.03–21.08.33	Discovery program promo: *American Chopper*
21.08.33–21.08.36	Discovery Channel ident
21.08.36–21.26.31	Program: *Europe's richest people* (Segment 2)
21.26.31–21.26.34	Discovery Channel ident
21.26.34–21.26.59	Advertising: Munich, film
21.26.59–21.27.24	Advertising: Citibank
21.27.24–21.27.54	Advertising: Dell, computer
21.27.54–21.27.57	Advertising: Discovery Channel ident
21.27.57–21.28.57	Program: *Discovery Channel Short Film*
21.28.57–21.46.05	Program: *Europe's richest people* (Segment 3)
21.46.05–21.46.08	Discovery Channel ident
21.46.08–21.46.38	Advertising: India Incredible, travel destination
21.46.38–21.46.41	Discovery Channel ident

21.46.41–21.47.55	Program: *Together TV*
21.47.55–21.47.58	Discovery Channel ident
21.47.58–21.52.16	Program: *Europe's richest people* (Segment 4)
21.52.16–21.52.19	Discovery Channel ident
21.52.19–21.52.49	Advertising: MatPrat, promotion of food
21.52.49–21.53.24	Advertising: Mercedes-Benz, car
21.53.24–21.53.54	Advertising: MatPrat, promotion of food
21.53.54–21.53.57	Discovery Channel ident
21.53.57–21.56.48	Program: *Endangered Languages*
21.56.48–21.59.13	Program: *Discovery Channel Short Films*
21.59.13–21.59.43	Discovery program promo: *Brainiac*
21.59.43–21.59.59	Discovery program intro
21.59.59–22.06.04	Program: *The Greatest Ever: Bombers* (Segment 1)
22.06.04–22.06.07	Discovery Channel ident
22.06.07–22.06.37	Advertising: MatPrat , promotion of food
22.06.37–22.06.57	Advertising: Gjensidige, insurance
22.06.57–22.07.27	Advertising: MatPrat, promotion of food
22.07.27–22.07.57	Advertising: India Incredible, travel destination
22.07.57–22.08.00	Discovery Channel ident
22.08.00–22.08.30	Discovery program promo: *Myth Busters*
22.08.30–22.08.33	Discovery Channel ident
22.08.33–22.26.00	Program: *The Greatest Ever: Bombers* (Segment 2)
22.26.00–22.26.03	Discovery Channel ident
22.26.03–22.26.33	Advertising: GEmoney
22.26.33–22.26.56	Advertising: BMW, car
22.26.56–22.26.59	Discovery Channel ident
22.26.59–22.28.01	Program: *Endangered Languages*
22.28.01–22.28.04	Discovery Channel ident
22.28.04–22.44.39	Program: *The Greatest Ever: Bombers* (Segment 3)
22.44.39–22.44.42	Discovery Channel ident
22.44.42–22.45.12	Advertising: Dell, computer
22.45.12–22.45.42	Advertising: Incredible India, travel destination
22.45.42–22.45.45	Discovery Channel ident
22.45.45–22.47.46	Program: *Endangered Languages*
22.47.46–22.47.49	Discovery Channel ident
22.47.49–22.53.47	Program: *The Greatest Ever: Bombers* (Segment 4)
22.53.47–22.53.50	Discovery Channel ident
22.53.50–22.56.21	Program: *Together TV*
22.56.21–22.59.45	Program: *Discovery Channel Short Film*
22.56.45–23.00.00	Discovery program intro

DISCOVERY CHANNEL NORWAY, 20.00.00–23.00.00, 2 FEBRUARY, 2006

20.00.00–20.08.07	Program: *Myth Busters* (Segment 1)

20.08.07–20.08.11	Discovery Channel ident
20.08.11–20.08.31	Advertising: Gjensidige, insurance
20.08.31–20.09.01	Advertising: GEmoney
20.09.01–20 09.31	Advertising: Dell, computers
20.09.31–20.09.34	Discovery Channel ident
20.09.34–20.10.04	Discovery program promo: *American Chopper*
20.10.04–20.10.06	Discovery Channel ident
20.10.06–20.27.40	Program: *Myth Busters* (Segment 2)
20.27.40–20.27.43	Discovery Channel ident
20.27.43–20.28.03	Advertising: Munich, film, Universal
20.28.03–20.28.33	Advertising: Citibank, loans
20.28.33–20.28.58	Advertising: KIA, car
20.28.58–20.29.13	Advertising: Microsoft
20.29.13–20.29.16	Discovery Channel ident
20.29.16–20.30.16	Program: *Endangered Language*
20.30.16–20.30.19	Discovery Channel ident
20.30.19–20.47.06	Program: *Myth Busters* (Segment 3)
20.47.06–20.47.09	Discovery Channel ident
20.47.09–20.47.19	Advertising: Fisherman's Friend
20.47.19–20.47.44	Advertising: BMW, car
20.47.44–20.47.47	Discovery Channel ident
20.47.47–20.48.17	Discovery program promo: *Myth Busters*
20.48.17–20.48.20	Discovery Channel ident
20.48.20–20.52.54	Program: *Myth Busters* (Segment 4)
20.52.54–20.52.59	Discovery Channel ident
20.52.59–20.53.29	Advertising: Netcom, mobile telephony
20.53.29–20.53.59	Advertising: Dell
20.53.59–20.54.29	Advertising: Incredible India, travel destination
20.54.29–20.54.34	Discovery Channel ident
20.54.34–20.55.46	Program: *Together TV*
20.55.46–21.00.02	Program: *Discovery Channel Short Film*
21.00.02–21.00.17	Discovery program intro
21.00.17–21.09.45	Program: *Forensic Detectives* (Segment 1)
21.09.45–21.09.48	Discovery Channel ident
21.09.48–21.10.18	Advertising: Munich, film
21.10.18–21.10.53	Advertising: Mercedez-Benz, car
21.10.53–21.11.13	Advertising: Gjensidige, insurance
21.11.13–21.11.43	Advertising: GEmoney
21.11.43–21.11.46	Discovery Channel ident
21.11.46–21.12.16	Discovery program promo
21.12.16–21.12.19	Discovery Channel ident
21.12.19–21.28.35	Program: *Forensic Detectives* (Segment 2)
21.28.35–21.28.38	Discovery Channel ident
21.28.38–21.29.08	Advertising: Dell, computers
21.29.08–21.29.11	Discovery Channel ident
21.29.11–21.29.41	Discovery program promo: *The Greatest Ever*

21.29.41–21.29.44	Discovery Channel ident
21.29.44–21.45.42	Program: *Forensic Detectives* (Segment 3)
21.45.42–21.45.45	Discovery Channel ident
21.45.45–21.46.15	Advertising: MatPrat, promotion of food
21.46.15–21.46.40	Advertising: KIA, car
21.46.40–21.47.10	Advertising: MatPrat , promotion of food
21.47.10–21.47.40	Advertising: Incredible India, India travel destination
21.47.40–21.47.43	Discovery Channel ident
21.47.43–21.50.34	Program: *Endangered Languages*
21.50.34–21.50.37	Discovery Channel ident
21.50.37–21.56.08	Program: *Forensic Detectives* (Segment 4)
21.56.08–21.56.11	Discovery Channel ident
21.56.11–21.57.12	Program: *Endangered Languages*
21.57.12–22.00.37	Program: *Discovery Channel Short Film*
22.00.37–22.00.52	Discovery program intro/ ident
22.00.52–22.08.38	Program: *The FBI Files* (Segment1)
22.08.38–22.08.41	Discovery Channel ident
22.08.41–22.08.56	Advertising: Microsoft (Norwegian voice over)
22.08.56–22.08.59	Discovery Channel ident
22.08.59–22.09.29	Discovery program promo: *The Greatest Ever*
22.09.29–22.09.32	Discovery Channel ident
22.09.32–22.25.30	Program: *FBI Files* (Segment 2)
22.25.30–22.25.33	Discovery Channel ident
22.25.33–22.25.58	Advertising: BMW, car
22.25.58–22.26.28	Advertising: Incredible India, travel destination
22.26.28–22.26.31	Discovery Channel ident
22.26.31–22.27.01	Discovery program promo: *American Chopper*
22.27.01–22.27.04	Discovery Channel ident
22.27.04–22.43.43	Program: *FBI Files* (Segment 3)
22.43.43–22.43.46	Discovery Channel ident
22.43.46–22.44.16	Advertising: Citibank, loans
22.44.16–22.44.46	Advertising: Dell, computers
22.44.46–22.45.11	Advertising: KIA, car
22.45.11–22.47.14	Program: *Endangered Languages*
22.47.14–22.47.17	Discovery Channel ident
22.47.17–22.53.07	Program: *FBI Files* (Segment 4)
22.53.07–22.53.10	Discovery Channel ident
22.53.10–22.53.30	Advertising: Munich, film
22.53.30–22.54.00	Advertising: Netcom, mobile telephony
22.54.00–22.54.03	Discovery Channel ident
22.54.03–22.55.58	Program: *Together TV*
22.55.58–22.59.23	Program: *Discovery Channel Short Film*
22.59.23–22.59.53	Discovery program promo: *Myth Busters*
22.59.53–23.00.08	Discovery Channel ident

DISCOVERY CHANNEL NORWAY,
20.00.00–23.00.00, 3 FEBRUARY, 2006

20.00.00–20.07.30	Program: *Myth Busters* (Segment 1)
20.07.30–20.07.33	Discovery Channel ident
20.07.33–20.07.53	Advertising: Gjensidige, insurance
20.07.53–20.08.23	Advertising: GEmoney
20.08.23–20.08.43	Advertising: Telenor Mobil, mobile telephony
20.08.43–20.08.46	Discovery Channel ident
20.08.46–20.09.16	Discovery program promo: *Myth Busters*
20.09.16–20.09.19	Discovery Channel ident
20.09.19–20.27.10	Program: *Myth Busters* (Segment 2)
20.27.10–20.27.13	Discovery Channel ident
20.27.13–20.27.33	Advertising: Munich, film, Universal
20.27.33–20.28.03	Advertising: Citibank, loans
20.28.03–20.28.13	Advertising: Fisherman's Friend
20.28.13–20.28.38	· Advertising: KIA, car
20.28.38–20.29.08	Advertising: Microsoft
20.29.08–20.29.11	Discovery Channel ident
20.29.11–20.30.11	Program: *Endangered Languages*
20.30.11–20.30.14	Discovery Channel ident
20.30.14–20.47.28	Program: *Myth Busters* (Segment 3)
20.47.28–20.47.31	Discovery Channel ident
20.47.31–20.48.01	Advertising: Dell, computers
20.48.01–20.48.04	Discovery channel ident
20.48.04–20.49.59	Program: *Together TV*
20.49.59–20.50.03	Discovery channel ident
20.50.03–20.54.35	Program: *Myth Busters* (Segment 4)
20.54.35–20.54.38	Discovery Channel ident
20.54.38–20.54.58	Advertising: Telenor Mobil, mobile telephony
20.54.58–20.55.28	Advertising: Skoda, car
20.55.28–20.55.58	Advertising: Incredible India, travel destination
20.55.58–20.56.01	Discovery Channel ident
20.56.01–20.57.01	Program: *Endangered Languages*
20.57.01–20.59.56	Program: *Discovery Channel Short Films*
20.59.56–21.00.11	Discovery program intro ident
21.00.11–21.23.31	Program: *Brainiac* (Segment 1)
21.23.31–21.23.34	Discovery Channel ident
21.23.34–21.23.44	Advertising: Fisherman's Friend
21.23.44–21.24.09	Advertising: KIA, car
21.24.09–21.24.29	Advertising: Telenor Mobil, mobile telephony
21.24.29–21.25.31	Program: *Endangered Languages*
21.25.31–21.25.34	Discover Channel ident
21.25.34–21.41.01	Program: *Brainiac* (Segment 2)

21.41.01–21.41.04	Discovery Channel ident
21.41.04–21.41.34	Advertising: Dell, computers
21.41.34–21.42.04	Advertising: Incredible India, travel destination
21.42.04–21.42.07	Discovery Channel ident
21.42.07–21.44.38	Program: *Together TV*
21.44.38–21.44.41	Discovery Channel ident
21.44.41–21.52.35	Program: *Brainiac* (Segment 3)
21.52.35–21.52.38	Discovery Channel ident
21.52.38–21.53.08	Advertising: Skoda, car
21.53.08–21.53.11	Discovery Channel ident
21.53.11–21.56.01	Program: *Endangered Languages*
21.56.01–21.59.41	Program: *Discovery Channel Short Film*
21.59.41–22.00.11	Discovery program promo: *American Chopper*
22.00.11–22.00.26	Discovery program ident
22.00.26–22.09.13	Program: *Indian Larry* (Segment 1)
22.09.13–22.09.16	Discovery Channel ident
22.09.16–22.09.46	Advertising: Munich, film
22.09.46–22.09.49	Discovery Channel ident
22.09.49–22.10.19	Discovery program promo: *American Chopper*
22.10.19–22.10.22	Discovery Channel ident
22.10.22–22.24.40	Program: *Indian Larry* (Segment 2)
22.24.40–22.24.43	Discovery Channel ident
22.24.43–22.25.03	Advertising: Telenor Mobil, mobile telephony
22.25.03–22.25.28	Advertising: BMW, car
22.25.28–22.25.58	Advertising: Citibank, loan
22.25.58–22.26.28	Advertising: Incredible India, travel destination
22.26.28–22.26.31	Discovery Channel ident
22.26.31–22.27.01	Discovery program promo: *The Greatest Ever*
22.27.01–22.27.04	Discovery Channel ident
22.27.04–22.43.01	Program: *Indian Larry* (Segment 3)
22.43.01–22.43.04	Discovery Channel ident
22.43.04–22.43.34	Advertising: MatPrat, promotion of food
22.43.34–22.44.04	Advertising: Dell, computers
22.44.04–22.44.29	Advertising: KIA, car
22.44.29–22.44.59	Advertising: MatPrat, promotion of food
22.44.59–22.44.02	Discovery Channel ident
22.44.02–22.46.16	Program: *Together TV*
22.46.16–22.46.19	Discovery Channel ident
22.46.19–22.53.31	Program: *Indian Larry* (Segment 4)
22.53.31–22.53.34	Discovery Channel ident
22.53.34–22.54.04	Advertising: Microsoft
22.54.04–22.54.07	Discovery Channel ident
22.54.07–22.56.07	Program: *Endangered Languages*
22.56.07–22.59.47	Program: *Discovery Channel Short Film*
22.59.47–23.00.02	Discovery program intro ident

DISCOVERY CHANNEL NORWAY,
20.00.00–23.00.00, 4 FEBRUARY, 2006

20.00.00–20.23.36	Program: *Building the Winter Games*, Ep. 2 (Segment 1)
20.23.36–20.23.39	Discovery Channel ident
20.23.39–20.23.59	Advertising: Munich, film
20.23.59–20.24.29	Advertising: Citibank, loans
20.24.29–20.24.39	Advertising: Fishermans Friend
20.24.39–20.24.42	Discovery Channel ident
20.24.42–20.25.43	Program: *Endagered language*
20.25.43–20.25.46	Discovery Channel ident
20.25.46–20.42.46	Program: *Building the Winter Games*, Ep. 2 (Segment 2)
20.42.46–20.42.49	Discovery Channel ident
20.42.49–20.43.09	Advertising: Gjensidige, insurance
20.43.09–20.43.12	Discovery Channel
20.43.12–20.45.42	Program: *Together TV*
20.45.42–20.45.45	Discovery Channel ident
20.45.45–20.51.58	Program: *Building the Winter Games*, Ep. 2 (Segment 3)
20.51.58–20.52.01	Discovery Channel ident
20.52.01–20.52.31	Advertising: Incredible India, travel destination
20.52.31–20.52.34	Discovery Channel ident
20.52.34–20.55.34	Program: *Endangered Language*
20.55.34–20.59.50	Program: *Endangered Languages*
20.59.50–21.00.05	Discovery program intro ident
21.00.05–21.25.04	Program: *American Chopper* (Segment 1)
21.25.04–21.25.07	Discovery Channel ident
21.25.07–21.25.27	Advertising: Gjensidige, insurance
21.25.27–21.25.30	Discovery Channel ident
21.25.30–21.26.00	Discovery program promo: *The Greatest Ever*
21.26.00–21.26.03	Discovery Channel ident
21.26.03–21.42.42	Program: *American Chopper* (Segment 2)
21.42.42–21.42.45	Discovery Channel ident
21.42.45–21.42.55	Advertising: Fishermans Friend
21.42.55–21.43.20	Advertising: KIA, car
21.43.20–21.43.40	Advertising: Telenor Mobil, mobile telephony
21.43.40–21.44.10	Advertising: Incredible India, travel destination
21.44.10–21.44.13	Discovery Channel ident
21.44.13–21.46.08	Program: *Together TV*
21.46.08–21.46.11	Discovery Channel ident
21.46.11–21.52.40	Program: *American Chopper* (Segment 3)
21.52.40–21.52.43	Discovery Channel ident
21.52.43–21.53.13	Advertising: Skoda, car

21.53.13–21.53.17	Discovery Channel ident
21.53.17–21.56.11	Program: *Together TV*
21.56.11–21.59.36	Program: *Discovery Channel Short Films*
21.59.36–21.59.51	Discovery program intro/ ident
21.59.51–22.06.58	Program: *Rides* (Segment 1)
22.06.58–22.07.01	Discovery Channel ident
22.07.01–22.07.21	Advertising: Gjensidige, insurance
22.07.21–22.07.24	Discovery Channel ident
22.07.24–22.07.54	Discovery program promo: *Europe's Richest People*
22.07.54–22.07.57	Discovery Channel ident
22.07.57–22.25.45	Program: *Rides* (Segment 2)
22.25.45–22.25.48	Discovery Channel ident
22.25.48–22.26.08	Advertising: Telenor Mobil, mobile telephony
22.26.08–22.26.38	Advertising: Wasa, food
22.26.38–22.27.08	Advertising: Incredible India, travel destination
22.27.08–22.27.11	Discovery Channel ident
22.27.11–22.27.41	Discovery program promo *The Greatest Ever*
21.27.41–22.27.44	Discovery Channel ident
22.27.44–22.45.12	Program: *Rides* (Segment 3)
22.45.12–22.45.15	Discovery Channel ident
22.45.15–22.45.45	Advertising: Netcom, mobile telephony
22.45.45–22.46.10	Advertising: BMW, car
22.46.10–22.46.40	Advertising: Citibank
22.46.40–22.46.50	Advertising: Fisherman's Friend
22.46.50–22.46.53	Discovery Channel ident
22.46.53–22.49.47	Program: *Together TV*
22.49.47–22.49.50	Discovery Channel ident
22.49.50–22.54.33	Program: *Rides* (Segment 4)
22.54.33–22.54.36	Discovery Channel ident
22.54.36–22.56.36	Program: *Endangered Languages*
22.56.36–23.00.01	Program: *Discovery Channel Short Film*

DISCOVERY CHANNEL NORWAY, 20.00.00–23.00.00, 5 FEBRUARY, 2006

20.00.00–20.06.57	Program: *American Chopper* (Segment 1)
20.06.57–20.07.00	Discovery Channel ident
20.07.00–20.07.30	Discovery program promo: *American Chopper*
20.07.30–20.07.33	Discovery Channel ident
20.07.33–20.24.42	Program: *American Chopper* (Segment 2)
20.24.42–20.24.45	Discovery Channel ident
20.24.45–20.25.45	Program: *Endangered Languages*

20.25.45–20.25.48	Discovery Channel ident
20.25.48–20.42.27	Program: *American Chopper* (Segment 3)
20.42.27–20.42.30	Discovery Channel ident
20.42.30–20.43.00	Advertising: Skoda, car
20.43.00–20.43.15	Advertising: Microsoft
20.43.15–20.43.18	Discovery Channel ident
20.43.18–20.46.18	Program: *Endangered Languages*
20.46.18–20.46.22	Discovery Channel ident
20.46.22–20.52.52	Program: *American Chopper* (Segment 4)
20.52.52–20.52.57	Discovery Channel ident
20.52.57–20.53.17	Advertising: Telenor Mobil, mobile telephony
20.53.17–20.53.42	Advertising: BMW, car
20.53.42–20.54.12	Advertising: Incredible India, travel destination
20.54.12–20.54.15	Discovery Channel ident
20.54.15–20.56.10	Program: *Together TV*
20.56.10–20.59.51	Program: *Discovery Channel Short Film*
20.59.51–21.00.56	Discovery program intro ident
21.00.56–21.01.16	Advertising: Sponsored by pokerrooms.com
21.01.16–21.08.48	Program: *Myth Busters* (Segment 1)
21.08.48–21.08.53	Advertising: Sponsored by pokerrooms.com
21.08.53–21.08.56	Discovery Channel ident
21.08.56–21.09.06	Advertising: Fishermans Friend
21.09.06–21.09.09	Discovery Channel ident
21.09.09–21.09.39	Discovery program promo: *American Chopper*
21.09.39–21.09.42	Discovery Channel ident
21.09.42–21.09.47	Advertising: Program is sponsored by pokerooms.com
21.09.47–21.27.30	Program: *Myth Busters* (Segment 2)
21.27.30–21.27.35	Advertising: Program is sponsored by pokerooms.com
21.27.35–21.27.38	Discovery Channel ident
21.27.38–21.28.08	Advertising: Microsoft
21.28.08–21.28.28	Advertising: Telenor Mobil, mobile telephony
21.28.28–21.28.31	Discovery Channel ident
21.28.31–21.29.01	Discovery program promo: *Brainiac*
21.29.01–21.29.04	Discovery Channel ident
21.29.04–21.29.09	Advertising: Program is sponsored by pokerooms.com
21.29.09–21.45.37	Program: *Myth Busters* (Segment 3)
21.45.37–21.45.42	Advertising: Program is sponsored by pokerooms.com
21.45.42–21.45.45	Discovery Channel ident
21.45.45–21.46.15	Advertising: Netcom, mobile telephony
21.46.15–21.46.40	Advertising: BMW, car
21.46.40–21.47.10	Advertising: Incredible India, travel destination
21.47.10–21.47.13	Discovery Channel ident
21.47.13–21.50.13	Program: *Endangered Languages*
21.50.13–21.50.16	Discovery Channel ident

21.50.16–21.50.21	Advertising: Program is sponsored by pokerrooms.com
21.50.21–21.54.45	Program: *Myth Busters* (Segment 4)
21.54.45–21.54.55	Advertising: Program is sponsored by pokerooms.com
21.54.55–21.54.58	Discovery Channel ident
21.54.58–21.55.28	Advertising: Citibank, loans
21.55.28–21.55.48	Advertising: Telenor Mobil, mobile telephony
21.55.48–21.55.51	Discovery Channel ident
21.55.51–21.56.21	Discovery program promo: *The Greatest Ever*
21.56.21–21.59.46	Program: *Discovery Channel Short Film*
21.59.46–22.00.01	Discovery program intro ident
22.00.01–22.00.11	Advertising: Program sponsored by pokerrooms.com
22.00.11–22.08.37	Program: *The Science of Lance Armstrong* (Segment 1)
22.08.37–22.08.42	Advertising: Program sponsored by pokerrooms.com
22.08.42–22.08.45	Discovery Channel ident
22.08.45–22.09.15	Discovery program promo: *Brainiac*
22.09.15–22.09.18	Discovery Channel ident
22.09.18–22.09.23	Advertising: Program sponsored by pokerrooms.com
22.09.23–22.26.44	Program: *The Science of Lance Armstrong* (Segment 2)
22.26.44–22.26.49	Advertising: Program sponsored by pokerrooms.com
22.26.49–22.26.52	Discovery Channel ident
22.26.52–22.27.22	Advertising: Citibank, loans
22.27.22–22.27.32	Advertising: Fishermans Friend
22.27.32–22.28.02	Advertising: Incredible India, travel destination
22.28.02–22.28.05	Discovery Channel ident
22.28.05–22.29.05	Program: *Endangered Languages*
22.29.05–22.29.08	Discovery Channel ident
22.29.08–22.29.13	Advertising: Program sponsored by pokerrooms.com
22.29.13–22.43.51	Program: *The Science of Lance Armstrong* (Segment 3)
22.43.51–22.43.56	Advertising: Program sponsored by pokerrooms.com
22.43.56–22.43.59	Discovery Channel ident
22.43.59–22.44.24	Advertising: KIA, car
22.44.24–22.44.44	Advertising: Telenor Mobil, mobile telephony
22.44.44–22.45.14	Advertising: Wasa, food
22.45.14–22.45.17	Discovery Channel ident
22.45.17–22.45.47	Discovery program promo: *The Greatest Ever* (machines)
22.45.47–22.45.50	Discovery Channel ident
22.45.50–22.45.55	Advertising: Program sponsored by pokerrooms.com
22.45.55–22.52.35	Program: *The Science of Lance Armstrong* (Segment 4)
22.52.35–22.52.45	Advertising: Program is sponsored by pokerrooms.com

22.52.45–22.52.48	Discovery Channel ident
22.52.48–22.53.08	Advertising: Munich, film, Universal
22.53.08–22.53.38	Advertising: Microsoft
22.53.38–22.53.41	Discovery Channel ident
22.53.41–22.56.31	Program: *Endangered Languages*
22.56.31–22.59.57	Program: Discovery Channel Short Film
22.59.57–23.00.12	Discovery program intro ident

DISCOVER CHANNEL UK, 20.00.00–23.00.00, 30 JANUARY, 2006

20.00.00–20.06.40	Program: *Southern Chopper* Episode (segment 1)
20.06.40–20.07.00	Discovery program promo: *American Chopper*
20.07.00–20.07.30	Advertising: KIA, car
20.07.30–20.08.00	Advertising: AXA BBP Healthcare
20.08.00–20.08.30	Advertising: Can't Read Word: UK printing services
20.08.30–20.09.00	Advertising: Lee, clothing
20.09.00–20.09.10	Advertising: Car insurance
20.09.10–20.09.40	Advertising: Vision Express, health care
20.09.40–20.10.00	Advertising: Egypt's Red Sea Riviera, travel destination.
20.10.00–20.10.20	Discovery program promo: *American Chopper* and *The Garage*
20.10.20–20.27.40	Program: *Southern Chopper*, Episode 5 (segment 2)
20.27.40–20.27.55	Discovery program promo for *American Chopper*
20.27.55–20.28.00	Discovery ident
20.28.00–20.28.30	Advertising: Herbalessens Shampoo
20.28.30–20.28.40	Advertising: Sainsburys, food
20.28.40–20.29.30	Advertising: US film studios
20.29.30–20.30.00	Advertising: Oxfam membership
20.30.00–20.30.30	Advertising: Mazda, car
20.30.30–20.30.45	Discovery program promo: *Trouble Trouble*, on Discovery Real Time
20.30.45–20.31.00	Discovery ident
20.31.00–20.47.30	Program: *Southern Chopper*, Episode 5 (segment 3)
20.47.30–20.47.50	Discovery program promo: *The Worlds Strangest UFO Stories*
20.47.50–20.48.00	Discovery Ident
20.48.00–20.48.30	Advertising: Pegeout, car
20.48.30–20.48.45	Advertising: Sainsburys, food
20.48.45–20.49.15	Advertising: Churchill, car insurance
20.49.15- 20.49.45	Advertising: Turkeytravel holidays
20.49.45–20.50.15	Advertising: Fosters beer

20.50.15–20.50.45	Advertising: AXA BBP Healthcare
20.50.45–20.50.55	Advertising: Dolmio, food
20.50.55–20.51.05	Discovery program promo: *American Chopper*
20.51.05–20.51.10	Discovery ident
20.51.10–20.57.40	Program: *Southern Chopper*, Episode 5 (segment 4)
20.57.40–20.57.45	Discovery Europe Networks ident
20.57.45–20.57.50	Discovery Channel ident
20.57.50–20.58.20	Advertising: Turkeytravel, travel destination
20.58.20–20.58.50	Advertising: Seat, car
20.58.50–20.59.30	Advertising: Grime and Lime, cleaning liquid
20.59.30–20.59.45	Advertising: Yellow Pages
20.59.45–21.00.15	Advertising: Car insurance online
21.00.15–21.00.45	Discovery Channel ident
21.00.45–21.09.20	*American Chopper* (Segment 1)
21.09.20–21.09.35	Discovery program promo: *The Garage*
21.09.35–21.09.40	Discovery Channel ident
21.09.40–21.10.10	Advertising: Carlsberg Beer
21.10.10–21.10.30	Advertising: Kellogs, food
21.10.30–21.11.00	Advertising: Kwikfit Tire and Exhaust for cars
21.11.00–21.11.20	Advertising: Stakeholder Saving, bank service
21.11.20–21.11.50	Advertising: Lee, clothing
21.11.50–21.12.10	Advertising: Tesco, food
21.12.10–21.12.40	Advertising: Seat, car
21.12.40–21.12.55	Discovery program promo: *My Greek Kitchen*, on Discovery Travel & Living
21.12.55–21.13.00	Discovery Channel ident
21.13.00–21.29.10	Program: *American Chopper* (Segment 2)
21.29.10–21.29.25	Discovery program promo: *Myth Busters* on Discovery Channel
21.29.25–21.29.30	Discovery Channel ident
21.29.30–21.30.00	Advertising: Dolmio, food
21.30.00–21.30.30	Advertising: Xbox, Dead or Alive 4, computer game
21.30.30–21.30.50	Advertising: Burger King: Cheese Burger, food
21.30.50–21.31.00	Advertising: ALDI, supermarket
21.31.00–21.31.30	Advertising: Swiftcover.com, car insurance online
21.31.30–21.32.00	Advertising: Volkswagen, car
21.32.00–21.32.03	Discovery Channel ident
21.32.03–21.47.45	Program: *American Chopper* (segment 3)
21.47.45–21.48.00	Discovery promo for *The Garage* on Discovery Channel
21.48.00–21.48.02	Discovery Channel ident
21.48.02–21.48.42	Advertising. Direct Line, car insurance
21.49.42–21.49.12	Advertising: NatWest, banking services
21.49.12–21.49.32	Advertising: Egypt's Red Sea Riviera Resort, travel destination

21.49.32–21.50.02	Advertising: KIA, car
21.50.02–21.50.32	Advertising: McDonalds, food
21.50.32–21.51.02	Advertising: CISCO, computer security
21.51.02–21.51.12	Discovery promo for *The Garage*
21.51.12–21.51.14	Discovery Channel ident
21.51.14–21.56.50	Program: *American Chopper* (Segment 4)
21.56.50–21.56.52	Discovery Channel ident
21.56.52–21.56.32	Advertising: Ireland, travel destination
21.56.32–21.57.02	Advertising: TISCALI, Internet service provider
21.58.02–21.58.32	Advertising: ARGOS, retail catalogue
21.58.32–21.58.52	Advertising: Bernard Mathew, food
21.58.52–21.59.22	Advertising: Pedegree, dog food
21.59.22–21.59.40	Discovery program promo/ intro: *The Garage*
21.59.40–22.05.10	Program: *The Garage* (segment 1)
22.05.10–22.05.28	Discovery program promo: *Myth Busters* on Discovery Channel
22.05.28–22.05.30	Discovery Channel ident
22.05.30–22.05.50	Advertising: Egypt's Red Sea Riviera, travel destination
22.05.50–22.06.50	Advertising: Rover, car
22.06.50–22.07.10	Advertising: Kwickfit, car services
22.07.10–22.07.30	Advertising: Rimmel London, cosmetics
22.07.30–22.08.00	Advertising: ING Direct, banking services
22.08.00–22.08.30	Advertising: Kellogs, food
22.08.30–22.08.50	Discovery program promo: *My Greek Kitchen* on Discovery Travel & Living
22.08.50–22.08.52	Discovery Channel ident
22.08.52–22.25.55	Program: *The Garage* (Segment 2)
22.25.55–22.26.25	Discovery program promo: *Building the Winter Games*
22.26.25–22.26.26	Discovery Channel ident
22.26.26–22.26.36	Advertising: Tango Clear, food
22.26.36–22.27.06	Advertising: Weetabix, food
22.27.06–22.27.16	Advertising: Bernard Mathews, food
22.27.16–22.27.46	Advertising: First Choice
22.27.46–22.28.16	Advertising: ARGOS, retail catalogue
22.28.16–22.28.46	Advertising: Muller, food
22.28.46–22.28.56	Advertising: Weetabix, food
22.28.56–22.29.00	Discovery Channel ident
22.29.00–22.46.00	Program: *The Garage* (Segment 3)
22.46.00–22.46.15	Discovery program promo: *Myth Busters* on Discovery Channel
22.46.15–22.46.18	Discovery Channel ident
22.46.18–22.46.48	Advertising: Kellogs, food
22.46.48–22.47.18	Advertising: Corsa, car

22.47.18–22.47.48	Advertising: Muller, food
22.47.48–22.48.08	Advertising: Dipers
22.48.08–22.48.38	Advertising: Pizza Hut, food
22.48.38–22.48.48	Advertising: Tango, food
22.48.48–22.48.58	Advertising: Vauxhall, car
22.48.58–22.49.18	Advertising: Mini Baby Bell, food
22.49.18–22.49.28	Discovery program promo
22.49.28–22.49.30	Discovery Channel ident
22.49.30–22.56.00	Program: *The Garage* (Segment 4)
22.56.00–22.56.02	Discovery Channel ident
22.56.02–22.56.22	Advertising: OralB Toothbrush
22.56.22–22.56.52	Advertising: Rajasthan, travel destination
22.56.52–22.57.22	Advertising: Washing powder
22.57.22–22.57.42	Advertising: Munich, film
22.57.42–22.58.12	Advertising: British Gas, energy
22.58.12–22.58.32	Advertising: Fixodent Neutral
22.58.32–22.58.50	Discovery promo for next program
22.58.50–23.00.00	Program: *FBI Files* about crime case in Detroit

DISCOVER CHANNEL UK, 20.00.00–23.00.00, 31 JANUARY, 2006

20.00.00–20.10.45	Program: *How It is Made* (Segment 1)
20.10.45–20.11.02	Discovery Promo: *The Worlds Strangest UFO Stories* on Discovery Channel
20.11.02–20.11.05	Discovery Channel ident
20.11.05–20.11.35	Advertising: Think! Driving campaign
20.11.35–20.12.05	Advertising: Co-op, supermarket
20.12.05–20.12.25	Advertising: Senokot digestive
20.12.25–20.13.05	Advertising: Grime and Lime, cleaning liquid
20.13.05–20.13.25	Advertising: Munich, film
20.13.25–20.13.35	Advertising: Yoplati, food
20.13.35–20.14.05	Advertising: McDonalds, food
20.14.05–20.14.35	Advertising: AXA BBP
20.14.35–20.14.45	Discovery program promo *How It is Made*
20.14.45–20.14.50	Discovery Channel ident
20.14.50–20.25.50	Program: *How It is Made 2* (Segment 2)
20.25.50–20.25.05	Discovery program promo: *American Chopper*
20.25.05–20.25.10	Discovery ident
20.25.10–20.25.50	Advertising: Pegeuot, car
20.26.50–20.27.30	Advertising: Port Aventura, Spain, travel destination
20.27.30–20.27.40	Advertising: Yoplati, food

20.27.40–20.28.10	Advertising: Kellogs, food
20.28.10–20.28.15	Discovery program promo: *The Gargage*
20.28.15–20.28.45	Discovery promo introducing the next program
20.28.45–20.39.35	Program: *How It is Made 2* (Segment 3)
20.39.35–20.40.05	Discovery promo for *Building the Winter Games* program
20.40.05–20.40.10	Discovery ident
20.40.10–20.40.40	Advertising: Kellogs, food
20.40.40–20.41.10	Advertising: AXA BBP Healthcare
20.41.10–20.41.50	Advertising: Oxfam membership
20.41.50–20.42.00	Advertising: Mullers, food
20.42.00–20.42.30	Advertising: XBox: Dead or Alive 4 game, computer game
20.42.30–20.43.30	Advertising: AOL
20.43.30–20.43.40	Advertising: Esure.com, car insurance
20.43.40–20.44.00	Discovery program promo: *My Greek Kitchen*, on Discovery Travel & Living
20.44.00–20.44.10	Discovery program promo: *Dirty Jobs*
20.44.10–20.44.12	Discovery Channel ident
20.44.12–20.55.15	Program: *How It is Made*
20.55.15–20.55.20	Discovery ident
20.55.20–20.55.50	Advertising: Sainsbury, supermarket
20.55.50–20.56.00	Advertising: Centerparcs.co.uk
20.56.00–20.56.30	Advertising: Toilet detergent
20.56.30–20.57.00	Advertising: Seat, car
20.57.00–20.57.20	Advertising: Mini Baby Bells cheese, food
20.57.20–20.57.40	Discovery program promo: *Dirty Jobs*
20.57.40–20.06.00	Program: *Dirty Jobs* (Segment 1)
21.06.00–21.06.29	Discovery program promo: *Building the Winter Games*
21.06.29–21.06.30	Discovery Channel ident
21.06.30–21.06.50	Advertising: Toilet cleaning liquid
21.06.50–21.07.10	Advertising: Jersey, travel destination
21.07.10–21.07.40	Advertising: Muller, food
21.07.40–21.07.50	Advertising: Homebase, home and garden products
21.07.50–21.08.10	Advertising: Munich, film
21.08.10–21.09.10	Advertising: AOL
21.09.10–21.09.30	Advertising: Imodium
21.09.30–21.09.33	Discovery Channel ident
21.09.33–21.25.55	Program: *Dirty Jobs* (Segment 2)
21.25.55–21.26.10	Discovery program promo: *American Chopper*
21.26.10–21.26.12	Discovery Channel ident

21.26.12–21.26.42	Advertising: Pedegree, dog food
21.26.42–21.27.12	Advertising: toilet detergent
21.27.12–21.27.32	Advertising: Kellogs food
21.27.32–21.28.02	Advertising: British Gas, energy
21.28.02–21.28.22	Advertising: Cleenex
21.28.22–21.28.42	Advertising: Mini Baby Bell cheese, food
21.28.42–21.28.45	Discovery Channel ident
21.28.45–21.45.10	Program: *Dirty Jobs* (Segment 3)
21.45.10–21.45.15	Discovery program promo: *The Garage*
21.45.15–21.45.20	Discovery Channel ident
21.45.20–21.45.50	Advertising: Burger King, food
21.45.50–21.46.30	Advertising: Port Aventura, Spain, travel destination.
21.46.30–21.47.00	Advertising: New Zealand Lamb, food
21.47.00–21.47.30	Advertising: Oxfam membership
21.47.30–21.48.30	Advertising: AOL
21.48.30–21.48.50	Discovery program promo *Trouble Trouble* on Discovery Real Time
21.48.50–21.49.00	Discovery program promo *The Blasters*
21.49.00–21.49.02	Discovery Channel ident
21.49.02–21.54.57	Program: *Dirty Jobs* (Segment 4)
21.54.57–21.55.12	Discovery program promo for *American Chopper* in Europe
21.55.12–21.55.15	Discovery Channel ident
21.55.15–21.55.35	Advertising: Catsand
21.55.35–21.56.05	Advertising: ING Direct, bank services
21.56.05–21.56.35	Advertising: CISCO, computer network safety
21.56.35–21.56.55	Advertising: Munich, film
21.56.55–21.57.15	Advertising: Quorn sausages, food
21.57.15–21.57.45	Advertising: Jaguar car
21.57.45–21.58.03	Discovery program promo *The Blaster*
21.58.03–22.06.53	Program: *The Blasters* (Segment 1)
22.06.53–22.06.58	Discovery program promo: *The Garage*
22.06.58–22.07.00	Discovery Channel ident
22.07.00–22.07.20	Advertising: Toilent liquid washer
22.07.20–22.07.30	Advertising: Bisto gravy, food
22.07.30–22.08.00	Advertising: Churchill, car insurance
22.08.00–22.08.30	Advertising: Whiskas, cat food
22.08.30–22.09.30	Advertising: AOL
22.09.30–22.09.50	Advertising: Cleenex
22.09.50–22.10.00	Advertising: Sainsbury, supermarket
22.10.00–22.10.05	Discovery Channel ident
22.10.05–22.27.15	Program: *The Blasters* (Segment 2)
22.27.15–22.27.30	Discovery program promo: *American Chopper*
22.27.30–22.27.33	Discovery Channel ident

22.27.33–22.28.03	Advertising: Seat, car
22.28.03–22.28.33	Advertising: Flora margarine, food
22.28.33–22.29.03	Advertising: Co-op, supermarket
22.29.03–22.29.13	Advertising: esure.com, car insurance
22.29.13–22.29.33	Advertising: AMOY, food
22.29.33–22.29.43	Advertising: Lanacane skin cream
22.29.43–22.30.03	Advertising: Sheeba, cat food
22.30.03–22.30.05	Discovery Channel ident
22.30.05–22.46.23	Program: *The Blasters* (Segment 2)
22.46.23–22.46.52	Discovery program promo: *The Garage*
22.46.52–22.46.55	Discovery Channel ident
22.46.55–22.47.15	Advertising: Cleenex
22.47.15–22.47.35	Advertising: Mini pringles, food
22.47.35–22.47.45	Advertising: Yoplati, food
22.47.45–22.48.05	Advertising: Munich, film
22.48.05–22.49.05	Advertising: AOL
22.49.05–22.49.35	Advertising: Dolmio, food
22.49.35–22.49.55	Advertising: Mini Baby Bell, food
22.49.55–22.50.25	Discovery program promo: *RSPCA*, Animal Planet
22.50.25–22.50.35	Discovery program promo: *FBI Files*
22.50.35–22.50.37	Discovery indent
22.50.37–22.54.07	Program: *The Blasters* (Segment 3)
22.54.07–22.54.22	Discovery program promo: *The Worlds Strangest UFO Stories*, on Discovery Channel
22.54.22–22.54.25	Discovery Channel ident
22.54.25–22.54.55	Advertising: Ahead biscuits, food
22.54.55–22.55.00	Advertising: Star, celebrity magazine
22.55.00–22.55.10	Advertising: Homebas, home and garden products
22.55.10–22.55.30	Advertising: Andrex, toilet paper
22.55.30–22.56.30	Advertising: AOL
22.56.30–22.56.35	Advertising: Star, celebrity magazine
22.56.35–22.56.55	Advertising: AMOY, food
22.56.55–22.57.00	Discovery program promo: *The Worlds Strangest UFO Stories* on Discovery Channel
22.57.00–22.57.25	Discovery program promo intro: *FBI files*
22.57.25–23.00.00	Program: *FBI files*

DISCOVERY CHANNEL UK, 20.00.00–23.00.00, 1 FEBRUARY, 2006

20.00.00–20.06.44	Program: *The Greatest Ever—Helicopters*, (Segment 1)
20.06.44–20.06.59	Discovery promo for *American Chopper* in Europe

20.06.59–20.07.02	Discovery Channel ident
20.07.02–20.07.32	Advertising: Landrover, car
20.07.32–20.07.42	Advertising: Knorr, food
20.07.42–20.08.12	Advertising: AXA, health insurance
20.08.12–20.08.22	Advertising: clothes washing liquid
20.08.22–20.08.52	Advertising: Law offices of James Sokolove
20.08.52–20.09.02	Advertising: Bonjella, pain relief
20.09.02–20.09.32	Advertising: The Independent, newspaper
20.09.32–20.10.02	Advertising: Capital One, credit card
20.10.02–20.10.05	Discovery Channel ident
20.10.05–20.27.35	Program: *The Greatest Ever—Helicopters* (Segment 2)
20.27.35–20.27.51	Discovery program promo: *The Garage*
20.27.51–20.27.52	Discovery Channel ident
20.27.52–20.28.22	Advertising: Jaffa Cakes, food
20.28.22–20.28.42	Advertising: Sanex, detergent
20.28.42–20.29.12	Advertising: Incredible India, travel destination
20.29.12–20.29:42	Advertising: Sheelas Wheels, car insurance
20.29.42–20.30.12	Advertising: BMW, car
22.30.12–20.30.22	Advertising: Bisto, food
22.30.22–20.30.52	Discovery program promo, *RSPCA*, on Animal Planet,
20.30.52–20.30.54	Discovery Channel ident
20.30.54–20.48.25	Program: *The Greatest Ever—Helicopters* (Segment 3)
20.48.25–20.48.40	Discovery Promo: *The Worlds Strangest UFO Stories*, on Discovery Channel.
20.48.40–20.48.42	Discovery Channel ident
20.48.42–20.49.12	Advertising: Corsa, car
20.49.12–20.49.42	Advertising: Vision Express, eye examination
22.49.42–20.50.12	Advertising: TISCALI, broadband services
20.50.12–20.50.52	Advertising: Abbey, Bank of England, banking service
20.50.52–20.51.22	Advertising: Heinz, food
20.51.22–20.51.32	Advertising: T-Zone, skin cream
20.51.32–20.51.42	Advertising: Corsa, Vauxhail, car
20.51.42–20.51.52	Discovery program promo: *Monster Move*
20.51.52–20.51.55	Discovery Channel ident
20.51.55–20.57.12	Program: *The Greatest Ever—Helicopters* (Segment 4)
20.57.12–20.57.27	Discovery promo for *American Chopper* in Europe
20.57.27–20.57.30	Discovery Channel ident
20.57.30–20.58.00	Advertising: V8, food
20.58.00–20.58.30	Advertising: Activia, food

20.58.30–21.00.00	Advertising: Jaguar, car
21.00.00–21.06.53	Program: *Monster Move* (Segment 1)
21.06.53–21.07.08	Discovery program promo: *The Garage*
21.07.08–21.07.10	Discovery Channel ident
21.07.10–21.07.40	Advertising: Actinie, food
21.07.40–21.08.10	Advertising: Renewex, skin cream
21.08.10–21.08.50	Advertising: Sheelas Wheels, car insurance
21.08.50–21.09.10	Advertising: Mini Pringles, food
21.09.10–21.09.40	Advertising: Finish, washing up powder
21.09.40–21.10.10	Advertising: Citroen, car
21.10.10–21.10.30	Discovery program promo: *OverHaul*
21.10.30–21.28.50	Program: *Monster Move* (Segment 2)
21.28.50–21.29.20	Discovery program promo: *Building the Winter Games*
21.29.20–21.29.22	Discovery Channel ident
21.29.22–21.29.52	Advertising: Sainsbury, supermarket
21.29.52–21.30.22	Advertising: Astra, car
21.30.22–21.30.42	Advertising: RAC, car service
21.30.42–21.31.02	Advertising: Fairy, cleaning spray
21.31.02–21.31.12	Advertising: Gavison, heartburn relief
21.31.12–21.31.32	Advertising: Senokot, digestion relief
21.31.32–21.31.42	Advertising: First Direct, bankin service
21.31.42–21.31.52	Advertising: Astra, car
21.31.52–21.31.56	Advertising: Discovery Channel ident
21.31.56–21.49.53	Program: *Monster Move* (Segment 3)
21.49.53–21.50.08	Discovery program promo: for *American Chopper* in Europe
21.50.08–21.50.10	Discovery Channel ident
21.50.10–21.50.40	Advertising: Jaffa Cakes, food
21.50.40–21.51.10	Advertising: The Independent, newspaper
21.51.10–21.51.40	Advertising: Muller, food
21.51.40–21.52.10	Advertising: Incredible India, travel destination
21.52.10–21.52.40	Advertising: Youngs, food
21.52.40–21.53.10	Advertising: Mazda, car
21.53.10–21.53.20	Discovery program promo: *Mega Builders*
21.53.20–21.53.24	Discovery Channel ident
21.53.24–21.57.25	Program: *Monster Move* (Segment 4)
21.57.25–21.57.40	Discovery program promo: *The Garage* on Discovery Channel
21.57.40–21.57.43	Discovery Channel ident
21.57.43–21.58.13	Advertising: Clario Diesel, car
21.58.13–21.58.43	Advertising: Fairy, washing liquid
21.58.43–21.59.13	Advertising: Not available
21.59.13–21.59.43	Advertising: Daz, washing powder
21.59.43–22.00.13	Advertising: CISCO, Internet security

22.00.13–22.00.33	Discovery intro promo
22.00.33–22.09.26	Program: *Mega Builders* (Segment 1)
22.09.26–22.09.41	Discovery program promo: *The Strangest UFO's*
22.09.41–22.09.44	Discovery Channel ident
22.09.44–22.10.14	Advertising: Astra, car
22.10.14–22.10.44	Advertising: ARIEL, washing powder
22.10.44–22.11.04	Advertising: FIXODENT
22.11.04–22.11.24	Advertising: Andrex, toilet paper
22.11.24–22.11.54	Advertising: TISCALI, broadband service
22.11.54–22.12.24	Advertising: Virgin Credit Card
22.12.24–22.12.36	Advertising: Ariel, washing powder
22.12.36–22.12.46	Advertising: Astra, car
22.12.46–22.12.48	Discovery Channel ident
22.12.48–22.28.48	Program: *Mega Builders* (Segment 2)
22.28.48–22.29.03	Discovery Channel promo: *American Chopper* in London
22.29.03–22.29.06	Discovery Channel ident
22.29.06–22.29.46	Advertising: Directline, insurance
22.29.46–22.30.16	Advertising: The Independet, newspaper
22.30.16–22.30.36	Advertising: AmbiPur, toilet liquid
22.30.36–22.31.06	Advertising: Tresemme, shampoo
22.31.06–22.31.36	Advertising: Citroen, car
22.31.36–22.31.56	Discovery program promo: *Trouble Trouble* on Discovery Real Time
22.31.56–22.31.59	Discovery Channel ident
22.31.59–22.47.15	Program: *Mega Builders* (Segment 3)
22.47.15–22.47.30	Discovery program promo: *The Garage*
22.47.30–22.47.33	Discovery Channel ident
22.47.33–22.48.03	Advertising: The Independent, newspaper
22.48.03–22.48.33	Advertising: Renault, car
22.48.33–22.49.03	Advertising: Kingsmill, food
22.49.03–22.49.33	Advertising: Youngs, food
22.49.33–22.50.03	Advertising: Whiskas, cat food
22.50.03–22.50.33	Advertising: Options, food
22.50.33–22.50.43	Discovery Channel and program promo: *FBI Files*
22.50.43–22.50.46	Discovery Channel ident
22.50.46–22.56.48	Program: *Mega Builders* (Segment 4)
22.56.48–22.56.51	Discovery Channel ident
22.56.51–22.57.11	Advertising: Real People, magazine
22.57.11–22.57.31	Advertising: ASDA, supermarket
22.57.31–22.58.01	Advertising: Incredible India, travel destination
22.58.01–22.58.21	Advertising: Nestle, cereal
22.58.21–22.58.51	Advertising: Pedigree, dog food,
22.58.51–22.58.21	Advertising: Huyndai, car

| 22.59.21–22.59.36 | Discovery Channel and program promo: *The Garage* |
| 22.59.36–23.00.00 | Discovery program promo/ intro: *FBI Files* |

DISCOVER CHANNEL UK, 20.00.00–23.00.00, 2 FEBRUARY, 2006

20.00.00–20.11.19	Program: *How It is Made*
20.11.19–20.11.34	Discovery program promo for American Chopper
20.11.34–20.11.36	Discovery Channel ident
20.11.37–20.11.47	Advertising: Washing detergent
20.11.47–20.12.17	Advertising: Jaffa Cakes, food
20.12.17–20.12.47	Advertising: AOL, Internet service provider
20.12.47–20.13.17	Advertising: The Careers Advice
20.13.17–20.13.47	Advertising: Incredible India, travel destination
20.13.47–20.13.57	Advertising: PC world, computers
20.13.57–20.14.37	Advertising: Abbey, Bank of England, mortgage
20.14.37–20.15.07	Advertising: Land Rover, car
20.15.07–20.15.16	Discovery program promo: *How It is Made*
20.15.16–20.15.19	Discovery Channel ident
20.15.19–20.26.11	Program: *How It is Made*
20.26.11–20.26.26	Discovery program promo: *The Garage*
20.26.26–20.26.29	Discovery Channel ident
20.26.29–20.26.59	Advertising: Actinie,
20.26.59–20.27.20	Advertising: Not available
20.27.20–20.28.00	Advertising: Sheela's Wheels, car insurance
20.28.00–20.28.30	Advertising: Clio, car
20.28.30–20.29.00	Discovery program promo: *Building the Winter Games*
20.29.00–20.29.17	Discovery program promo/intro to *How It is made*
20.29.17–20.40.38	Program: *How It is Made 2* (Segment 1)
20.40.38 –20.40.53	Discovery program promo: *The Worlds Strangest UFO* on Discovery Channel
20.40.53–20.40.55	Discovery Channel ident
20.40.55–20.41.25	Advertising: Police
20.41.25–20.41.55	Advertising: Activia
20.41.55–20.42.25	Advertising: Herbalessens shampoo
20.42.25–20.42.55	Advertising: Lloyds TSB, loans
20.42.55–20.43.25	Advertising: Rajasthan, travel destination
20.43.25–20.43.55	Advertising: British Gas, energy
20.43.55–20.44.25	Advertising: Jaguar, car

20.44.25–20.44.45	Discovery program promo: *Trouble Trouble* on Discovery Real Time
20.44.45–20.45.49	Discovery program promo: *Transplanting a human face*
20.45.49–20.55.51	Program: *How It is Made 2*
20.55.51–20.56.05	Discovery program promo: *American Chopper*
20.56.05–20.56.08	Discovery Channel ident
20.56.08–20.56.38	Advertising: toilet liquid detergent
20.56.38–20.57.08	Advertising: Incredible India, travel destination
20.57.08–20.57.38	Advertising: Vision express, sight examination
20.57.38–20.58.08	Advertising: Sainsbury, supermarket
20.58.08–20.58.38	Discovery promo for *Building the Winter Games* program
20.58.38–20.59.00	Discovery program promo: *Face Race*
20.59.00–21.04.56	Program: *Face Race*, (Segment 1)
21.04.56–21.05.11	Discovery program promo: *The Garage*
21.05.11–21.05.14	Discovery Channel ident
21.05.14–21.05.44	Advertising: KIA Rio Diesel, car
21.05.44–21.06.04	Advertising: Chocolate
21.06.04–21.06.34	Advertising: Activia
21.06.34–21.07.04	Advertising: washing up powder
21.07.04–21.07.34	Advertising: V8, food
21.07.34–21.08.04	Advertising: The Careers Advice
21.08.04–21.08.12	Advertising: Not available due to technical problems
21.08.12–21.08.36	Discovery program promo: *Overhaul* on Discovery Real Time
21.08.36–21.08.38	Discovery Channel ident
21.08.38–21.25.10	Program: *Face Race* (Segment 2)
21.25.10–21.25.25	Discovery program promo: *Building the Winter Games* program
21.25.25–21.25.27	Discovery Channel ident
21.25.27–21.25.57	Advertising: Jaffa Cakes, food
21.25.57–21.26.07	Advertising: ARGOS, retail catalogue
21.26.07–21.26.27	Advertising: Enterprise, car rental
21.26.27–21.26.57	Advertising: AA, car insurance
21.26.57–21.27.27	Advertising: Whiskas, cat food
21.27.27–21.27.57	Advertising: Skoda, car
21.27.57–21.28.00	Discovery Channel ident
21.28.00–21.44.00	Program: *Face Race* (Segment 3)
21.44.00–21.44.15	Discovery promo American Chopper
21.44.15–21.44.18	Discovery Channel ident
21.44.18–21.44.28	Advertising: Dolmio, food
21.44.28–21.44.58	Advertising: Sanitary towels
21.44.58–21.46.28	Advertising: UBS, financial services

21.46.28–21.46.48	Advertising: RAC, car insurance
21.46.48–21.47.18	Advertising: Heinz, food
21.47.18–21.47.48	Advertising: British Gas, energy
21.47.48–21.47.18	Advertising: BMW, car
21.47.18–21.47.27	Discovery program promo: *Psychic Witness*
21.47.27–21.47.30	Discovery Channel ident
21.47.30–21.56.16	Program: *Face Race* (Segment 4)
21.56.16–21.56.29	Discovery program promo: *The Garage*
21.56.29–21.56.33	Discovery Channel ident
21.56.33–21.57.03	Advertising: Sheeba, cat food
21.57.03–21.57.23	Advertising: Actimel, food
21.57.23–21.57.33	Advertising: PC world, computers
21.57.33–21.58.13	Advertising: Sheebas Wheels, car insurance
21.58.13–21.58.23	Advertising: Bisto, food
21.58.23–21.59.03	Advertising: Honda, cars
21.59.03–21.59.18	Discovery program promo: *American Chopper*
21.59.18–21.59.37	Discovery program promo intro: *Psychic Witness*
21.59.37–22.07.18	Program: *Psychic Witness* (Segment 1)
22.07.18 -22.07.33	Discovery program promo: *Building the Winter Games*
22.07.33–22.07.35	Discovery Channel ident
22.07.35–22.08.05	Advertising: Kia Rodeo, car
22.08.05–22.08.35	Advertising: Incredible India, travel destination
22.08.35–22.09.05	Advertising: Pricedot TV, TV shopping
22.09.05–22.09.25	Advertising: ASDA, car insurance
22.09.25–22.09.35	Advertising: washing liquid
22.09.35–22.10.05	Advertising: Brother, printer
22.10.05–22.10.35	Advertising: Wholegrain, food
22.10.35–22.10.38	Discovery Channel ident
22.10.38–22.27.20	Program: *Psychic Witness* (Segment 2)
22.27.20–22.27.34	Discovery program promo: *The Worlds Strangest UFO Stories* on Discovery Channel
22.27.34–22.27.37	Discovery Channel ident
22.27.37–22.28.07	Advertising: Whiskas, cat food
22.28.07–22.28.47	Advertising: Direct Line, car insurance
22.28.47–22.29.17	Advertising: Old El Paso, food
22.29.17–22.29.37	Advertising: Curry, sales electronics
22.29.37–22.30.07	Advertising: Renault, car
22.30.07–22.30.37	Discovery program promo: *RSPCA*, on Animal Planet
22.30.37–22.30.40	Discovery Channel ident
22.30.40–22.46.52	Program: *Psychic Witness* (Segment 3)
22.46.52–22.47.06	Discovery program promo: *The Garage* on Discovery Channel
22.47.06–22.47.08	Discovery Channel ident

22.47.08–22.47.28	Advertising: Smile, toothpaste
22.47.28–22.47.58	Advertising: British Gas, energy
22.47.58–22.48.38	Advertising: Sheeba Wheels, car insurance
22.48.38–22.49.08	Advertising: Fairy, washing powder
22.49.08–22.49.38	Advertising: Jaffa Cakes, food
22.49.38–22.50.08	Advertising: Renault, car
22.50.08–22.50.18	Discovery Channel promo
22.50.18–22.50.20	Discovery Channel ident
22.50.20–22.55.57	Program: *Psychic Witness* (Segment 4)
22.55.57–22.56.26	Discovery program promo: *The Worlds Strangest UFO Stories* on Discovery Channel
22.56.26–22.56.29	Discovery Channel ident
22.56.29–22.56.59	Advertising: Cheerios, food
22.57.00–22.57.30	Advertising: Heinz, food
22.57.30–22.58.00	Advertising: Incredible India, travel destination
22.58.00–22.58.30	Advertising: Go Ahead, food
22.58.30–22.59.00	Advertising: Hyundai, car
22.59.00–22.59.30	Discovery program promo: *Building the Winter Games*
22.59.30–23.00.00	Discovery intro to *FBI files*

DISCOVER CHANNEL UK, 20.00.00–23.00.00, 3 FEBRUARY, 2006

20.00.00–20.08.52	Program: *Mega Builders* (Segment 1)
20.08.52–20.09.22	Discovery program promo: *The Garage*
20.09.22–20.09.24	Discovery Channel ident
20.09.24–20.09.54	Advertising: Kellogs, food
20.09.54–20.10.26	Advertising: Virgin Credit Card
20.10.26–20.10.46	Advertising: Jersey, travel destination
20.10.46–20.11.16	Advertising: Brother, printer
20.11.16–20.11.56	Advertising: Abbey, Bank of England, mortgage
20.11.56–20.12.26	Advertising: Land Rover, car
20.12.26–20.12.46	Discovery program promo: *Trouble Trouble* on Discovery Real Time
20.12.46–20.12.48	Discovery Channel ident
20.12.48–20.28.49	Program: *Mega Builders* (Segment 2)
20.28.49–20.29.04	Discovery program promo: *American Chopper*
20.29.04–20.29.07	Discovery Channel ident
20.29.07–20.29.37	Advertising: McDonalds, food
20.29.37–20.29.47	Advertising: Sunday Express, newspaper
20.29.47–20.30.17	Advertising: Incredible India, travel destination
20.30.17–20.30.47	Advertising: Davidhoff, fragrance
20.30.47–20.31.07	Advertising: British Gas, energy

20.31.07–20.31.37	Advertising: Jaguar, car
20.31.37–20.31.40	Discovery Channel ident
20.31.40–20.46.55	Program: *Mega Builders* (Segment 3)
20.46.55–20.47.25	Discovery program promo: *The Garage* on Discovery Channel
20.47.25–20.47.28	Discovery Channel ident
20.47.28–20.47.38	Advertising: Sunday Express
20.47.38–20.47.48	Advertising: CenterParcs, holiday parks
20.47.48–20.48.18	Advertising: Bodyform, sanetary towls
20.48.18–20.48.48	Advertising: Loyds TSB, banking services
20.48.48–20.49.18	Advertising: DFS, furniture
20.49.18–20.49.28	Advertising: DVD Corps Bride, film
20.49.28–20.49.58	Advertising: Revels, food
20.49.58–20.50.28	Advertising: Mazda, car
20.50.28–20.50.38	Discovery program promo: *FBI Files*
20.50.38–20.50.40	Discovery Channel ident
20.50.40–20.56.43	Program: *Mega Builders* (Segment 4)
20.56.43–20.57.13	Discovery program promo for *Building the Winter Games*
20.57.13–20.57.16	Discovery Channel ident
20.57.16–20.57.46	Advertising: KIA, car
20.57.46–20.58.06	Advertising: Imodium
20.58.06–20.58.36	Advertising: Activia, food
20.58.36–20.59.06	Advertising: O2, telephony
20.59.06–20.59.36	Advertising: Harpic, toilet fragrance
20.59.36–20.59.46	Advertising: Bisto, food
20.59.46–21.00.02	Discovery program promo/intro: *FBI files*
21.00.02–21.07.48	Program: *FBI Files* (Segment 1)
21.07.48–21.08.18	Discovery program promo: *The Worlds Strangest UFO Stories* on Discovery Channel.
21.08.18–21.08.21	Discovery Channel ident
21.08.21–21.08.51	Advertising: Comfort, washing liquid
21.08.51–21.09.21	Advertising: Actimel
21.09.21–21.09.41	Advertising: 3, mobile telephony
21.09.41–21.10.11	Advertising: Garnier, skin cream
21.10.11–21.10.21	Advertising: MFI.co.uk
21.10.21–21.10.51	Advertising: Kellogs, food
21.10.51–21.11.21	Advertising: Citroen, car
21.11.21–21.11.41	Discovery program promo: *Overhaulin* on Discover Real Time
21.11.41–21.11.44	Discovery Channel ident
21.11.44–21.27.41	Program: *FBI Files* (Segment 2)
21.27.41–21.28.11	Discovery program promo: *Building the Winter Games* on Discovery Channel
21.28.11–21.28.14	Discovery Channel ident

21.28.14–21.28.34	Advertising: Colgate, toothpaste
21.28.34–21.28.44	Advertising: Thompson, travel agency
21.28.44–21.29.14	Advertising: Branston Beans, food
21.29.14–21.29.44	Advertising: Virgin Credit Card
21.29.44–21.30.14	Advertising: Muller, food
21.30.14–21.30.44	Advertising: Jaguar, cars
21.30.44–21.30.47	Discovery Channel ident
21.30.47–21.47.26	Program: *FBI Files* (Segment 3)
21.47.26–21.47.28	Discovery Channel ident
21.47.28–21.47.58	Discovery Promo: *The Worlds Strangest UFO Stories*, on Discovery Channel
21.47.58–21.48.00	Discovery Channel ident
21.48.00–21.48.20	Advertising: Colgate, toothpaste
21.48.20–21.48.50	Advertising: Dolmio, food
21.48.50–21.49.00	Advertising: ALDI, sparkling water
21.49.00–21.49.20	Advertising: Enterprise, car rental
21.49.50–21.50.20	Advertising: Keloggs, food
21.50.20–21.51.00	Advertising: Pegeout, car
21.51.00–21.51.10	Discovery program promo: *On The Run*
21.51.10–21.51.13	Discovery Channel ident
21.51.13–21.57.02	Program: *FBI Files* (Segment 4)
21.57.02–21.57.32	Discovery program promo: *The Garage* on Discovery Channel.
21.57.32–21.57.36	Discovery Channel ident
21.57.36–21.57.56	Advertising: DryNites, nappies
21.57.56–21.58.26	Advertising: incredible India, travel destination
21.58.26–21.58.56	Advertising: Cisco Systems, Internet security
21.58.56–21.59.26	Advertising: Fairy, washing up powder
21.59.26–22.00.06	Advertising: Honda, car
22.00.06–22.00.21	Discovery program promo/intro: *On the Run*,
22.00.21–22.08.53	Program: *On the Run* (Segment 1)
22.08.53–22.09.08	Discovery program promo: *American Chopper* in Europe on Discovery Channel.
22.09.08–22.09.11	Discovery Channel ident
22.09.11–22.09.41	Advertising: KIA, car
22.09.41–22.10.41	Advertising: AOL, Internet service provider
22.10.41–22.11.01	Advertising: Always
22.11.01–22.11.21	Advertising: Fixodent
22.11.21–22.11.51	Advertising: Pedigree, dog food
22.11.51–22.12.11	Advertising: 3, mobile telephony
22.12.11–22.12.13	Discovery Channel ident
22.12.13–22.29.27	Program: *On the Run* (Segment 2)
22.29.27–22.29.57	Discovery Promo: *The Worlds Strangest UFO Stories*, Sunday at 10 on Discovery Channel (US interviewees and UK voice over).

22.29.57–22.29.59	Discovery Channel ident
22.29.59–22.30.29	Advertising: Citroen, car
22.30.29–22.30.49	Advertising: Johnston's, baby wipe
22.30.49–22.31.19	Advertising: Incredible India: travel destination
22.31.19–22.31.29	Advertising: Sunday Express, newspaper
22.31.29–22.31.59	Advertising: Whiskas, cat food
22.31.59–22.32.29	Advertising: Pizza Hut, food
22.32.29–22.32.49	Discovery program promo, *Trouble Trouble*, on Discovery Real Time
22.32.49–22.32.52	Discovery Channel ident
22.32.52–22.49.08	Program: *On the Run* (Segment 2)
22.49.08–22.49.38	Discovery program promo: *The Garage*, on Discovery Channel
22.49.38–22.49.41	Discovery Channel ident
22.49.41–22.50.11	Advertising: Citroen, car
22.50.11–22.50.31	Advertising: Smile, toothpaste
22.50.31–22.50.51	Advertising: Pringles, food
22.50.51–22.51.01	Advertising: washing liquid
22.51.01–22.51.31	Advertising: Bodyform, sanitary towel
22.51.31–22.51.41	Advertising: Sunday Express, newspaper
22.51.41–22.52.11	Advertising: Kings Mills, food
22.52.11–22.52.41	Advertising: Kellogs, food
22.52.41–22.52.51	Discovery program promo: *Psychic Witness*
22.52.51–22.52.54	Discovery Channel ident
22.52.54–22.56.53	Program: *On the Run* (Segment 3)
22.56.53–22.57.23	Discovery program promo: *Building the Winter Games*
22.57.23–22.57.27	Discovery Channel ident
22.57.27–22.57.57	Advertising: Suzuki, car
22.57.57–22.58.17	Advertising: Tesco, supermarket
22.58.17–22.58.37	Advertising: Not available
22.58.37–22.59.17	Advertising: Egg, banking services
22.59.17–22.59.57	Advertising: Cheesy heads, food
22.59.57–23.00.12	Discovery program promo/intro: *Psychic Witness*

DISCOVERY CHANNEL UK, 20.00.00–23.00.00, 4 FEBRUARY, 2006.

20.00.00–20.09.07	Program: *American Chopper* (Segment 1)
20.09.07–20.09.22	Discovery program promo: *The Garage*, on Discovery Channel
20.09.22–20.09.25	Discovery Channel ident
20.09.25–20.09.45	Advertising: Sanex, skin spray

20.09.45–20.10.05	Advertising: Johnstons, bady cream
20.10.05–20.10.15	Advertising: Knorr, food
20.10.15–20.10.45	Advertising: Wholegrain, food
20.10.45–20.10.55	Advertising: The Sun, newspaper
20.10.55–20.11.05	Advertising: Thompson, travel agency
20.11.05–20.11.35	Advertising: Loyds TSB, financial services
20.11.35–20.11.45	Advertising: The National Lottery
20.11.45–20.11.55	Advertising: Muller, food
20.11.55–20.12.25	Advertising: Jaguar, car
20.12.25–20.12.28	Discovery Channel ident
20.12.28–20.28.27	Program: *American Chopper* (Segment 2)
20.28.27–20.28.42	Discovery program promo: *The Worlds Strangest UFO Stories*, on Discovery Channel
20.28.42–20.28.45	Discovery Channel ident
20.28.45–20.29.15	Advertising: Cheerio, food
20.29.15–20.29.45	Advertising: Haagen Daz, food
20.29.45–20.30.05	Advertising: Andrax, toilet paper
20.30.05–20.30.25	Advertising: The Sun, newspaper
20.30.25–20.30.35	Advertising: Bisto, food
20.30.35–20.31.15	Advertising: Pegeout, car
20.31.15–20.31.35	Discovery program promo: *Trouble Trouble*, on Discovery Real Time
20.31.35–20.31.38	Discovery Channel ident
20.31.38–20.49.04	Program: *American Chopper* (Segment 3)
20.49.04–20.49.21	Discovery program promo: *The Garage* on Discovery Channel
20.49.21–20.49.24	Discovery Channel ident
20.49.24–20.49.54	Advertising: KIA, car
20.49.54–20.50.04	Advertising: Argos
20.50.04–20.50.34	Advertising: British Gas, energy
20.50.34–20.51.04	Advertising: Daily Mail, newspaper
20.51.04–20.51.44	Advertising: Port Aventura, Spanish holiday resort
20.51.44–20.52.24	Advertising: Cheese snack, food
20.52.24–20.52.34	Discovery program promo: *American Chopper*
20.52.34–20.52.37	Discovery Channel ident
20.52.37–20.56.36	Program: *American Chopper* (Segment 4)
20.56.36–20.57.21	Discovery program promo for *Building the Winter Games*
20.57.21–20.57.24	Discovery Channel ident
20.57.24–20.57.54	Advertising: Citroen, car
20.57.54–20.58.24	Advertising: Activia, yogurt
20.58.24–20.58.54	Advertising: Incredible India, travel destination
20.58.54–20.59.34	Advertising: Egg, banking services
22.59.34–20.59.54	Advertising: TESCO, food
20.59.54–21.00.10	Discovery program promo/intro: *The Garage*

21.00.10–21.05.42	Program: *The Garage* (Segment 1)
21.05.42–21.05.57	Discovery program promo: *American Chopper*, on Discovery Channel
21.05.57–21.06.00	Discovery Channel ident
21.06.00–21.06.30	Advertising: ING Direct, banking services
21.06.30–21.07.00	Advertising: Incredible India, travel destination
21.07.00–21.07.30	Advertising: AXA, healthcare
21.07.30–21.08.00	Advertising: Oxfam, membership
21.08.00–21.08.30	Advertising: Virgin Credit Card
21.08.30–21.09.00	Advertising: Land Rover, car
21.09.00–21.09.04	Discovery Channel ident
21.09.04–21.26.05	Program: *The Garage* (Segment 2)
21.26.05–21.26.20	Discovery program promo: *Building the Winter Games*
21.26.20–21.26.23	Discovery Channel ident
21.26.23–21.26.53	Advertising: Fairy, washing up powder
21.26.53–21.27.23	Advertising: British Gas, energy
21.27.23–21.27.53	Advertising: Law firm
21.27.53–21.28.23	Advertising: Daz, washing powder
21.28.23–21.28.53	Advertising: Land Rover, car
21.28.53–21.28.56	Discovery Channel ident
21.28.56–21.45.56	Program: The *Garage* (Segment 3)
21.45.56–21.46.11	Discovery program promo: *American Chopper*
21.46.11–21.46.15	Discovery Channel ident
21.46.15–21.46.45	Advertising: Flora, food
21.46.45–21.47.15	Advertising: Max Factor, cosmetics
21.47.15–21.47.45	Advertising: DFS, furniture
21.47.45–21.48.15	Advertising: O2, telephony
21.48.15–21.48.45	Advertising: Old El Paso, food
21.48.45–21.49.15	Advertising: Skoda, car
21.49.15–21.49.25	Discovery program promo: *Strangest UFO stories*
21.49.25–21.49.28	Discovery Channel ident
21.49.28–21.55.56	Program: *The Garage* (Segment 4)
21.55.56–21.56.26	Discovery Promo: *The Worlds Strangest UFO Stories*, on Discovery Channel
21.56.26–21.56.29	Discovery Channel ident
21.56.29–21.56.59	Advertising: Wholegrain, food
21.56.59–21.57.29	Advertising: Actime
21.57.29–21.58.59	Advertising: Jaguar, car
21.58.59–21.59.19	Discovery Channel program promo: *My Greek Kitchen*, on Discovery Travel & Living.
21.59.19–21.59.37	Discovery program promo/intro: *The Worlds Strangest UFO Stories*
21.59.37–22.06.40	Program: *The Worlds Strangest UFO Stories* (Segment 1)

22.06.40–22.06.55	Discovery program promo: *American Chopper*
22.06.55–22.06.58	Discovery Channel ident
22.06.58–22.07.28	Advertising: Revels, food
22.07.28–22.07.58	Advertising: Incredible India, travel destination
22.07.58–22.08.28	Advertising: V8, food
22.08.28–22.08.58	Advertising: Virgin credit card
22.08.58–22.09.18	Advertising: The Sun, newspaper
22.09.18–22.09.58	Advertising: Pegeout, car
22.09.58–22.10.00	Discovery Channel ident
22.10.00–22.27.04	Program: *The Worlds Strangest UFO Stories* (Segment 2)
22.27.04–22.27.19	Discovery program promo
22.27.19–22.27.22	Discovery Channel ident
22.27.22–22.27.52	Advertising: Happy, building insurance
22.27.52–22.28.22	Advertising: Daz, food
22.28.22–22.28.52	Advertising: Wholegrain, food
22.28.52–22.29.52	Advertising: Honda, car
22.29.52–22.29.55	Discovery Channel ident
22.29.55–22.46.07	Program: *The Worlds Strangest UFO Stories* (Segment 3)
22.46.07–22.46.22	Discovery program promo: *Building the Winter Games*
22.46.22–22.46.25	Discovery Channel ident
22.46.25–22.46.55	Advertising: Whiskas, cat food
22.46.55–22.47.25	Advertising: Astra, car
22.47.25–22.47.55	Advertising: British Gas, energy
22.47.55–22.48.25	Advertising: Capital One, credit card
22.48.25–22.48.55	Advertising: Actimel
22.48.55–22.49.05	Advertising: Astra, car
22.49.05–22.49.25	Advertising: The Sun, newspaper
22.49.25–22.49.45	Discovery Channel program promo: *My Greek Kitchen*, on Discovery Travel & Living
22.49.45–22.49.55	Discovery program promo: *Deadliest Catch*
22.49.55–22.49.59	Discovery Channel ident
22.49.59–22.55.24	*The Worlds Strangest UFO Stories* (Segment 4)
22.55.24–22.55.54	Discovery program promo: *The Worlds Strangest UFO* on Discovery Channel
22.55.54–22.55.57	Discovery Channel ident
22.55.57–22.56.27	Advertising: Seat, car (UK voice over)
22.56.27–22.56.57	Advertising: Branston, food
22.56.57–22.57.27	Advertising: Fairy, washing up powder
22.57.27–22.57.57	Advertising: The Independent, newspaper
22.57.57–22.58.27	Advertising: Tiscali, Internet service
22.58.27–22.58.45	Discovery program promo/ intro: *Deadliest Catch*
22.58.45–23.00.00	Program: *Deadliest Catch*.

DISCOVERY CHANNEL UK,
20.00.00–23.00.00, 5 FEBRUARY, 2006

20.00.00–20.06.56	Program: *Myth Busters* (Segment 1)
20.06.56–20.07.11	Discovery program promo: *American Chopper*
20.07.11–20.07.14	Discovery Channel ident
20.07.14–20.07.44	Advertising: AA car insurance
20.07.44–20.08.14	Advertising: AOL Broadband
20.08.14–20.08.44	Advertising: Cancer Research UK
20.08.44–20.09.14	Advertising: Kellogs, food
20.09.14–20.09.44	Advertising: ING savings account
20.09.44–20.10.14	Advertising: Jaguar, car
20.10.14–20.10.18	Discovery Channel ident
20.10.18–20.26.45	Program: *Myth Busters* (Segment 2)
20.26.45–20.27.00	Discovery program promo: *The Garage*, on Discovery Channel
20.27.00–20.27.04	Discovery Channel ident
20.27.04–20.27.34	Advertising: Nestle, food
20.27.34–20.28.04	Advertising: Youngs, food
20.28.04–20.28.34	Advertising: Love It! magazine
20.28.34–20.29.04	Advertising: Go Ahead, food
20.29.04–20.29.34	Advertising: Land Rover, car
20.29.34–20.29.38	Discovery Channel ident
20.29.38–20.46.10	Program: *Myth Busters* (Segment 3)
20.46.10–20.46.25	Discovery program promo: *The Worlds Strangest UFO Stories*, on Discovery Channel
20.46.25–20.46.28	Discovery Channel ident
20.46.28–20.46.58	Advertising: Mars, food
20.46.58–20.47.28	Advertising: Kellogs, food
20.47.28–20.47.58	Advertising: Fairy, washing up powder
20.47.58–20.48.28	Advertising: DAZ, washing powder
20.48.28–20.48.58	Advertising: Go Ahead, food
20.48.58–20.49.48	Discovery program promo: *Over Haulin*, on Discovery Real Time
20.49.48–20.49.58	Discovery program promo: *American Chopper*
20.49.58–20.50.01	Discovery Channel ident
20.50.01–20.57.14	Program: *Myth Busters* (Segment 4)
20.57.14–20.57.29	Discovery program promo: *American Chopper*
20.57.29–20.57.32	Discovery Channel ident
20.57.32–20.57.52	Advertising: Maltesers, food
20.57.52–20.58.22	Advertising: Jaffa Cakes, food
20.58.22–20.58.52	Advertising: Incredible India, travel destination
20.58.52–20.59.02	Advertising: Finish, washing up powder
20.59.02–20.59.32	Advertising: Actimel

20.59.32–21.00.02	Advertising: Toyota, car
21.00.02–21.00.32	Discovery program promo: *Building the Winter Games*
21.00.32–21.00.46	Discovery program promo/intro: *American Chopper*
21.00.46–21.09.18	Program: *American Chopper* (Segment 1)
21.09.18–21.09.48	Discovery program promo: *UFO stories*, on Discovery Channel.
21.09.48–21.09.51	Discovery Channel ident
21,09.51–21.10.21	Advertising: KIA, car
21.10.21–21.10.41	Advertising: Pringle, food
21.10.41–21.11.01	Advertising: Always, sanetary towel
21.11.01–21.11.31	Advertising: CentreParcs, parks
21.11.31–21.12.01	Advertising: O2, telephone
21.12.01–21.12.31	Advertising: Go Ahead, food
21.12.31–21.12.51	Advertising: Tesco, food
21.12.51–21.13.12	Discovery program promo: *Trouble Trouble*, on Discovery Real Time .
21.13.12–21.13.15	Discovery Channel ident
21.13.15–21.29.24	Program: *American Chopper* (Segment 2)
21.29.24–21.29.41	Discovery program promo: *The Garage,* on Discovery Channel
21.29.41–21.29.43	Discovery Channel ident
21.29.43–21.30.13	Advertising: BMW, car
21.30.13–21.30.43	Advertising: Jaffa Cakes, food
21.30.43–21.31.03	Advertising: RAC, car service
21.31.03–21.31.13	Advertising: ALDI, supermarket
21.31.13–21.31.43	Advertising: Kellogs, food
21.31.43–21.32.13	Advertising: Whiskas, cat food
21.32.13–21.32.43	Discovery program promo: *Building the Winter Games*, on Discovery Channel
21.32.43–21.32.46	Discovery Channel ident
21.32.46–21.48.28	Discovery program *American Chopper* (Segment 3)
21.48.28–21.48.58	Discovery Promo; *The Worlds Strangest UFO Stories*, on Discovery Channel
21.48.58–21.49.02	Discovery Channel ident
21.49.02–21.49.32	Advertising Cisco Systems, Internet security
21.49.32–21.50.02	Advertising: Mars, food
21.50.02–21.50.32	Advertising: Incredible India, travel destination
21.50.32–21.51.02	Advertising: Skoda, car
21.51.02–21.51.12	Advertising: Corpose Bride, film
21.51.12–21.51.42	Advertising: Virgin Credit Card
21.51.42–21.51.52	Advertising: PC World, electronics
21.51.52–21.52.02	Advertising: The Sun, newspaper
21.52.02–21.52.32	Discovery promo: *Building the Winter Games*

21.52.32–21.52.42	Discovery program promo: *The World's Strangest UFO*
21.52.42–21.52.45	Discovery Channel ident
21.52.45–21.58.21	Program, *American Chopper* (Segment 4)
21.58.21–21.58.36	Discovery program promo: *The Garage*, on Discovery Channel.
21.58.36–21.58.39	Discovery Channel ident
21.58.39–21.59.09	Advertising: Activia
21.59.09–21.59.29	Advertising: Enterprise, car rental
21.59.29–21.59.59	Advertising: Youngs, food
21.59.59–22.00.29	Advertising: Go Ahead, food
22.00.29–22.01.09	Advertising: Pegeout, car
22.01.09–22.01.39	Discovery program promo: *Building the Winter Games*, on Discovery Channel
22.01.39–22.01.56	Discovery program prom/intro: *The Worlds Strangest UFO stories*
22.01.56–22.06.55	Program: *The Worlds Strangest UFO Stories* (Segment 1)
22.06.55–22.07.10	Discovery program promo: *The Garage*, on Discovery Channel
22.07.10–22.07.13	Discovery Channel ident
22.07.13–22.07.33	Advertising: Colgate, toothbrush
22.07.33–22.08.02	Advertising: Actimel, food
22.08.02–22.08.12	Advertising: ALDI, food
22.08.12–22.08.42	Advertising: Toyota, car
22.08.42–22.09.12	Advertising: Head & Shoulders, shampoo
22.09.12–22.09.42	Advertising: Kellogs, food
22.09.42–22.10.12	Advertising: Capital One, credit card
22.10.12–22.10.42	Discovery program promo: *Building the Winter Games*, on Discovery Channel
22.10.42–22.10.45	Discovery Channel ident
22.10.45–22.28.09	Discovery program: *The Worlds Strangest UFO stories* (Segment 2)
22.28.09–22.28.24	Discovery program promo: *American Chopper*
22.28.24–22.28.27	Discovery Channel ident
22.28.27–22.28.57	Advertising: Whiskas, cat food
22.28.57–22.29.27	Advertising: Wales, travel destination
22.29.27–22.29.57	Advertising: Nestle, Shreddies, food
22.29.57–22.30.27	Advertising: Kingsill, food
22.30.27–22.30.57	Advertising: Hyundai, car
22.30.57–22.31.27	Discovery program promo: *RSPCA*, on Animal Planet
22.31.27–22.31.31	Discovery Channel ident
22.31.31–22.48.49	Program: *The Worlds Strangest UFO stories* (Segment 3)

22.48.49–22.49.04	Discovery program promo: *The Garage*, on Discovery Channel
22.49.04–22.49.08	Discovery Channel ident
22.49.08–22.49.38	Advertising: Comfort Pure, fabric softener
22.49.38–22.50.08	Advertising: Jaffa Cakes, food
22.50.08–22.50.28	Advertising: Hugo Boss, fragrance (UK voice over)
22.50.28–22.50.58	Advertising: Philadelphia, cheese (UK actors and voice over)
22.50.58–22.51.38	Advertising: Pegeout, car (UK text)
22.51.38–22.52.08	Advertising: Branston, baked beans (UK voice over)
22.52.08–22.52.23	Discovery program promo: *American Chopper* in England
22.52.23–22.52.27	Discovery Channel ident
22.52.27–22.58.30	Program: *The Worlds Strangest UFO stories* (Segment 4) Imagery experts examining videos of UFO's Produced by Mentorn—A television corporation company for Discovery Networks Europe. (UK voice over) © Mentorn UFO's Limited and Strangest UFO's Stories Canada Inc. MMV
22.58.30–22.59.00	Discovery program promo: *Building the Winter Games*, on Discovery Channel
22.59.00–22.59.02	Discovery Channel ident
22.59.02–22.59.13	Advertising: Lanacane, cosmetics
22.59.13–22.59.23	Advertising: The Sun, newspaper
22.59.23–22.59.53	Advertising: Velux, lighting
22.59.53–23.00.03	Advertising: The Little Polar Bear, film

Bibliography

Aaker, D. A. (2004) *Brand Portfolio Strategy: Creating Relevance, Differentiation, Energy, Leverage, and Clarity.* New York: Free Press.

Aaker, D. A. (1996) *Building strong brands.* New York: Free Press.

ABI Research (2008) Mobile TV Subscribers to Number 462 Million by 2012. January 24. http://www.abiresearch.com/abiprdisplay.jsp?pressid=1043 (accessed, September 2, 2008).

Alexander, A. and Owers, J. (2007) The Economics of Children's Television. pp. 57–74. In J. A. Bryant (ed.), *The Children's Television Community.* Mahwah, N.J.: Lawrence Erlbaum.

Amazon (2008) http://www.amazon.co.uk (accessed, September 17, 2008).

Artz, L. (2005) Monarchs, Monsters, and Multiculturalism: Disney's Menu for Global Hierarchy. pp. 75–98. In M. Budd, and M. H. Kirsch (eds), *Rethinking Disney: Private Control, Public Dimensions.* Middletown, CT: Wesleyan University Press.

Ascentmedia (2005) *Discovery Networks Europe opens state-of-the-art media transmission centre.* http://www.ascentmedia.co.uk/news/default.aspx?articleID =405&begindate=1/1/ 2005&enddate=12/31/2005 (accessed, 20 May, 2006).

AT&T Mobile TV (2008) http://www.wireless.att.com/learn/messaging-internet/ mobile-tv (accessed, 4 September, 2008).

Auletta, K. (2006) The Raid: How Carl Icahn Came up Short, Annals of Communications, *New Yorker,* Issue 20, March. http://www.newyorker.com/fact/ content/articles/060320fa_fact4 (accessed, 5 May, 2006).

Aversa, J. (1999) FCC Approves AT&T-TCI deal. *The Washington Post,* 17 February. http://www.washingtonpost.com/wp-srv/washtech/longterm/att_tci/att_tci. htm (accessed, 19 October, 2008).

Balmer, J. M.T. and Grey, E. R. (2003) Corporate Brands: What are They? What of Them? *European Journal of Marketing,* 37, 7/8: 972–997.

Barnes, B. (2006) As Ratings Plateau, Cable Networks Branch Out. *Wall Street Journal.* 25 November, pg. A.1.

Baruh, L. (2007) Read at Your Own Risk: Shrinkage of Privacy and Interactive Media. *New Media Society,* 9, 2: 187–211.

Barker, C. (1999) *Television, Globalisation and Cultural Identities.* Buckingham, UK: Open University Press.

Bauman, Z. (1998) *Globalization: The Human Consequences.* Cambridge.UK: Polity.

BBC (2005) *BBC Annual Reports and Accounts, 2004/2005.* http://www.bbcgovernors.co.uk/annreport/report05/BBC_2004_05.pdf (accessed, 13 September, 2005).

BBC (2004a) *The BBC's international role.* Submission to the Independent Panel on Charter Review, September. http://www.bbc.co.uk/thefuture/text/bbc_intlsubmission.html (accessed, 12 September, 2005).

BBC (2004b) *Review of the BBC's Royal Charter: BBC Response to DCMS Consultation*. http://www.bbc.co.uk/thefuture/text/dcms_response_complete.html (accessed, 20 May, 2006).

BBC (2004c) *Annual Report 2003/2004*. http://www.bbcgovernors.co.uk/annreport/report04.html#facts (accessed, 29 september, 2006).

BBC (2002a) *BBC and Discovery Communications, Inc. Sign the Deal of the Decade*, Press Release. http://www.bbc.co.uk/pressoffice/pressreleases/stories/2002/03_march/22/dcibbcdeal.shtml (accessed, 22 March, 2006).

BBC (2002b) *People + Arts and Animal Planet Celebrate Five Year Anniversary in Latin America With Record Ratings and Rapid Subscriber Growth*. http://www.bbc.co.uk/print/pressoffice/bbcworldwide/worldwidestories/pressreleases/2002/12_december/people_and_arts_animal_planet_anniversary.shtml (accessed, 28 February, 2008).

BBC Worldwide (2006) *Programme sales catalogue*.

BBC Worldwide (2005a) *Programme sales catalogue*.

BBC Worldwide (2005b) *BBC Showcase*. http://www.bbcworldwide.com/showcase2005 (accessed, 5 September, 2005).

BBC Worldwide (2005c) *Planet Earth set for Movie Release. Press Release*, February 28. http://www.bbc.co.uk/pressoffice/commercial/worldwidestories/pressreleases/2005/02_february/planet_earth_movie.shtml (accessed, 5 September).

BBC Worldwide (2005d) *Annual Review 2004/2005*. http://www.bbcworldwide.com/ annualreviews/review2005/bus_channels_03.htm (accessed, 11 May, 2006).

BBC Worldwide (2004) *Programme sales catalogue*.

BBC Worldwide (2003a) *Programme sales catalogue*.

BBC Worldwide (2003b) *Walking With . . . Brand is Monster Hit for the BBC Worldwide. Press release*, 15 June. http://www.bbc.co.uk/pressoffice/commercial/worldwidestories/pressreleases/2003/07_july/walking_with_brand.shtml (accessed, 2 September 2005).

BBC Worldwide (2002) *Programme sales catalogue*.

BBC Worldwide (1999) *Annual Report and Accounts 1998/1999*. http://www.bbcworldwide.com/aboutus/corpinfo/annualreps/report1999/pdfs/review.pdf (accessed, 9 September, 2005).

BBC Worldwide (1998) *BBC Worldwide Annual Reports and Accounts 97/98*. http://www.bbcworldwide.com/report/globalbr/globalbr.htm (accessed, 15 September, 2005).

Beatty, S. (2001) National Geographic Ventures Deeper Into Hostile World of Cable TV—It Teams Up With News Corp. To Battle Discovery Channel And Animal Planet Spinoff. *Wall Street Journal* (Eastern Edition), 7 August: B.1. (accessed, 5 March, 2006).

Beavis, S. (1998) BBC Teams up With Discovery; Communications Revolution Gathers Pace. *The Guardian*, 20 March, 25.

Bellamy, JR., R. and Chabin, J. B. (1999) Global Promotion and Marketing of Television. pp. 211–232. In S.T. Eastman, D.A. Ferguson and R.A. Klein (eds), *Promotion and Marketing for Broadcasting and Cable*. Third edition. Boston: Focal Press.

Bisson, G., Senior Analyst, *Screen Digest*, interview with author, 24 September, 2004.

Blind, S. and Hallenberg, G. (1996) *European Co-production in Film and Television*. Heidelberg: Universitatsverlag, C. Winter.

Bloomberg (2006) Malone's Liberty Seeks Buyer for Hotel-Video Unit, People Say. 30 March. http://www.bloomberg.com/apps/news?pid=10000087&sid=aiidF5 aHEBEM&refer=top_world_news (accessed, 4 May, 2006).

Bloomberg (2005) Nokia's Kallasvuo Says Reviving U.S. Fortunes Is a Top Priority. August 2. http://www.bloomberg.com/apps/news?pid=10000085&sid=a36 CRWoMK0VI (accessed, 6 September, 2006).

Blumler, J. G. (1999) Political Communication Systems All Change: A Response To Kees Brants. *European Journal of Communication*, 14, 2: 241–249.

Bonini, S. M. J., Mendonca, L. T. and Oppenheim, J. M (2006) When social issues become strategic. Executives ignore sociopolitical debates at their own peril. *McKinsey Quarterly*, No. 2. http://www.mckinseyquarterly.com/article_page. aspx?ar=1763&L2=21&L3=114 (accessed, 6 April, 2006).

Bonner, P. and Aston, L. (2003) Independent Television in Britain, Volume 6. *New Developments in Independent Television 1981–92: Channel 4, TV AM, Cable and Satellite*. Basingstoke, UK: Palgrave.

Born, G. (2004) *Uncertain Vision: Birt, Dyke and the Reinvention of the BBC*. London: Secker & Warburg.

Borton, J. (2004) Face-off: China's Tom Group vs Star TV. http://www.atimes.com/atimes/China/FK18Ad01.html (accessed, 6 March, 2008).

Boyd-Barrett, O. (2006) Cyberspace, globalization and empire. *Global Media and Communication*, 2, 1: 21–41.

Boyd-Barrett, O. (1998) Media Imperialism reformulated. pp. 157–176. In D. K. Thussu (ed.) *Electronic empires: global media and local resistance*. London: Arnold.

Brants, K. (1998) Who's Afraid of Infotainment? *European Journal of Communication*, 13, 3: 315–335.

Brown, D. (1998) *Regionalisation and Market Positioning for Pan-European Pay-TV*. London: FT Media and Telecoms.

Brown, M. (2003) Walking With Hybrids. *The Guardian*, 24 November. http://media.guardian.co.uk/mediaguardian/story/0,7558,1091644,00.html(accessed, 9 September, 2005).

Brown, R. (1993) New Frontiers for Discovery: Network will Expand Original Production as it Reaches New Outlets in Latin America, America, Europe and Asia. *Broadcasting & Cable*, October, 38.

Brunsdon, C. (2004) Life-Styling Britain: The 8–9 Slot on British Television. pp. 75–92. In L. Spigel and J. Olsson (eds), *Television After TV: Essays on a Medium in Transition*. Durham, NC: Duke University Press.

Brunsdon, C., Johnson, C., Moseley, R. and Wheatly, H. (2001) Factual Entertainment on British Television: The Midlands TV Research Group's '8–9 Project'. *European Journal of Cultural Studies*, 4, 1: 29–62.

Buerkle, T. (1998) BBC Heads Out (With a Guide) To New Frontier: TV in America. *International Herald Tribune*. www.iht.com/articles/1998/03/20/bbc.t.php (accessed, 23 March, 2006).

Burgi, M. (1995) Through the Wall. *Brandweek*. 12 June, p. 36.

Business Week (2005) *Global Brands, Special Report—The Best Global Brands*. August 1. http://www.businessweek.com/magazine/content/05_31/b3945098. htm (accessed, 6 September, 2006).

C21 Media (2004a) *Discovering France*. http://www.c21media.net (accessed, 8 November, 2004).

C21 Media (2004b) *Channel Profile—Discovery Europe: Pan-Regional, Interview With John Begert, VP of Content and Marketing, Discovery Networks Europe*. http://www.c21media.net (accessed, 28 October, 2004).

Caldwell, J. T. (2004) Industrial Geography Lessons: Socio-Professional Rituals and the Borderlands of Production Culture. pp. 163–190. In N. Couldry and A. McCarthy (eds), *MediaSpace: Place, Scale and Culture in a Media Age*. London: Routledge.

Caldwell, J. T. (1995) *Televisuality: Style, Crisis, and Authority in American Television*. New Brunswick, NJ: Rutgers University Press.

Carter, S., Managing Director, Pioneer Productions, UK, interview with author, London, 23 March, 2004.

Carugati, A. (2007) Discovery's Ricca. *World Screen*. October. http://www.worldscreen.com/interviewscurrent.php?filename=ricca1007.htm (accessed, 27 November, 2008).

Carugati, A. (2003) Discovery's Judith McHale. *World Screen*, October. http://www.worldscreen.com/interviewsarchive.php?filename=1003mchale.htm (accessed, 20 May, 2006).

Castells, M. (2000) The Rise of the Network Society, Vol 1. *The Information Age*. Oxford, UK: Blackwell.

Chalaby, J. K. (2005a) Towards an Understanding of Media Transnationalism. pp. 1–13. In J. K. Chalaby (ed.), *Transnational Television Worldwide: Towards a New Media Order*. London: I. B. Tauris.

Chalaby, J. K. (2005b) The Quiet Invention of a New Medium: Twenty Years of Transnational Television in Europe. pp. 43–65. In J. K. Chalaby (ed.), *Transnational Television Worldwide: Towards a New Media Order*. London: I. B. Tauris.

Chalaby, J. K. (2003) Television For a New Global Order. *Gazette*, 65, 6: 457–472.

Chalaby, J. K. (2002) Transnational Television in Europe—The Role of Pan-European Channels. *European Journal of Communication*, 17, 2: 183–203.

Chan, J. M. (2005) Trans-border Broadcasters and TV Regionalization in Greater China: Processes and Strategies. pp. 172–195. In J. K. Chalaby (ed.), *Transnational Television Worldwide: Towards a New Media Order*. London: I. B. Tauris.

Chan-Olmsted, S. and Kim, Y. (2002) The PBS Brand Versus Cable Brands: Assessing the Brand Image of Public Television in a Multichannel Environment. *Journal of Broadcasting & Electronic Media*, 46, 2: 300–320.

China Daily (2006) Sales of HDTV Sets to Jump. *China Daily*, 20 June. www.chinadaily.com.cn/bizchina/2006-06/20/content_621614.htm (accessed, 6 March, 2008).

Chris, C. (2007) Discovery's Wild Discovery: The Growth and Globalization of TV's Animal Genres. pp. 137–157. In S. Banet-Weiser, C. Chris, and A. Freitas (eds.), *Cable Visions: Television Beyond Broadcasting*. New York: New York University Press.

Chris, C. (2002) All Documentary, All the Time? Discovery Communications, Inc. and Trends in Cable Television. *Television and New Media*, 3, 1: 7–27.

Clark, N. (2004) MTV Expands its Reach in Germany. *International Herald Tribune*. 25 June. www.iht.com/articles/2004/06/25/viva_ed3_0.php (accessed, 7 October, 2008).

Clarke, S. (2003) Journey of Discovery Continues for Factual Giant With Deep Pockets. *TV International*, 16 July, 11, 14: 10.

Clarke, S. (1995) A European Original Lands on the Channel. *Variety*, New York, 3 April.

Collins, R. (2002) *Media and Identity in Contemporary Europe*. Bristol, UK: Intellect Books.

Collins, R. (1998) *From Satellite to Single Market: New Communication Technology and European Public Service Television*. London: Routledge.

Collins, R. (1990a) *Television: Policy and Culture*. London: Unwin Hyman Ltd.

Collins, R. (1990b) *Satellite television in Western Europe*. London: John Libbey.

Comer-Calder, N., Former Senior Vice President and General Manager, DNE, interview with author, London, 4 October, 2004.

Corner, J. (2002) Performing the Real: Documentary Diversions. *Television & New Media*, 3, 3: 255–269.

Corner, J. (2001) Form and Content in Documentary Study. pp. 125–126. In G. Creeber (ed.), *The Television Genre Book*. London: BFI Publishing.

Corner, J. (2000) What Can We Say About 'Documentary'? *Media, Culture & Society*, 22, 5: 681–688.

Corner, J. and Rosenthal, A. (2005) Introduction. pp. 1–16. In A. Rosenthal and J. Corner (eds), *New Challenges for Documentary*. Second edition. Manchester, UK: Manchester University Press.

Cottle, S. (2004) Producing Nature(s): On the Changing Production Ecology of Natural History TV. *Media, Culture & Society*, 26, 1: 81–101.

Cottle, S. (2003) Producing Nature(s): The Changing Production Ecology of Natural History TV. pp. 170–187. In S. Cottle (ed.), *Media organisation and production*. London: Sage.

Crandall, R. W. (1992) Cable Television. pp. 211–259. In B. Owen and S. Steven (eds), *Video Economics*. Cambridge, MA: Harvard University Press.

Croteau, D. and Hoynes, W. (2006) *The Business of Media: Corporate Media and the Public Interest*. Second Edition. Thousand Oaks, CA: Pine Forge Press.

Croteau, D. and Hoynes, W. (2001) *The Business of Media: Corporate Media and The Public Interest*. Thousand Oaks, CA: Pine Forge Press.

Crupi, A. (2007) Monster.com's Ad Pod Traps Viewers. *Adweek*, Dec 3, pg. 10.

Crupi, A. (2006a) Discovery, USA Net Enjoy Ratings Gains. *Media Week*, 28 February. http://www.mediaweek.com/mw/search/article_display.jsp?vnu_content_id=1002076520 (accessed, 18 March, 2006).

Crupi, A. (2006b) NYT Co. to Sell Discovery Times Back to Discovery. *Mediaweek*, 17 April.

Curran, J. (2002) *Media and Power*. London: Routledge.

Dahlgren, P. (2000) Key trends in European television. pp. 23–34. In J. Wieten, G. Murdock, and P. Dahlgren (eds), *Television Across Europe—A Comparative Introduction*. London: Sage.

Davies, P. (2002) *New Media Market*, 8 February, 20, 5.

Davis, W. (1999) *The European TV Industry in the 21st Century*. London: Informa Publishing.

Dawson, M. (2007) Little Players, Big Shows: Format, Narration, and Style on Television's New Smaller Screens. *Convergence*, 13, 3: 231–250.

Dawtrey, A. (1998) BBC, Discovery Allies in U.S. *Variety*. 20 March. http://www.variety.com/article/VR1117468973.html?categoryid=14&cs=1 (accessed, 1. December, 2008).

Dawtrey, A. (1993) Cabler to Spend $ 200 Mil to Produce Original Dox. *Variety*, 24 March. www.variety.com (accessed, 18 March, 2006).

DCGEP (2006) *Discovery Communications Global Education Partnership*. http://www.discoveryglobaled.org (accessed, 8 September, 2006).

DCMS (1998) *The Report of the Creative Industries Task Force Inquiry into Television Exports*. Department for Culture, Media and Sport, Creative Industries Programme. 20 March. http://www.culture.gov.uk/NR/rdonlyres/2BAEF3D8-C46B-43C7-918D-5B63B27BF56D/0/dcmstvexports1998.pdf (accessed, 2 November, 2007).

Deans, J. (1998) BBC's Voyage of Discovery. *Broadcast*, 16 January, pp. 22–24.

Dhc (2006) *10-K*. Discovery Holding CO filed this Form 10-K on 03/23/06 United States Securities and Exchange Commission, Washington, D.C. 20549. http://ir.discoveryholding.com (accessed, 22 April, 2006).

Discovery (2008a) http://dsc.discovery.com (accessed, 19 August, 2008).

Discovery (2008b) Discovery at a Glance. 11 August. http://corporate.discovery.com/media/pdf/discovery-at-a-glance.pdf (accessed, 13 October, 2008).

Discovery (2008c) International Networks: Latin America and the Iberian Peninsula. http://corporate.discovery.com/brands/intl_networks/intl_networks.html (accessed, 3 march, 2008).

Discovery (2008d) Discovery Digital Media. http://corporate.discovery.com/ brands/digital-media/ (accessed, 17 October, 2008).

Discovery (2007a) Discovery Acquires Howstuffworks.com. http://corporate.discovery.com/news/press/07q4/hsw101507.html (accessed, 8 September, 2008).

Discovery (2007b) Discovery to Close Retail Stores. 17 May. http://corporate.discovery.com/discovery-news/discovery-communications-close-retail-stores/ (accessed, 17 October, 2008).

Discovery (2007c) Discovery Networks U.S. Hispanic Group Announces New Programming Slate for Discovery En Espanol. May 16. http://corporate.discovery.com/news/press/07q2/espanol051607.html" http://corporate.discovery.com/news/press/07q2/espanol051607.html (accessed, 17 October, 2008).

Discovery (2006a) www.discovery.com (accessed, 20 August, 2006.).

Discovery(2006b) *Discovery Communications Expands Mobile Content Services in Europe.* http://corporate.discovery.com/news/press/06q1/021506.html (accessed, 12 March, 2006).

Discovery (2005a) *Discovery Communications Launches Global Showcase for Lance Armstrong and the Discovery Channel Pro Cycling Team*, Press Release. http://corporate.discovery.com/news/press/05q2/050601r.html (accessed, 15 March, 2006).

Discovery (2005b) *Discovery Communications Forms Global New Media Group, New Senior Management Appointments Round Out Team Focused on Growth Efforts Worldwide.* Press Release, 24 October. http://corporate.discovery.com/ news/press/05q4/ 051024r.html (accessed, 8 October, 2006).

Discovery (2004a) *Job Description 'Reversioning Specialist',* Careers@Discovery. http://secured. Kenexa.com/discoveryv4/newhr/jobdesc.asp?ID=1723 (accessed, 2 November, 2004).

Discovery (2004b) *Careers@Discovery.* http://secured.kenexa.com/discoveryv4/ newhr/default.asp (accessed, 2 November, 2004).

Discovery (2003a) *Discovery Networks Europe Announces Increased Channel Offering in Italy.* 29 May. www.discovery.com (accessed, 28 July, 2003).

Discovery (2003b) *Discovery, UNESCO, and UN Works Mark International Mother Language Day With a Celebration of Cultural Diversity*, Press Release, 11 February. www.discovery.com (accessed: 5 August, 2003).

Discovery Campus (2006) *Discovery Campus.* www.discovery-campus.de (accessed, 21 May, 2006).

Discovery Channel Asia (2008) *Corporate Profile.* http://www.discoverychannelasia.com/_includes/corporate/index.shtml (accessed, 28 February, 2008).

Discovery Education (2008) http://www.discoveryeducation.com (accessed, 7 September, 2008).

Discovery letter to the EU Commission (2003) *Review of the Television Without Frontiers Directive, response from Discovery Networks Europe,* July. http:// europa.eu.int/comm/avpolicy/regul/review-twf2003/wc_dne.pdf (accessed, 4 April, 2006).

Discovery Mediapack (2004) *Global Specials.* http://mediapack.discoveryeurope.com/programming/global_q1.shtml (accessed, 20 May, 2006).

Discovery Mediapack (2003a) *All Feeds—Discovery Networks Europe.* http://mediapack.discoveryeurope.com/distribution/index.shtml (accessed, 20 May, 2006).

Discovery Mediapack (2003b) *Company History.* http://mediapack.discoveryeurope.com/corporate/company_history.shtml (accessed, 10 October, 2006).

Discovery Mediapack (2003c) *Viewer Profile: Sex.* http://mediapack.discoveryeurope.com/research/sex.shtml (accessed, 10 October, 2006).

Discovery Mediapack (2003d) *Viewer Profile: Socio-Economic.* http://mediapack.discoveryeurope.com/research/socio-economic.shtml (accessed, 12 October, 2006).

Disney (2006) *Form 10–K*. Annual Report Pursuant to Section 13 or 15(d) of the Securities Exchange Act of 1934, for the Fiscal Year Ended September 30, 2006 Commission File Number 1-11605, United States Securities and Exchange Commission, Washington, D.C. 20549, http://corporate.disney.go.com/investors/index.html (accessed, 26 February, 2007).

Doane, D. (2003) An alternative perspective on brands: markets and morals. Pp. 185–198, in R. Clifton and J. Simmons (eds.) *Brands and Branding*. New York. Bloomberg Press.

Dow Jones Sustainability Indexes (2004) www.sustainability-indexes.com (accessed September 9, 2004).

Dox (1997) Forum interviews—Chris Haws, Discovery UK. 14, December.

Eao (2005) *Yearbook: Television Channels—Programme Production and Distribution*, 5.

Economist, The (1998) Come in, the water's lovely, 3 January, 63.

Eisenberg, D. (2003) TV's Unlikely Empire. *Time*. New York, March, 161, 9: 54–56.

Emery, D., Former Managing Director, BBC Worldwide, UK, interview with author, London, 16 May 2003.

European Commission (1989) *Council Directive 89/552/EEC of 3, October 1989*. Council Directive of 3 October 1989 on the coordination of certain provisions laid down by law, regulation or administrative action in Member States concerning the pursuit of television broadcasting activities (89/552/EEC) The Council of the European Communities. http://europa.eu.int/smartapi/cgi/sga_doc?smartapi!celexapi!prod!CELEXnumdoc&lg=EN&numdoc=31989L0552&model=guichett (accessed, 4. April, 2006).

European Commission (1984) *Television without Frontiers. Green Paper on the Establishment of the Common Market for Broadcasting, Especially by Satellite and Cable*. COM (84) 300, 14 June 1984. Introduction; Parts One, Two and Three, 47. http://aei.pitt. edu/archive/00001151/01/TV_frontiers_gp_pt_1_3. pdf (accessed, 5 May, 2005).

European Television Guild (2003) Discovery: Coping with Europe's differences. www.europeantelevisionguild.com/newsclips/nclips23.html (accessed, 11 November 2003).

Everhart Bedford, K. (2000) Strike up the Brand! PBS Tuning up its Image as Carole Feld Moves On. *Current*, March 20. http://www.current. org/pbs/pbs005feld.html (accessed, 25 December, 2004).

FBI Files, Introduction, Discovery Channel UK, 31 January, 2006.

Flynn, B. (1992) Small is Profitable? TBI Niche Channels. *Television Business International*, February, pp. 31–35.

Forbes (2005) Shanghai Media Group to Expand Digital TV, Form JV With Discovery, AFX News Limited. http://www.forbes.com/home_asia/feeds/afx/2005/06/12/afx2088614.html (accessed, 1 December, 2008).

Forrester, C. (2003a) Discovery Communications: 'Growing, Growing, Growing . . .'. *Transnational Broadcasting Studies*, TBS 11, Fall–Winter. www.tbsjournal.com/Archieves/Fal03/Forrester.html (accessed, 19 October, 2008).

Forrester, C. (2003b) Searching for Documentary Crowd Pleasers—And in HDTV. *European Television Guild*. http://www.europeantelevisionguild.com/pages/news/archive/13072003searchingfordocumentary.htm (accessed, 6 September, 2006).

Fortune (2006) High Hopes, Low Wages, 17 April.

Franklin, B. (1997) *Newszak and News Media*. London: Arnold.

Freeman, M. (2004) Brand Plays On. *Variety*, 29 March–4 April, 394: 7: B1, B4. (accessed, April 15, 2009).

Fürsich, E. (2003) Between Credibility and Commodification: Nonfiction Entertainment as a Global Media Genre. *International Journal of Cultural Studies*, 6: 2: 131–153.

Garcia Canclini, N. (1995) *Hybrid Cultures: Strategies for Entering and Leaving Modernity.* Minneapolis: University of Minnesota Press.

Goggin, G. (2006) *Cell Phone Culture: Mobile Technology in Everyday Life.* London: Routledge.

Gorard, J. (2004) *Branding Across Platforms—Have We Given it a Thought?,* J. Gorard, Director Marketing, BBC World, at Frames 2004: Global Convention On the Business of Entertainment, FICCI. http://www.ficciframes.com/frames2006/Archive/2003/synopsis/branding.htm (accessed, 15 March, 2006).

Gough, P. J. (2008) Ted Koppel, Discovery Parting Ways. *Reuters.*25 November. http://www.reuters.com/article/televisionNews/idUSTRE4AP04S20081126 (accessed, 27 November, 2008).

Grove, C. (2000) Hendricks Leads Global Discovery Mission. *Variety,* 20 November, 381, 1: 33.

Grover, R. (2004) Is John Malone Out to Circle the Globe? *Business Week,* March 16. www.businessweek.com/bwdaily/dnflash/mar2004/nf20040316_7536_db042.htm (accessed, 4 May, 2006).

Guider, E. (2002) Discovery Enters Beijing. *Variety,* 4 June. http://www.variety.com/article/VR1117867976.html?categoryid=1236&cs=1&query=discovery+network+asia (accessed, 4 March, 2008).

Guider, E. (1997) Mip Makes for Strange Bedfellows. *Variety,* 14 April. http://www.variety.com/story.asp?l=vstory&a=VR1117434798&c=38&cs=1 (accessed, 8 November, 2003).

Gunther, M. (2006) Mr. MTV Grows Up, *Fortune.* Europe Edition, 17 April, vol. 153, issue 7. pp. 76–84.

Habermas, J. (2001) Why Europe Needs a Constitution. *New Left Review.* http://www.newleftreview.net/NLR24501.shtml#_edn18 (accessed, 29 March, 2006).

Hafez, K. (2007) *The Myth of Media Globalization.* Cambridge, UK: Polity.

Hall, L. (2005) The Building of a Great Brand. *Discovery at 20 Special Commemorative of Advertising Age.* 4 April, C14. http://www.adage.com/custom-programs/pr/discovery.pdf (accessed, 15 March, 2006).

Hamelink, C. J. (1983) *Cultural Autonomy in Global Communications.* New York: Longman.

Harrie, E. (2009) *The Nordic Media Market 2009: Media Companies and Business Activities.* First edition. Gothenburg: Nordicom.

Harris Interactive (2006) *Discovery Ranks Number One for Quality Among all Media and TV Brands in 2006 Equitrend® Brand Study.* 20 June. http://www.harrisinteractive.com/ news/newsletters/clientnews/2006_DiscoveryCommunications.pdf (accessed, 4 October, 2006).

Hatch, M. J. and Schultz, M. (2003) Bringing the Corporation into Corporate Branding. *European Journal of Marketing,* 37, 7–8: 1041–1064.

Havens, T. (2006) *Global Television Marketplace.* London: BFI.

Held, D. and McGrew, A,. (2007) *Globalization/Anti-Globalization: Beyond the great divide.* Second Edition. Cambridge, UK: Polity.

Hendricks, J. (1999) *Speech to the Royal Television Society in London, England.,* 20 April.

Hendricks, J. (1996) *The Worldview Address,* Edinburgh International Television Festival, August, 4.

Hertz, N. (2003) *Global Corporations Fear For Their Brands.* http://www.last-wizards.com/pages/modules.php?name=News&file=article&sid=42, Posted on 3 January (accessed, 3 January, 2005).

Hewes, J., Deputy Chief Executive and Head of International Production, Wall to Wall, UK, interview with author, London, 23 March, 2004.

Higgins, J. M. (1999) Discovery's big stretch. *Broadcasting & Cable,* 25 January. 129, 4: pg. 106.

Hill, A. (2005) *Reality TV: Audiences and Popular Factual Television*. London: Routledge.

Hoffmann Meyer, M., Chief Executive for Co-productions and Documentaries, TV2 Denmark, interview with author, 20 January, 2006.

Holtzberg D. and Rofekamp, J. (2002) *The Current State of the International Marketplace For Documentary Films. 30 January* (with revisions made on 20 April, 2002). An earlier version of the article was published in the documentary film magazine Dox, published by the European Documentary Network. http://www.centerforsocialmedia.org/documents/currentstate.pdf (accessed, 21 April, 2009).

Humphreys, P. and Lang, M. (1998) Digital Television Between the Economy and Pluralism. pp. 9–35. In J. Steemers (ed.), *Changing Channels—The Prospect for Television in a Digital World*. Luton, UK: University of Luton Press.

Ibef (2005) US Companies in India: Discovery Communications India, 8 September. http://www.ibef.org/artdisplay.aspx?cat_id=432&art_id=7510 (accessed, 3 March, 2008).

Indiantelevision (2008) Indiantelevision.com's Interview With Discovery India senior VP, GM Rahul Johri, 21 July. http://www.indiantelevision.com/interviews/y2k8/executive/rahul_johri_int.php (accessed, 19 august, 2008).

Indiantelevision (2007) Discovery, Visa to Explore Olympic Cities With Chinese Filmmakers. 14 May. (accessed, 17 October, 2008).

Indiantelevision (2006) Discovery Most Watched Channel in Asia Among Movers & Shakers: Pax Survey. 10 July. http://www.indiantelevision.co.in/headlines/y2k6/july/july94.htm (accessed, 17 October, 2008).

Informa Media (2006) New Polish Pay TV Lands Discovery Chs. 25 September. http://www.informamedia.com/itmgcontent/imed/search/articles/1158930547906.html (accessed, 28 September, 2008).

Informa Media (2003) Survival of the Fittest. 1 March. http://www.informamedia.com/itmgcontent/imed/search/articles/1034683122764.html (accessed, 20 May, 2006).

Informa Media (2002) Holding Steady. 1 September. http://www.informamedia.com/itmgcontent/imed/search/articles/1031300998973.html (accessed 3 January, 2007).

Interbrand (2005) *BusinessWeek/Interbrand Annual Ranking of the 100 Top Global* Brands, Press Release. http://www.interbrand.com/best_brands_2005.asp (accessed, 23 March, 2006).

Iosifidis, P., Steemers, J. and Wheeler, M. (2005) *European Television Industries*. London: BFI.

Jacobs, R. D. and Klein, R. A. (1999) Cable Marketing and Promotion. pp. 127–152. In S. T. Eastman, D. A. Ferguson, and R. A. Klein (eds), *Promotion and Marketing for Broadcasting and Cable*. Third edition. Boston: Focal Press.

Jin, D. Y. (2007) Transformation of the World Television System Under Neoliberal Globalization, 1983 to 2003. *Television & New Media*; 8, 3: 179.

Juniper Research (2008) Mobile Entertainment Service Market to Increase Threefold to $64bn by 2012. 23 January. http://juniperresearch.com/shop/viewpressrelease.php?pr=73 (accessed, 17 October, 2008).

Kalagian, T. (2007) Programming Children's Television: The Cable Model. pp. 147–164. In J. A. Bryant (ed.), *The Children's Television Community*. Mahwah, N.J.: Lawrence Erlbaum.

Katz, R., (1996) The World According to Hendricks, *Multichannel News*, 7 October pp. 1, 32.

Katz, Y. (2005) *Media Policy for the 21st Century in the United States and Western Europe*. Cresskill, NJ: Hampton Press.

Kehaulani Goo, S. (2006) N.Y. Times to Quit Discovery News Channel. *The Washington Post*, 14 April, D04. http://www.washingtonpost.com/wp-dyn/content/article/2006/04/13/AR2006041301778.html (accessed 1 December, 2008).

Keighron, P. (2002) Deal of the Decade. *Broadcast*, 5 April, 15.

Keller, K. L. (2003) *Strategic Brand Management: Building, Measuring, and Managing Brand Equity*. Second edition. Upper Saddle River, NJ: Prentice Hall.

Kellner, D. (2003) Media Culture and the Triumph of the Media Spectacle. *Media Spectacle*. http://www.gseis.ucla.edu/faculty/kellner/papers/mediaspectaclein-tro.htm (accessed, 8 October, 2006).

Kilborn, R. (2003) *Staging the Real: Factual TV Programming in the Age of Big Brother*. Manchester, UK: Manchester University Press.

Kilborn, R. and Izod, J. (1997) *An Introduction to Television Documentary— Confronting Reality*. Manchester, UK: Manchester University Press.

Klaassen, A. (2006) This is the Discovery We've Been Looking for. *Advertising Age*, Midwest region edition, Chicago, 16 October, 77, 42: 4.

Klein, N. (2002) *Brand USA America's Attempt to Market Itself Abroad Using Advertising Principles is Destined to Fail*. Originally published in *Los Angles Times*, Sunday, March 10. http://www.commondreams.org/views02/0310-06.htm (accessed, 27 February, 2006).

Kotler, P. and Keller K. L. (2006) *Marketing Management*. Twelfth edition. Upper Saddle River, NJ: Prentice Hall.

Kraidy, M. M. (2005) *Hybridity, or The Cultural Logic of Globalization*. Philadelphia: Temple University Press.

Krätke, S. (2003) Global Media Cities in a World-wide Urban Network. *European Planning Studies*, 11, 6: 605–628.

Kung-Shankleman, L. (2000) *Inside the BBC and CNN: Managing Media Organisations*. London: Routledge.

Kurtz, H. (2006) Ted Koppel and 'Nightline' Crew Turn Down HBO For Discovery Deal. *The Washington Post*, Thursday, 5 January, C0. http://www.washingtonpost.com/wp-dyn/content/article/2006/01/04/AR2006010400665.html (accessed, 22 April, 2006).

Leonard, D. (2008) Tommy Lee Saves the Planet! *CNN Money*. http://money.cnn.com/2008/05/14/news/companies/planet_earth.fortune/index.htm (accessed, 2 December, 2008).

Levin, G. (2008a) Another Sweeping Nature Special When 'Planet' Freezes Over. *USA Today*. http://www.usatoday.com/life/television/news/2008-04-08-fro-zen-planet_N.htm (Accessed, 26 November, 2008).

Levin, G. (2008b) Planet Green TV Network Pushes Environmentalism. *USA Today*. http://www.usatoday.com/life/television/news/2008-03-30-planet-green_N.htm (accessed, 28 November, 2008).

Levitt, T. (1983) The Globalization of Markets. *Harvard Business Review*, 61: 92–102.

Lewyn, M. (1992) John Hendricks: The Conscience of Cable TV. *Business Week*, 31 August. http://www.businessweek.com/archives/1992/b328165.arc.htm?campaign_id=search (accessed, 11 October, 2006).

Li, K. (2006) Update 2—News Corp Reaches Deal With Liberty Media on DirecTV. 22 December. http://www.reuters.com/article/idUSN2227191820061222 (accessed, 19 October, 2008).

Liberty Global (2008) www.lgi.com (accessed, 19 October, 2008).

Lindemann, J. (2004) The Financial Value of Brands. pp. 27–46 in R. Clifton, J. Simmons, and A. Sameena (eds.) Brands and Branding. Princeton, NJ: Bloomberg Press.

Littleton, C. (1996) Cable Targets Global 'Niche' Brand. *Broadcasting & Cable*, 1 July: 56.

Litman, B. R. (1998) The Economics of Television Networks: New Dimensions and New Alliances. Pp. 131–150 in A. Alexander, J. Owers and R. Carveth, (eds) *Media Economics: Theory and Practice*. Second edition. Mahwah, N.J.: Lawrence Erlbaum.

Lury, C. (2004) *Brands: The Logos of the Global Economy*. London: Routledge.

Major, R. (2003) Discovery Seeks to Update Brand With UK as ìTest-Bedî. *New Media Markets*, 28 March.

Marketing Charts (2007) Affluent Consumers in Latin America Like Discovery Channel, Google. http://www.marketingcharts.com/television/affluent-consumers-in-latin-america-like-discovery-channel-google-1103/ (accessed, 28 February, 2008).

McElvouge, L. (2000) The Doyen of Discovery. *The Television Book*. London: Royal Television Society.

McElvouge, L. (1998a) The Race For Factual Domination Begins. *Television Business International, May*: 40.

McElvouge, L. (1998b) US Networks Continue Expansion. *Television Business International*, September: 17.

McElvouge, L. (1997) Battle of The 'Most Trusted' Media Brands. *Television Business International*, February/March: 14.

McKelvy, P. and Deluca, T. (2003) Wrangling Data. *Millimeter*. 33, 10: 57.

McMurria, J. (2004) Global Channels. pp. 38–41. In J. Sinclair (ed.), *Contemporary World Television*. London: BFI.

Mega Builders introduction, Discovery Channel UK, 3 February, 2006.

Mermigas, D. (2005) Bowled over: What the alphabet soup of digital media spells for top firms. *The Hollywood Reporter*, 30 November. www.hollywoodreporter.com/thr/film/feature_display.jsp?vnu_content_id=1001572632 (accessed, 5 May, 2006).

Meza, E. (2003) ProSieben, Discovery 'Spacemen' in Orbit. *Variety*, 26 March. www.variety.com/article/VR1117883674?categoryid=1601&cs+1&s+h&p+0 (accessed, 3 September, 2005).

Miller, S. (2004) Discovery. *Broadcasting & Cable*, 28 June, 44.

Miller, T., Govil, N., McMurria, J., Maxwell, R. and Wang, T. (2005) *Global Hollywood 2*. London: BFI.

Mitchell, K. and Granger, R. (1993) In a new world, networks seek to own their shows. *Multichannel News*, 7 June, pp. 38, 42.

Mittell, J. (2004) *Genre and Television: From Cop Shows to Cartoons in American Culture*. New York: Routledge.

Mobile TV Nokia (2005) Consumers Also Want to Watch TV Programs on Their Mobile. 30 August. http://www.mobiletv.nokia.com/news/showNews/?id=53(accessed, 17 October, 2008).

Mooij, M. de (2005) *Global Marketing and Advertising—Understanding Cultural Paradoxes*. Second edition. London: Sage Publications.

Moragas Spà, M. de and Lòpez, B. (2000) Decentralization Processes and 'Proximate Television' in Europe. pp. 33–51. In G. Wang, J. Servaes and A. Goonasekera (eds), *The New Communications Landscape. Demystifying media globalisation*. Routledge: London.

Morley, D. (2006) Globalisation and Cultural Imperialism Reconsidered: Old Questions in New Guises. pp. 30–43. In J. Curran and D. Morley (eds), *Media and Cultural Theory*. London: Routledge.

Morley, D. and Robins, K. (1995) *Spaces of Identity—Global Media, Electronic Landscapes and Cultural Boundaries*. London: Routledge.

Moran, A. (1998) *Copycat Television: Globalization, Program Formats, and Cultural Identity*. Luton, UK: University of Luton Press.

Moss, L. (2008) Discovery, BBC Team Again for 'Frozen Planet' TV Event for 2012. *Multichannel News*, 4 September. http://www.multichannel.com/article/CA6549399.html (accessed, 26 November, 2008).

Moss, L. (2002) Discovery, BBC Extend Global Pact. *Multichannel News*, 25 March. http://www.multichannel.com/article/CA203774.html (accessed, 11 February, 2005).

Murray, S. (2005) Brand Loyalties: Rethinking Content Within Global Corporate Media. *Media, Culture and Society*, 27, 3: 415–435.

National Geographic Channel (2006) Milestones. http://www.ngc.tv/info/milestones.aspx (accessed, 16 March, 2006).

Nederveen Pieterse, J. (2004) *Globalization and Culture: Global Melange*. Lanham, MD: Rowman and Littlefield.

Nederveen Pieterse, J. (2001) Hybridity, So What? The Anti-Hybridity Backlash and the Riddles of Recognition. *Theory, Culture & Society*, 18, 2–3: 219–245.

Nederveen Pieterse, J. (1995) Globalization as Hybridization pp. 45–68. In M. Featherstone, S. Lash and R. Robertson (eds), *Global Modernities*. London: Sage.

New York Times (2008) www.nytimes.com/auth/login?URI=/2008/09/17/dining/17diet.html&OQ=_rQ3D5Q26refQ3DhealthQ26orefQ3DsloginQ26orefQ3DsloginQ26orefQ3Dslogin&refuse_cookie_error=show_error (accessed, September 17, 2008).

New York Times Company, The Investor Relations (2002) *Discovery Civilization Channel to be Renamed 'Discovery Times Channel'*. Press Release, December 2. http://www.corporate-ir.net/ireye/ir_site.zhtml?ticker=NYT&script=411&layout=-6&item_id= 361066&sstring=discovery~times (accessed, 22 March, 2006)

News Corp (2008) United States Securities And Exchange Commission Washington, DC 20549 FORM 10-K Annual Report Pursuant To Section 13 Or 15(d) Of The Securities Exchange Act Of 1934. http://www.newscorp.com/investor/annual_reports.html (accessed, 19 October, 2008).

Nichols, B. (2001) *Introduction to Documentary*. Bloomington: Indiana University Press.

Nokia (2006) *Discovery Communications and Nokia Announce Global Collaboration*. http://press.nokia.com/PR/200603/1039650_5.html, March 16 (accessed, 19 March, 2006).

Observer, The (2004) 'Swamp Alligator' With a Taste for Conservation. Sunday, December 5. www.guardian.co.uk/media/2004/dec/05/broadcasting.rupertmurdoch1 (accessed, 19 October, 2008).

Ofcom (2007) The Future of Children's Television Programming. Consultation published, October, 3. http://www.ofcom.org.uk/consult/condocs/kidstv/ (accessed, 11 June, 2008).

Ofcom (2004) *Ofcom Review of Public Service Television Broadcasting (PSB)—Phase 1, Supporting Documents—Volume 2, The current system, Appendices B: Genre Definitions*. www.ofcom.org.uk (accessed, 14 February, 2005).

Ohmae, K. (2005) *The Next Global Stage: Challenges and Opportunities in our Borderless World*. Upper Saddle River, NJ: Wharton School Publishing.

Olins, W. (1999) *Trading Identities: Why Countries and Companies are Taking on Each Others' Role*. London: The Foreign Policy Centre.

One TV World (2006) Cable Network Profiles. Discovery Channel (US). http://www.onetvworld.org/tmpls/network/06profiles/161.pdf (accessed, 6 September, 2006).

Orgad, S. (2006) This Box Was Made for Walking: How Will Mobile Television Transform Viewers' Experience and Change Advertising? Nokia and the Department of Media and Communications, London School of Economics. http://www.mobiletv.nokia.com/resources/files/RD1910NokiaGlobal_lowres.pdf (accessed, 2 September, 2008).

Osborne, M. (2002) Discovering New Talent in Mainland China. *Variety*, 6 April. http://www.variety.com/article/VR1117864911.html?categoryid=19&cs=1&query=Discovering+New+Talent (accessed, 4 March, 2008).

O'Shaughnessy, J. (2002) Q&A: John Hendricks, Discovery Communications, Inc. *Hollywood Reporter*, 9 December. http://www.hollywoodreporter.com/thr/article_display.jsp?vnu_content_id=1775860 (accessed, 15 March, 2006).

Osterhammel, J. and Petersson, N. P. (2005) *Globalization: A Short History.* Princeton, NJ: Princeton University Press.

Owen, B. M. and Wildman, S. S. (1992) *Video Economics.* Cambridge, MA: Harvard University Press.

Owers, J., Carveth, R. and Alexander, A. (1998) An Introduction to Media Economics Theory and Practice. pp. 1–44. In A. Alexander, J. Owers and R. Carveth (eds), *Media Economics: Theory and Practice.* Second edition. Mahwah, NJ: Lawrence Erlbaum.

Papathanassopoulos, S. (2002) *European Television in the Digital Age—Issues, Dynamics and Realities.* Cambridge, UK: Polity.

Pedleton, J. (1992) U.S. Cablers Plugging Into Europe. *Variety*, 15 October. http://www.variety.com/article/VR101144.html?categoryid=18&cs=1&query=u%2E s%2E+cablers+plugging+into+europe (accessed, 19 October, 2008).

Peers, M. (1997) Discovery Ups and Downs: Cash Flow Jumps 26%. *Variety*, 26 February. http://www.variety.com/vstory/VR1117435606.html?categoryid=38 &cs=1&query=%22Cash+flow+jumps%22 (accessed, 19 October, 2008).

Petrozzello, D. (1998) Bite-Sized Branding in Digital Age. *Broadcasting & Cable*, 4 May, 128, 19: 88–92.

Pinto, A. (2005) Indiantelevision.com's Interview With Discovery Networks India MD Deepak Shourie. *Indian Television.com,* 26 December. http://www.indiantelevision.com/interviews/y2k5/executive/deepak_shourie.htm (accessed, 3 March, 2007).

PIXAR (2007) http://www.pixar.com (accessed, 17 October, 2008).

Price, M. E. (1995) *Television, The Public Sphere and National Identity.* Oxford, UK: Clarendon Press.

PWC (2005) Big Bets for the U.S. Cable Industry. *Technology Forecast Publication*, 1–37. http://www.pwc.com/em/pdfs/cablev4-x.pdf (accessed, 21 February, 2005).

Rantanen, T. (2005a) *The Media and Globalization.* London: Sage.

Rantanen, T. (2005b) An Interview With Anthony Giddens. *Global Media and Communications*, 1, 1: 63–77.

Reguly, E. (1997) A Hometown Boy With Global Vision. *The Times*, 2 August, 25.

Reynolds, M. (2000) Discovery Seeks Mammoth Appeal—Raising the Mammoth—Company Business and Marketing, *Cable World, 6 March*. http://www.findarticles.com/p/articles/mi_m0DIZ/is_10_12/ai_60589458 (accessed, 4 April, 2006).

Ritzer, G. (2004) *The McDonaldization of Society.* Revised New Century Edition. Thousand Oaks, CA: Pine Forge Press.

Robertson, R. (1995) Glocalization: Time–Space and Heterogeniety–Homogeniety. pp. 25–44. In M. Featherstone, S. Lash and R. Robertson (eds), *Global Modernities*. London: Sage.

Robertson, R. (1992) *Globalization: Social Theory and Global Culture.* London: Sage.

Robichaux, M. (2002) *Cable Cowboy: John Malone and The Rise of The Modern Cable Business.* Hoboken, NJ: John Wiley.

Robinson, J. (2006) BBC Finds a Treasure in Planet Earth. *The Observer*, 9 April. http://observer.guardian.co.uk/business/story/0,,1749763,00.html (accessed, April 9, 2006).

Roe, K. and De Meyer, G. (2001) One Planet—One Music? MTV and Globalization. pp. 33–44. In A. Gebesmair and A. Smudits (eds), *Global Repertoires: Popular Music Within and Beyond the Transnational Music Industry.* Aldershot, UK: Ashgate Publishing.

Roe, K. and De Meyer, G. (2000) Music Television: MTV–Europe, pp. 141–157 in J. Wieten, G. Murdock, and P. Dahlgren (eds.) *Television Across Europe–A Comparative Introduction*. London: Sage.

Romano. A. (2004) Extreme Discovery. *Broadcasting & Cable*, May, 134, 18: 24–25.

Roost, F. (2005) Synergy City: How Times Square and Celebration Are Integrated Into Disney's Marketing Cycle. pp. 261–298. In M. Budd and M. H. Kirsch (eds), *Rethinking Disney: Private Control, Public Dimensions*. Middletown, CT: Wesleyan University Press.

Schiller, H. (1985) Electronic Information Flows: New Basis for Global Dominations? pp. 11–20. In P. Drummond and R. Patterson (eds), *Television in Transition: Papers from the First International Television Studies Conference*. London: BFI.

Schlesinger, P. (2001) Tensions in the Construction of European Media Policies. pp. 95–115. In N. Morris and S. Waisbord (eds), *Media and Globalization: Why the State Matters*. Lanham, MD: Rowman & Littlefield.

Scholte, J. A. (2000) *Globalization: A Critical Introduction*. London: Macmillan.

Scott, K. D. and White, A. M. (2003) Unnatural History? Deconstructing the *Walking with Dinosaurs* Phenomenon. *Media, Culture and Society*, 25, 3: 315–332.

Screen Digest (2005) Sex and Shopping Drive New Television Launches as Europe Sees a Record Boom in New TV Channels. http://www.screendigest.com/press/releases/FHAN-6G7BXG/pressRelease.pdf (accessed, 9 November, 2005).

Screen Digest (2003a) TV Channel Launches in Europe are on the Up—So are Closures. 20 May.

Screen Digest (2003b) Number of Channels by Genre: Documentaries', May: 154–156.

Screen Digest (2002) Documentary Channels in the US. February: 63.

Senior Executive (1), DNE, interview with author, London, 12 May, 2004.

Senior Executive (2), DNE, interview with author, London, 30 July, 2003.

Seidenberg, S., Documentary television producer, interview with author, London, 14 July, 2003.

Shen Lawfirm (2005) *Shenlaw Bulletin*, Vol. I, 2, February. http://shenlawfirm.com/bull/2.pdf (accessed, 21 April, 2006).

Shi, A. (2005) The Taming of the Shrew: Global Media in a Chinese Perspective. *Global Media and Communication*, 1, 1: 33–36.

Shin, A. (2006) Google Earth to Get Discovery Video. *Washington Post*, April 7; D04. http://www.washingtonpost.com/wp-dyn/content/article/2006/04/06/AR2006040601925_pf.html (accessed, 28 November, 2008).

Sinclair, J. (2005) International Television Channels in the Latin American Audiovisual Space. pp. 196–215. In J. K. Chalaby (ed.) *Transnational Television Worldwide; Towards a New Media Order* London. I. B. Tauris.

Sinclair, J. (2003) "The Hollywood of Latin America": Miami as Regional Center in Television Trade. *Television & New Media*, 4, 3: 211.

Singer, A., Creative Director, West Park Productions, UK, interview with author, London, 16 June, 2004.

Siklos, R. (2006) With a Mogul's Touch, a Chinese Media Man Connects to the West. *New York Times*, 16 January. http://www.nytimes.com/2006/01/16/business/media/16shanghai.html?_r=1 (accessed, 1 December, 2008).

Smith, A. D. (1995) *Nations and Nationalism in a Global Era*. Cambridge, UK: Polity Press.

Snider, M. (2008) Full-Length Shows, Even Movies, Growing on Cellular. *USA Today*, 23 April. http://www.usatoday.com/tech/wireless/phones/2008-04-21-download-mobile_N.htm (accessed, 4 September, 2008).

Snoddy, R. (2002) Teaming Up for Wild Success. *The Times*, 22 March, 20.

Sparks, C. (2005) The Problem of Globalization. *Global Media and Communication*, 1, 1: 20–23.

Sparks, C. (1998) Is There a Global Public Sphere? Pp. 108–124 in D. K. Thussu (ed.), *Electronic Empires: Global Media and Local Resistance*. London: Arnold.

Sreberny, A. (2000) The Global and the Local in International Communication. pp. 93–119. In J. Curran and M. Gurevitch (eds), *Mass Media and Society*. London: Arnold.

Steemers, J. (2004) *Selling Television: British Television in the Global Marketplace*. London: BFI.

Steen Müller, T. Managing Director, European Documentary Network, Denmak, interview with author, Prague, 21 June, 2003.

Stelter, B. (2008) Discovery Starts 'Green' Cable Channel. 2 June.http://www.iht.com/articles/2008/06/02/technology/adco,php (accessed, 28 November, 2008).

Sterling, C. H. and Kittross, J. M. (2002) *Stay Tuned: A History of American Broadcasting*. Third Edition. Mahwah: Lawrence Erlbaum.

Straubhaar, J. D. and Duarte, L. G. (2005) Adapting US Transnational Television Channels to a Complex World: From Cultural Imperialism to Localization to Hybridization. pp. 216–253. In J. K. Chalaby (ed.), *Transnational Television Worldwide: Towards a New Media Order*. London: I. B. Tauris.

Syvertsen, T. (2003) Challenges to Public Television in the Era of Convergence and Commercialization, *Television & New Media*, 4, 2: 155–175.

Taylor, J., Former Managing Director, Discovery Networks Europe, UK, interview with author, London, 18 June, 2003.

Taylor, J. (2002) Reflections on the Industry From the Factual Frontline. *New Media Markets*, February, 20, 4: 6.

TBI (2005) Explosive Start for Supervolcano. *Television Business International Buyers Briefing*, 30 March.

Telecoms (2006) Discovery Communications Expands Mobile Content Services in Europe. 16 February. http://www.telecoms.com/itmgcontent/tcoms/search/articles/20017336499.html (accessed, 20 August, 2008).

Telecoms (2005) Just the Facts. 1 September. http://www.telecoms.com/itmgcontent/ tcoms/search/articles/1126892721514.html?page=4 (accessed, 25 March, 2006).

Television Research Partnership, Colwell, T. and Price, D. (2005) *Rights of Passage—British Television in the Global Market*, commissioned by British Television Distributors' Association (BTDA). In September 2004 the BTDA became part of Pact, the trade body for UK independent producers and rights holders. http://www.pact.co.uk/uploads/file_bank/1698.pdf (accessed, 6 September, 2006).

Thal-Larsen, P. (2003) Taking on the Real World. *Financial Times*, 23 September. pp. 8–9.

The Greatest Ever: Bombers, Discovery Channel Norway, 1 February, 2006.

The World's Strangest UFO Stories, Introduction, Discovery Channel UK, 5 February, 2006.

Third World and Environment Broadcasting Project (2003) The World on The Box: International Issues in News and Factual Programs on UK Television 1975–2003. Carried out by The Communication and Media Research Institute (CAMRI), University of Westminster, UK. http://www.ibt.org.uk/3WE/Research/WorldontheBoxTop.htm (accessed, 5 October, 2005).

Thussu, D. K. (2007) *News as Entertainment: The Rise of Global Infotainment*. London: Sage.

Thussu, D. K. (2006) *International Communication: Continuety and Change*. Second edition. London: Arnold.

Thussu, D. K. (2005) The Transnationalization of Television: The Indian Experience. pp. 156–172. In J. K. Chalaby (ed.), *Transnational Television Worldwide: Towards a New Media Order.* London: I. B. Tauris.

Thussu, D. K. (2000) *International Communication: Continuety and Change.* London: Arnold.

Thussu, D. K. (1999) Privatizing the Airwaves: The Impact of Globalization on Broadcasting in India Media Culture Society; 21; 125–131.

Thussu, D. K. (1998) Introduction. pp. 1–9. In D. K. Thussu (ed.), *Electronic empires: global media and local resistance.* London: Arnold.

TNS-Gallup (2008) Seertall uke 38. Norge. http://www.tns-gallup.no/default. aspx?did=9081613 (accessed, 13 October, 2008).

TNS-Gallup TV-Meter (2008) Seertal uge 38 (15 September–21 September, 2008).

Tobin, A. (1999) New paths to Discovery. *Cable & Satellite Europe*, November, 10.

Tomlinson, J. (1999) *Globalisation and Culture.* Cambridge, UK: Polity.

Tunstall, J. (1993) *Television Producers.* London: Routledge.

Tunstall, J. (1977) *The Media are American.* New York: Columbia Press.

Tunstall, J. and Machin, D. (1999) *The Anglo-American Media Connection.* Oxford, UK: Oxford University Press.

Turow, J. (2006) *Niche Envy: Marketing Discrimination in the Digital Age.* Cambridge, MA: MIT Press.

UNESCO (2003) *UNESCO Teams with Discovery Communications and UN to Promote Languages.* 13 February. http://www.unesco.org (accessed, 18 August, 2003).

Urry, J. (2003) *Global Complexity.* Cambridge, UK: Polity Press.

Variety (1993) Discovery Buys Remainder of Europe Stake. 8 January. http://www. variety.com (accessed, 23 April, 2009).

Venturelli, S. (1998) *Liberalizing the European Media: Politics, Regulation, and the Public Sphere.* Oxford, UK: Clarendon Press.

Verrier, R. (2005) Canada Rolls Credits on a Slump. *Los Angeles Times,* 23 October. http://www.latimes.com/classified/jobs/career/cl-fi-hollycanada23oct23,0,617730. story?coll=la-class-employ-career (accessed, 26 April, 2006).

Volkmer, I. (1999) *News In the Global Sphere—A study of CNN and its Impact on Global Communication.* Luton, UK: University of Luton Press.

Vranica, S. (2007) New Ads Take On TiVO: Tie-Ins to TV Shows Aim to Prevent Fast-Forwarding. *Wall Street Journal,* New York, Oct 5: pg. b.4.

Waisbord, S. (2004) McTV: Understanding the Global Popularity of Television Formats. *Television & New Media,* 5, 4: 359–383.

Washington Post, The (2005) Discovery Communications Inc. http://www.washingtonpost.com/wp-srv/business/post200/2005/DISC.html (accessed, 7 October, 2006).

Weprln, A. (2008) *Ted Koppel, Discovery End Partnership Early.* Variety, 25 November. http://www.broadcastingcable.com/article/159873-Ted_Koppel_Discovery_End_Partnership_Early.php (accessed, 15 April, 2009).

Whitefield, M. (1999) Miami-Based Discovery Communications Shapes Television in Latin America. Knight Ridder/Tribune Business News, 14 August. http://findarticles.com/p/articles/mi_hb5553/is_199908/ai_n22420492/ (accessed, 17 April, 2009).

Williams, M. (1998) Voyage Embarks on 2-Year Discovery Deal, Cablers to Bow Programming Block. *Variety,* 5 December. www.variety.com/article/VR1117481069.html?categoryid=14&cs=1&query=Voyage+embarks+on+2%2Dyear+Discovery+deal (accessed, 28 November, 2008).

Willis, J. (2004) *Behind the Scenes, interview with Julie Willis, SVP, Discovery Channel Marketing.* http://media.dsc.discovery.com/knowmore/home.html (accessed, 16 August, 2004).

Winslow, G. (2004) Wild Times for Natural History. *Television Business International*, 1 October.

Index

A

Aaker, D. A. 55, 56, 58
ABC, 20, 24, 131
ABI Research, 44
acquisitions, 25, 29, 44, 73, 74, 80,
    102, 120
Advance/Newhouse Communication, 23
advertising,
    and broadcasting, 37
    and Discovery, 26, 27, 37-39,
        109–111, 115–117
    and narrowcasting, 11, 17, 40, 41,
        97, 104
    and television audience, 40, 97
    in the digital media environment, 43,
        47
    global target audience segments, 10, 11
Adweek (magazine), 47
Africa, 60, 62, 106, 115, 123, 136
Al-Jazeera, 138
Alexander, A., 20, 41
Amazon.com, 43, 46, 54, 56, 149
American Chopper, 3, 39, 78, 114,
    139–141
Animal Planet, 23, 26, 30, 44, 60–63,
    85, 86, 87
animation, 93, 118, 119, 120, 129
Argentina, 41, 61
Artz, L., 93, 119
Asia,
    and Discovery, 2, 3, 19, 45, 59, 122,
        126
    and television audience, 41
    and the television sector, 31, 32
    cable distribution, 22
Aston, L., 25
AT&T, 22, 45
Auletta, K., 22
Australia, 22, 59, 74, 120

Aversa, J., 22

B

BBC America, 62, 85, 87
BBC (British Broadcasting Corpora-
    tion), *see* BBC
    and brand, 49, 62, 65, 86
    and Discovery, 62, 84–95, 129,
    factual television programming, 90,
        99–101, 141
    license fee, 84, 92
    Natural History Unit, 86, 94
    Rights Agency, 90
    The Ten Most Memorable Factual
        Programs, 95
BBC World, 11, 17, 32
BBC Worldwide,
    and Animal Planet, 30, 85, 86, 87
    and branding, 68, 84, 86
    and factual television programming,
        86–88
    and joint venture with Discovery,
        3,26, 84–95, 129
    and People+Arts, 30, 61, 62
    and programmes sales, 87–89, 92
Balmer, J. M.T., 55, 56
Barker, C., 24
Barnes, B., 43
Baruh, L., 46
Bauman, Z., 2
Beatty, S., 75
Beavis, S., 85
Bell, M., 136
Bellamy, JR., R., 50, 51 and 57
Best Global Brands, 64
Big Brother, 14, 82, 116
Bisson, G., 98
Blasters, The, 114, 140
Blind, S., 75, 79

blockbuster logic, 3, 91, 93
Bloomberg, 22, 64
Blu Ray, 43
Blue Planet, 3, 68, 92, 94, 129
Blumler, J. G., 137
Bonini, S. M., 72
Bonner, P., 25
Born, G., 14, 90, 129
Borton, J., 32
Boyd-Barrett, O., 9, 149
brands,
    and diversification, 55
    global factual television, 3, 89, 91
    media, 51, 53, 56
    most valuable, 64
    and loyalty, 55, 57
    online, 54
    ranking, 53, 54
    television, 50–53
    as intangibles, 49, 50, 71
Brants, K., 137
Brazil, 29, 30, 41, 61, 81
Break the Addiction: An Inconvenient Truth, 150
British Broadcasting Corporation, *see* BBC
broadband, 22, 43, 45, 58
broadcasting,
    in Europe, 37
    in the Nordic region, 34–36, 100
    in the UK, 24, 25, 100, 104
    in the US, 19, 20, 24
Broadcasting & Cable (magazine), 23
Brown, D., 25, 27, 104
Brown, M., 94
Brown, R., 2
Brunsdon, C., 14, 137
Buerkle, T., 62
Building the Winter Games, 114, 128, 141, 148
Burgi, M., 32
Business Week (magazine), 62, 64

C
C21 Media, 27, 105
Caldwell, J. T., 6
Canada, 42, 61, 74, 83, 116, 120
Carter, S., 20, 76, 78, 89, 122
Cartoon Networks, 41
Carugati, A., 39, 108
Carveth, R., 20
Castells, M., 85
CBS, 20, 24

Chabin, J. B, 50, 51, 57
Chalaby, J. K., 11, 18, 24–26, 40, 57, 96, 103–105, 132, 144, 148
Chan, J. M., 32
Changing Rooms, 78, 81
Changing Sexes, 113, 136
Chan-Olmsted, S., 51, 52, 55
Channel 4, 74, 87, 98, 101
childrens television, 41, 42, 119, 120
China, 32, 103, 122, 131
China Daily, 32, 103
Chris, C., 14, 20–21, 23–24, 51, 58, 73–74, 78, 128, 131, 150
Clark, N., 102
Clarke, S., 26, 27, 77
CNBC, 11, 32, 45
CNN, 10, 11, 17–18, 32, 49, 139
Coca-Cola, 61, 64
Collins, R., 3, 16, 96, 97, 143
Comer-Calder, N., 21, 66, 75–77, 101, 103
communications infrastructure, 5, 22, 24, 25, 27–29, 32, 98
co-production of television programming, Anglo-American, 87, 88
    and BBC Worldwide/Discovery, 84–95
    and national broadcasters, 79
    and the National Geographic Channel, 89
    fiction, 88
    the rationale for, 79–83
Corner, J., 12, 75, 134–136, 137
Cottle, S., 92, 94
Cox Cable Communications, 21, 22, 23
Crandall, R. W., 19
Croteau, D., 19, 29, 24, 51, 85
Crupi, A., 38, 47, 57
culture, *see* televisual culture; globalization of culture; global culture
cultural heterogenization, 15–18, 142–144
    and language, 15, 16, 143
    and mobile telephony, 17
    and media content, 16, 142, 143
    and national culture, 16, 18, 143
    and television channels, 9, 10, 17, 143
    and factual television, 17, 143
cultural homogenization, 8–13, 133–140
    and brands, 10, 11, 133
    and cultural imperialism, 8, 9, 138, 149

and factual television, 11–13, 134–139
and television channels, 10
cultural hybridization, 13–15, 140–142
and art forms, 14
and language, 13, 15, 142
and national culture, 140, 141
and factual television, 13, 14, 140
and the telenovela, 15
and television programming, 14, 15
Curran, J., 16, 24

D

Dahlgren, P., 24
Davies, P., 40
Davis, W., 79
Dawson, M., 45
Dawtrey, A., 27, 86
DCGEP (Discovery Channel Global Education Partnership), 62
De Meyer, G., 10, 17, 18, 100, 102, 148
Deadliest Catch, 3, 125, 128, 140, 157
Deans, J., 85, 86, 89
Denmark, 34, 35, 100
Deluca, T., 81
DCMS (Department for Culture, Media and Sport, UK), 118, 120
Digitaltelevision distribution, 27, 28, 31, 40, 52
Dirty Jobs, 38, 43, 128, 140
Discovery Campus, 68, 133
Discovery Channel,
and audience, 37–39, 41, 89, 132
and branding, 65, 66
in China, 32
in Europe, 28–29
in Germany, 27
and Global Specials, 123–126, 128, 131, 136, 148
in India, 30, 31
in Latin America, 29, 30
in Norway, 109–117
in the UK, 109–117
in the US, 19–24, 78
and youtube.com, 44
Discovery Communications, 20–23, 44, 51, 74
Discovery en Espanol, 23, 102
Discovery Global Businesses and Brands, 63
Discovery Health Channel, 23, 40, 44, 53, 54, 131
Discovery Kids, 23, 29, 41, 131
Discovery Networks Asia, 31, 32

Discovery Networks Europe, 26–29, 63, 66, 98, 99, 101, 104, 105, 108, 109, 139
Discovery Networks India, 102
Discovery Networks International, 33, 57, 63, 107, 132
Discovery Networks Latin America/ Iberia, 29, 30
Discovery Networks US, 19–24, 40, 63, 84, 102, 132
Discovery Science Channel, 33
Discovery Times Channel, 56
Discovery Travel & Living, 30, 33
Discoverystore.com, 46, 63, 70
Discovery.com, 42, 43, 54, 69
Disney Channel, 24, 41, 51, 53, 93
Doane, D., 71
docu-drama, 14, 94, 140
docu-soap, 14, 78, 112, 114, 137, 138, 140, 146
documentaries,
demand for, 51, 75
and the BBC, 74, 76, 86, 87, 88, 90, 91, 129
and Discovery, 2, 13, 51, 74, 76, 78, 131, 134–136, 138
functions of, 11, 12, 134, 150, 151
television channels, 52, 98, 99
genre, 11, 14
production of, 68, 69, 79, 85–88, 90, 95
and the US, 20, 21, 51, 52, 78
and the UK, 17, 74, 76–77, 100
and Europe, 67, 98–101
and the Nordic region, 100, 110, 112
Dow Jones Sustainability Indexes, 71
Dox (magazine), 79
DR1, 34, 99, 100
Duarte, L. G., 13, 15, 29, 30
Dvd, 42, 43, 46, 48, 92

E

Eao (European Audiovisual Observatory), 99, 100
Economist, The (magazine), 89
Eisenberg, D., 64, 78
Emery, D., 26, 41, 65–66, 84, 85
ESPN, 24, 31, 41, 56
European Commission, 9, 82, 116, 149
European television sector,
and cable and satellite television channels, 9, 37, 41, 42, 96, 97
and cultural diversity, 10, 16, 17, 96, 97, 99–105

and deregulation, 22, 24, 81, 82
and import of television program-
    ming and film, 8, 9, 119, 120
Europe's Richest, 115, 116, 128, 140
Extreme Engineering
Everhart Bedford, K., 69

F

Face Race, 115, 116, 128, 136

factual formats, 14, 78, 81, 82
factual television, *see* factual entertain-
    ment, documentaries, docu-soap,
    docudrama, factual formats,
    reality TV
factual entertainment, and Discovery,
    52, 67, 76–79
    and infotainment, 11–13, 134, 137
    characteristics of, 12, 13, 113, 114
    the emergence of, 12, 77, 137
    the popularity of, 78, 137
FBI Files, 3, 114, 115
Financial Times, 34, 64, 78
Finland, 17, 35, 100
First Tuesday, 77
Flynn, B., 103
Forbes (magazine), 32
Forrester, C., 20, 22, 69, 80, 142
Fortune (magazine), 114
Fox Kids, 18, 98
France, 27, 68, 120
Franklin, B., 12
Freston, T., 34, 58
Frozen Planet, 92
Fürsich, E., 10, 13, 57, 75, 91, 130,
    138

G

Garage, The, 114, 115, 138, 141, 143
Garcia Canclini, N., 14
Germany, 17, 26, 68, 1002, 120
global culture, 1, 96, 147, 148
globalization, *see* also media globaliza-
    tion
    contested nature of, 1, 2, 5, 6
    of brands, 135, 136
    of culture, 2, 7, 8, 13, 15
    of labour, 83
    of production of factual television,
        79–81, 84–95
    of television programming distribu-
        tion, 81, 82, 132, 133, 135, 136,
        139
glocalization, 14, 141–143

Goggin, G., 44, 45
Google, 43, 54, 56, 64, 149
Gorard, J., 49
Gough, P. J., 131
Govil, N., 83
Granger, R., 51
Greatest Ever: Bomber, The, 3,
    113–115, 136, 140
Greatest Ever: Helicopters, The, 128,
    140
Grey, E. R., 55, 56
Grove, C., 69
Grover, R., 22
Guider, E., 32, 86
Gunther, M., 34, 58

H

Habermas, J., 139
Hafez, K., 16
Hall, L., 69, 79
Hallenberg, G., 75, 79
Hamelink, C. J., 8
Harrie, E., 35–37
Harris Interactive, 53, 54, 55
Hatch, M. J., 55
Havens, T., 119, 121
HBO, 39, 41
HD TV (High Definition TV), 23, 29,
    32, 33, 43
Held, D., 5
Hendricks, J., 1, 2, 20 – 22, 52, 57, 74,
    80, 129, 147
Hertz, N., 71
Hewes, J., 33, 130
Higgins, J. M., 23
Hill, A., 11, 13, 14, 137
History (television genre), 86, 88, 95,
    121
History Channel, 23, 53
Hoffmann Meyer, M., 129, 130
Holtzberg D., 75, 77
Hot Art, 108, 109, 141
Howstuffworks.com, 42, 44, 46
Hoynes, W., 19, 20, 24, 37, 51, 85
Humphreys, P., 68, 79, 93

I

Ibef, 31
India,
    and Discovery, 26, 30, 11, 59, 102
    and cable and television channels,
        30
    and cultural hybridity, 15
    and STAR TV, 31

Indiantelevision, 41, 102, 103
Industrial Revelations, 108, 109, 141
Informa Media, 29, 40
infotainment,
  and news, 11, 12
  and the factual television genre, 12,
    13, 137
  and the spectacular, 128, 129
  as a way to reach audiences, 128, 129
  global, 12, 128
Interbrand, 50, 62, 64, 71
Internet, the
  and advertising, 43, 44, 46
  and media content, 42, 43
  e-commerce, 46
  Top 25 Online Brands Ranked, 54
Iosifidis, P., 42, 119, 121
Italy, 28, 60
iTunes, 43, 149
Izod, J., 98

J

Jacobs, R. D., 21
Japan, 22, 32, 59, 92
Jin, D. Y., 32
Johnson, C., 14
joint venture, 24–26, 31, 32, 72
journalism, 9, 11–13, 123, 131,
  136–137
Juniper Research, 44

K

Kagan research, 40
Kalagian, T., 51, 93
Katz, R., 57
Katz, Y., 5
Kehaulani Goo, S., 57
Keighron, P., 87, 89, 90, 91
Keller, K. L., 49, 55, 56, 64, 71
Kellner, D., 128
Kika, 42
Kilborn, R., 13, 14, 98
Kittross, J. M., 20
Klaassen, A., 43
Klein, N., 70
Klein, R. A., 21
Koppel, T., 131
Kotler, P., 64, 71
Kraidy, M. M., 5, 13, 134
Krätke, S., 80
Kung Fu Monks, 90
Kung-Shankleman, L., 49, 51
Kurtz, H., 131

L

Lang, M, 68, 79, 93
Latin America, 29, 30, 41
Learning Channel, The, 27, 38, 53, 78,
  85, 94
Leonard, D., 40
Levin, G., 39, 92
Levitt, T., 10, 11
Lewyn, M., 21, 74
Li, K., 22
Liberty Global, 22, 149
Liberty Media, 21–24, 32, 34, 86, 149,
  150
Lindemann, J., 50
Litman, B. R., 19
Littleton, C., 51
localization, 18, 27, 96, 97, 101–111,
  141, 144
London, 27, 80, 86
Lòpez, B., 16
Lury, C., 50, 54, 55, 64, 70, 79

M

Machin, D., 22, 24
Major, R., 67
Malone, J., 21, 22
Marketing Charts, 41
Maxwell, R., 83
McDonaldization, 10, 139, 148
McDonalds, 10, 61, 64, 139
McElvouge, L., 19, 26, 27, 62, 86, 150
McGrew, A., 5
McKelvy, P., 81
McMurria, J., 83, 132
media globalization,
  and Discovery's televisual culture,
    132–151
  consequences of, 5, 145, 146
  definition of, 2, 5, 6
  deterritorialization, 7, 144, 149
  different theoretical articulations,
    6–18
Mega Builders, 114, 115, 128
Merchandising, 42, 79, 93
Mermigas, D., 22
Meza, E., 92
Miami, 27, 29, 30, 57
Microsoft, 43, 64, 70
Middle East, The
Miller, S., 62
Miller, T., 83
Mitchell, K., 51
Mobile Telephony, 3, 17, 42–46, 56,
  63, 92, 149

Monster.com, 47
Monster Garage, 78
Monster Move, 114, 140
Mooij, M. de., 148
MoragasSpà, M. de., 16
Moran, A., 14, 81
Morley, D., 7, 9, 10, 11, 144
Moseley, R. 14
Moss, L., 62, 87, 92
MSNBC, 45
MTV, 10, 17, 18,
Multichannel News, 57
Murdoch, R., 22
Murray, S., 58, 92, 93
Mythbusters, 2, 34, 38, 43, 47, 78, 111,
    112, 116, 139

N
NAFTA, 29
narrowcasting,
    and branding, 50–52
    and cable and satellite television
        channels, 11, 37, 40
    and Discovery Channel, 3, 11, 40,
        41, 97, 104, 134, 140
    and National Geographic Channel,
        40, 41
    in Asia, 41
    in Europe, 17, 41, 103
    in Latin America, 41
    of television genres, 41, 77, 120, 135
    in the US, 38, 37, 41
National Geographic Channel, 24, 31,
    40, 41, 51, 53, 65, 66, 74, 75,
    89, 98
Natural History (television genre), 3,
    73, 86–93, 129, 150
NBC, 20, 24,
Nederveen Pieterse, J., 1, 5, 7, 14–16,
    142, 144, 149
Netherlands, 25, 104, 15, 108
New York Times, The (newspaper), 56, 57
news, 10–13
News and Current Affairs (television
    genre), 87, 88
News Corporation,
    and the National Geographic Chan-
        nel, 24
    in China, 32
    in India, 31
    in Latin America, 29, 30
    in the US, 22, 133
NHK, 68, 92, 94
Nichols, B., 134

Nickelodeon, 24, 41, 51
Nielsen Media, 37, 38
Nike, 50, 54, 55, 79
Nokia, 17, 45, 64
Nordic region, 35–37, 100, 105
NOVA, 20, 87
Norway, 36, 110–116, 128, 134,
    143
NRK, 34, 36, 42, 56, 79, 100

O
Observer, The, 22
Ofcom, 42, 112–114, 135
Ohmae, K., 5
Olins, W., 71
Olympics, The, 103, 114, 123, 128,
    131, 148
One Alliance, 31
One TV World, 38–39
Orgad, S., 45
Osborne, M., 32
O'Shaughnessy, J., 57
Osterhammel, J., 1
Owen, B. M., 19
Owers, J., 41

P
Pan-European,
    brands, 11
    targeting of television audience, 11,
        96–99, 103, 104
    television channels, 96–99
Papathanassopoulos, S., 37, 51
PBS (Public Broadcasting Service, US),
    22, 52, 55, 69
Pedleton, J., 24, 25
Peers, M., 26
Petersson, N. P., 1
Petrozzello, D., 40
Pinto, A., 30
Pixar, 93, 120
Planet Earth, 3, 68, 92–94, 129
Planet Green, 23, 39, 44, 63
podcasts, 43
Poland, 60, 67
Pompeii: The Last Day, 94, 95
ProSieben, 91, 94
Public Service Broadcasting,
    in Denmark, 34, 35, 100
    in Europe, 96, 97
    in Finland, 35, 100
    in Norway, 34, 36, 42, 56, 100
    in Sweden, 36, 42, 100
    in the UK, 42, 56, 94, 100

R

Radio, 56, 58, 69
Rantanen, T., 1, 5, 7, 138, 145
Reagan, R., 19, 20
reality TV, 14, 78, 112, 137, 138, 140, 141
Reguly, E., 86
Reynolds, M., 69
Rights of Passage – British Television in The Global Market, 81, 88
Ritzer, G., 10, 139
Robertson, R., 14, 141, 147, 148
Robichaux, M., 21
Robins, K., 7, 10, 11, 144
Robinson, J., 92, 93, 94
Roe, K., 10, 17, 18, 68, 100, 102, 148
Rofekamp, J., 75, 77
Romano. A., 40
Roost, F., 61
Rosenthal, A., 12
Russia, 107

S

satellite technology, 5, 22, 25, 27, 50, 62
satellite television, 9, 21, 25, 27, 29, 30, 32, 42, 96, 97, 104
Schiller, H., 8, 149
Schlesinger, P., 9, 138
Scholte, J. A., 2
Schultz, M., 55
Scott, K. D., 91
Screen Digest, 16, 29, 52, 98, 99,
Seidenberg, S., 74, 79, 121, 122, 126
ShenLawfirm, 71
Shi, A., 32
Shin, A., 43
Siklos, R., 32
Sinclair, J., 29, 30, 41
Singer, A., 65, 66, 87, 88, 107, 127, 138
Smith, A. D., 17
Snider, M., 45
Snoddy, R., 94
Sony, 30, 31, 32, 50
Southern Chopper, 140, 141
Spain, 45, 61, 116
Sparks, C., 2, 133, 138
Sreberny, A., 9
Steemers, J., 78, 84, 87, 93, 105, 129, 132
Steen Müller, T., 130
Stelter, B., 39
Sterling, C. H., 20

Straubhaar, J. D., 13, 15, 29, 30
Strategic programming, 69, 93
Supervolcano, 94, 128, 140
Supersize Me, 150
Sweden, 36, 42, 45, 100
synergy, 42, 44, 46, 57, 93
Synovate, 41
Syvertsen, T., 82

T

Taylor, J., 20, 21, 25–27, 40, 74, 100, 101, 103
TBI/*Television Business International* (magazine), 94, 103
TCI (Tele-Communications, Inc.), 21, 22, 25, 86, 150
Telecoms, 27, 45
Telenovelas, 15
television, *see* advertising; broadcasting; European television sector; factual television; narrowcasting; satellite television; US
Television Research Partnership, 82, 88, 89, 118, 121
Television without Frontiers Directive, 82, 83, 116
televisual culture, 5–8, 132–151
    definition of, 6
    Discovery's, 132–144
    theoretical articulations of: *see* cultural heterogenization; cultural homogenization; cultural hybridization
televisuality, 6
Thal-Larsen, P., 33, 34, 65, 78, 129, 147
Third World and Environment Broadcasting Project, 8, 17, 143
Thussu, D. K., 5, 7, 11–13, 15, 24, 30, 31, 41, 42, 46, 47, 70, 99, 137
Time Warner, 22, 30, 84, 133
TiVo, 46, 47
TNS-Gallup, 34
Tobin, A., 104
TogetherTV, 110, 115, 136
Tomlinson, J, 5
Top 25 Online Brands, 54
Tour de France, 69, 70
Trading Spaces, 78
Treehugger.com, 39, 43, 44
Tunstall, J., 15, 22, 24, 77, 86
Turkey
Turow, J., 47
TV2 (Norway), 36

TV2 Denmark, 100, 129, 130

U

UK,
  and cable and satellite television
    channels in the, 25, 27, 104
  and television programming export,
    119–121
  broadcasters in the, 9, 94
UNESCO, 62, 110, 111, 115,
United States,
  and film and television export,
    119–121
  and media brands in the, 53, 54
  and media power, 9, 119–121, 141
  broadcasters in the, 19, 20, 24
  cable and satellite television channels
    originating from, 19, 20, 42,
    46, 52
Urry, J., 50

V

Variety (magazine), 24–27, 32, 150)
Venturelli, S., 82
Verrier, R., 83
Viacom, 22, 24, 30, 34, 58, 102, 133
Virgin, 50, 56
VIVA, 101, 102
VOD (Video-On-Demand), 43, 45, 46,
    56, 58
Volkmer, I., 139
Vranica, S., 47

W

Waisbord, S., 82, 139
Walking with Dinosaurs, 78, 91–93
Walking with Cavemen, 92, 94
Walking with . . . brand, 91–94

Wall Street Journal, 47
Wall to Wall, 14, 33, 81, 130
Walt Disney Company, 24, 30, 41, 51,
    55, 56, 58, 61, 84, 93, 120
Wang, T., 83
WAP (Wireless Application Protocol),
    45, 156
Washington Post, The (newspaper), 65,
    131
Watch with the World, 69, 70, 135,
    148
Weakest Link, The, 141
Weprin, A., 131
West Park Pictures, 65, 87, 88, 107, 127
western culture, 15
Wheatly, H., 14
Wheeler, M., 42, 119, 121, 131
White, A. M., 91, 214
Who Do You Think You Are, 14, 81
Who Wants to be a Millionaire?, 141
Whitefield, M., 29
Wildlife (television genre), 3, 87, 88,
    113, 129
Wildman, S. S., 19
Williams, M., 27
Willis, J., 55
Winslow, G., 68, 92
World's Strangest UFO Stories, The,
    113, 128, 140,

Y

Yahoo, 43, 54, 56
YLE, 100
YouTube, 43, 44

Z

ZDF, 68, 92
Zee TV, 15, 31, 138